The Lost Apple

The Lost Apple

Operation Pedro Pan,
Cuban Children in the U.S.,
and the Promise of a Better Future

María de los Angeles Torres

Beacon Press, Boston

BEACON PRESS
25 Beacon Street, Boston, Massachusetts 02108-2892
www.beacon.org

Beacon Press books
are published under the auspices of
the Unitarian Universalist Association of Congregations.

07 06 05 04 03 8 7 6 5 4 3 2 1

Text design by Isaac Tobin

Library of Congress Cataloging-in-Publication Data
Torres, María de los Angeles.
  The lost apple : Operation Pedro Pan, Cuban children in the U.S.,
and the promise of a better future / María de los Angeles Torres.
p. cm.
Includes bibliographical references (p.).
  ISBN 0-8070-0232-1 (alk. paper)
  1. Refugee children—Cuba. 2. Refugee children—United States.
3. Refugee children—Services for—United States. I. Title.
HV640.5.C9T67 2003
  325′.21′083097291—dc21
                            2003002617

To the memory of Maria Piers, whose gift was the ability to remember and explain how children experience feelings

Contents

Prologue

LA MANZANA PERDIDA	THE LOST APPLE
Señora Santana,	Señora Santana,
¿por qué llora el niño?	why is the boy crying?
Por una manzana que se le ha perdido.	He has lost his apple.
Yo le daré una,	I will give him one,
yo le daré dos;	I will give him two;
una para el niño,	one for him
y otra para vos.	and one for you.
Yo no quiero una,	I don't want one,
yo no quiero dos.	I don't want two.
Yo quiero la mía,	I want the one
la que se perdió.[1]	that I lost.

—*Spanish nursery rhyme*

On Thanksgiving Day, 1999, a Cuban boy named Elián González was found tied to an inner tube off the coast of Florida. Rumor has it he was floating at sea for days after witnessing the drowning of his mother and ten other fellow rafters from Cuba. A pod of dolphins had gently nudged him to safety. As if fate needed to close a historical circle, at the very same moment that he was rescued, about fifty Cuban-American children refugees from another epoch were marking their arrival to the United States some forty years ago. The dramatic arrival of Elián would reopen the wounds of perhaps one of the most dramatic events in post-revolutionary Cuba, the unprecedented exodus in the early 1960s of more than 14,000 unaccompanied children that came to be known as Operation Pedro Pan.

Like most events that crossed the great ideological fault lines of the Cold War, Operation Pedro Pan spun contradictory myths. In Cuba, the exodus of more than 14,000 children was seen as an act of U.S. aggression upon the young Cuban revolution, a CIA plot to rob the nation of its future. For the United States, the young refugees were living proof of the horrors of communism, children who had to be saved and brought to freedom. Four decades later, Elián would become a symbol of those more than 14,000 Pedro Pans. The Cuban press, calling the Pedro Pans 14,000 Eliancitos,[2] portrayed Cuba's campaign to rescue Elián for the fatherland as a way to undo the injustice committed on the others. The Cuban poet Cintio Vitier even declared that "the innocence of a child would save the nation."

Not surprisingly, the same historical paradigm was present in the debate about Elián in the exile community, where the argument was that the Communists would take advantage of this boy's innocence to inculcate their diabolical materialist ideas.[3] Returning Elián to Cuba would challenge the very reason why more than one million Cubans had left the island. It would ignore the origins of the exile—where Operation Pedro Pan is the principal metaphor for the flight—from a regime so repressive that parents were willing to send their children into exile alone, not knowing whether they would ever be reunited. Elián became one more child to save; a line had been drawn in the sand in the battle against Fidel Castro who, forty years later, still controlled the island.

In a moment of political contestation, a child thus became a way to try to legitimize failed political choices. In Cuba, the dream of a utopian society had yielded to a corrupt and authoritarian regime. The new socialist man was never realized; instead, Marxist managers waited to take their turn in a new global capitalist economy, while other youths risked their lives floating to the United States on rickety rafts. In Miami, the exile community had failed in its *lucha*—the struggle—to topple the Castro government, its own political leadership anti-democratic and ineffective. For U.S. politicians running for the presidency, the child became a way to cater to voters.[4] Several congressional representatives even introduced a bill to grant him citizenship. For the U.S. media,

Elián, the poster child, was used to compete for television viewers. Elián provided a way for both sides to breathe life into a bankrupt politics.

In a sense, the Elián González saga was an attempt by two old antagonists to revive their distinct revolutionary visions—that they alone held the key to a better future for Cuba through the education of its children. The narrative shaping the struggle over Elián's future, really the contest over the destiny of Cuba, had been scripted during the 1959 revolution, a political event that tore apart the island nation and unleashed a struggle for the control of the hearts and minds of its children. Educating children became central to the revolutionary government's plans to create the "New Man," the prototype of a socialist society. The opposition, in turn, rallied behind the battle cry "Save the Children" and established an underground network to hurry them to safety, to a place where they could be taught democratic ways. Ironically, they also claimed that the children would be the building blocks of a New Society, for they would be the "New Men."

For the United States, the children became cannon fodder for the ideological battles of the Cold War. The best example of using Cuban children for their propaganda value can be found in a documentary commissioned by the U.S. government about Operation Pedro Pan made in English and Spanish. "Why would Mama and Papa send you alone to the United States?" asks the film's narrator in that higher-pitched voice that adults often use to speak to children. "Fidel Castro," he replies in a much lower, sinister tone. The documentary was titled *The Lost Apple,* after an old Spanish nursery rhyme, whose words simultaneously evoke desire and a loss of innocence.

This was not the first time that a nation's future was imagined through its progeny. Wars and social upheavals have long engendered myths of dramatic change, and such myths influence what happens to children. Children provoke a longing for our past, while opening a boundless future. In addition, they embody private and public pasts and futures. The Cuban nation itself was, in part, imagined by José Martí, poet and hero of the Cuban war of independence of the late

1800s, through his writings to and about children. *Los pinos nuevos* (the new pines), he wrote, would grow tall to replace the youth imprisoned by the Spaniards.

The Mexican nation reveres the young cadets, Los Niños Héroes, who gave up their lives defending their country against U.S. intervention, thus placing its heroic youths at the center of the search for national sovereignty. The Russian Revolution politically sanctified children who denounced their parents—who represented the past—and chose the revolution that symbolized the future.

Time and again, political struggles have been played out through refugee children.[5] During the Spanish Civil War, thousands of them were evacuated to the Soviet Union, France, and Mexico.[6] Jewish children in Nazi Germany were saved from death in concentration camps by a movement known as the Kindertransport.[7] British children were sent abroad during World War II.[8] And more than one thousand unaccompanied Hungarian minors were resettled in the United States after the 1956 uprising in Hungary.[9]

By a strange twist of history, many of these campaigns would come to bear in one way or another on the exodus of Cuban children. The ghosts of the Spanish Civil War would scare priests and parents in Revolutionary Cuba into thinking that their children would be safer elsewhere. Penny Powers, a British intelligence official who helped with the Kindertransport, would become the central coordinator for the underground's effort during Operation Pedro Pan; and Monsignor Bryan Walsh, who once helped to resettle Hungarian teenagers in the United States, would become a principal actor in the granting of visa waivers and U.S. resettlement of the Pedro Pan children.

There were other key participants, of course; Jim Baker, an American educator deeply enamored with Cuba who identified himself as an American-Cuban, indeed who felt he was an exile the day he and his family fled the island; the women of the underground thoroughly committed to the cause of saving children from indoctrination; and the Cuban parents themselves. All would be driven by the urgency to save children—not because they were in physical danger, but rather because *why did wanted to "save" cuban children*

they believed that the minds of children mattered to the future of a country and it was imperative that the children be saved from Communist brainwashing. They had all become heirs to a modernist proposal born of a post-revolutionary world that held that children's minds were the building blocks of future nations.

Almost two decades later, many Pedro Pans, myself included, would journey back to the island in search of explanations about the dramatic events that so deeply affected our lives. Instead, we found government officials eager to use our return as ammunition against our parents and against an exile community whose myth of origin included our flight from our homeland. This book is a culmination of my search for explanations, an attempt to piece together from disparate sources a more layered and perhaps more comprehensive account of our journey. I not only question government policies but also try to understand the philosophical framework within which government officials, activists, and parents were able to stage such a dramatic exodus of children, one which made them believe that family separations were necessary in order to protect the innocence of their children and the future of their nation.

Main Question: why did parents and political actors think it was necessary to stage the exodus of 14,000 cuban children?

Introduction

My mother's relatives lived in Yaguajay, a little town nestled between the sea and the foot of the Escambray Mountains in the Las Villas province of Cuba. Two or three times a year, my family took the five-hour drive from our home in Havana to visit them. In the summer of 1961, our trip had a secret purpose. We were coming to say good-bye. We were delivering some of our possessions: a fan, jewelry, photographs. We also brought our longhaired cat, Johnny, for safekeeping until our return. I sat next to Johnny's cage in the backseat; I can still recall the smell of his sweaty coat.

My parents, like thousands of Cubans, had supported the revolution at first; they hid rebels in our home, a risk that could have cost them their lives. In January 1959, the day the *rebeldes* marched into Havana, my father rushed home to pick me up so that we could greet them. When we reached the Avenida de los Presidentes, a wide avenue dotted with statues of Cuba's past presidents, he hoisted me onto his shoulders so that I could see over the crowd. People were jubilant—dancing, chanting, and reaching out to touch the bearded rebels in their olive green uniforms. One stopped in front of us and reached up to hug me; I was mesmerized by the red glass beads of the rosary that hung from his neck and the silver cross almost buried in his hairy chest. We honked our car horn all the way home. My father told me it was a day I must never forget.

But during the next two years, everything changed. Fidel Castro, once a popular hero in our family, became a ruler we feared. We stopped collecting trading cards featuring heroes of the revolution. I no longer rode my toy military jeep on the back patio, waving the red and black flag of the 26 of July Movement.[1] I had just turned six. Time was moving fast. Turmoil was increasingly becoming a part of our daily lives. Sirens were heard at all hours. Our familiar routines of playing in the park and going to the beach on Sundays were constantly disrupted by threats of bomb raids. Just months earlier, the government had shut down the schools, including mine, Nuestra Señora de Lourdes. There was constant confusion in the air. For reasons I only understood later, my parents decided to go into exile.

The quickest way for the family to depart was to send me to the United States with a visa waiver; I would then claim my parents and sisters, who would join me in a few months. I was to travel with my best friend, Xavier Arruza, also six years old. His older brothers were already in Miami. It was Xavier's father who had obtained the visa waiver for me. I was going to Miami, I was told, to stay with Nenita and Pucho Greer, my parents' friends. We started to pack my things. I felt a strange surge of excitement (I had never been on an airplane before) mixed with apprehension (I had never been separated from my parents). Secrecy shrouded my trip: no one was to know that I was leaving the country. My parents had not even told my younger sister, Alicia.

On July 30, just before dawn, my parents woke me and dressed me in the aqua blue and white checkered dress my grandmother had made for me, on which they pinned a piece of paper bearing my name and the name and phone number of our friends in Miami. They quietly loaded the car: a suitcase, a gray and red vinyl handbag, and my favorite doll. The sky was turning a pale orange pink as we drove to the airport.

Years would pass before I learned how many other children had left the island in the same fashion, to be reunited with their parents at an uncertain date. Some, in fact, never saw their parents again; others experienced long separations. Still others faced terrible hardship in foster homes or institutions. At the time, though, I knew only about my cousins, who arrived in the United States shortly after I did. On Sundays, we visited two of my cousins at a makeshift camp in south Dade County. Church officials in Havana had told their parents that their daughters would receive a *beca* (scholarship) to go to a good school in the United States. Instead they were sleeping in a large room filled with small cots squeezed so tightly together that they had to slide onto them from the pillow end. Later two cousins were shipped to a foster home in Albuquerque, New Mexico, and others to an orphanage in St. Louis, Missouri.

By mid-1961, most middle-class Cuban families knew of the semi-clandestine visa waiver program that had spurred this child migration. But no one spoke about it openly; everyone was sworn to secrecy, both on the island and in the United States. It wasn't until March 8, 1962, that the *Miami Herald* wrote about a secret effort called Operation Exodus that was bringing Cuban youth to the United States to save them from Fidel Castro's brainwashing. The *Herald* reported 8,000 had already arrived in South Florida.[2] In the next seven months, another 6,000 unaccompanied children would enter the United States. In total, between the years 1960 and 1962, more than 14,000 children entered the United States through the program that came to be known as Operation Peter Pan or, in its Spanish translation, *Operación Pedro Pan*.

There are many debates about the origin of the name. In Cuba it is referred to by its English name. A few years ago, I visited Noemi Booth, an English teacher who had worked at Ruston Academy in Havana and was still living in Cuba. When I told her that I was conducting research on Operation Pedro Pan, she quickly corrected me and said, "Here we refer to it as Operation *Peter Pan*."[3] In a book published in 1962, Ruby Hart Phillips, *New York Times* correspondent in Havana throughout the fifties, wrote about an American she knew who had helped hundreds of children leave Cuba, and someone had called his work Operation Peter Pan.[4] But Monsignor Walsh, one of the pivotal figures in the exodus, always called it *Pedro Pan* and told us that a local reporter had dubbed it as such. An article that appeared in the *Miami Herald* on March 9, 1962, states, "This is the underground railway in the sky—Operation Peter Pan. Maybe it should be Operation Pedro Pan."[5] A *New York Times* article May 27, 1962, would use the name again when it reported that 10,000 children were already in the United States and called it "the largest peacetime program for homeless refugee children in this country."[6] Nowhere did I find in government documents reference to Operation Peter Pan or Pedro Pan. The closest we have to an official name was the *Miami Herald*'s article dubbing it Operation Exodus and

El Rescate de la Niñez, listed in a CIA directory entitled *Counterrevolutionary Organizations.*

But the name caught on anyway. Walt Disney's version of Peter Pan had been released in the mid-fifties, and the idea of children in flight found a familiar popular imagery. Surely unbeknownst to those who helped popularize the name was the more ambivalent and complicated literary figure created by J. M. Barrie, the author of *Peter Pan.*[7] In the original story, when Wendy first meets Peter Pan and he tells her he has no mother, she feels "that she was in the presence of a tragedy."[8] Peter, who has innumerable adventures, can never have a family—it is "the one joy from which he must be forever barred."[9] Peter Pan, a boy who refused to grow up, spent his time luring children away from their parents to a frequently dangerous place called Neverland. There, Peter is the leader of the "lost boys," babies who fell from their cradles when their nurses neglected them. It is a place where children long for their mothers but slowly begin to forget their past. The tragic side of Peter Pan was a strange foreshadowing of what many children of Operation Pedro Pan would come to experience.

Despite the headlines about the unprecedented exodus of Cuban children, larger events overshadowed it, and Operation Pedro Pan soon faded from public attention. By October 1962, the world would be at the brink of nuclear war. The United States detected the Soviet Union's nuclear missiles on the island and demanded that they be removed. In turn, the Soviet Union demanded that the United States make a pledge of nonintervention in Cuba. As a result of the standoff, both Cuba and the United States banned travel to and from the island. The plight of these children—many whose parents had not been able to come to the United States—would be forgotten in the unfolding world drama.

Uncovering the Forbidden

The Cuban community in the United States is held together by the powerful collective belief that we had no choice but to flee the island. There is no stronger proof of this than the fact that parents, fearful of the

Communist government, sent their children abroad, alone. In effect, we, the children in exile, became living evidence of the terrible turn of events on the island. Leaving Cuba was a heroic deed. Living in exile was a patriotic sacrifice, and dying in exile was nearly elevated to an act of martyrdom. Miami's Little Havana cemetery is filled with Cuban flags, like a military cemetery.

The result has been an official narrative of the origins of the exile community that is imposed on all our experiences. The stories tell of a heroic flight from repression to freedom. Our exodus has even permeated the electoral arena, as political candidates in Miami list "Pedro Pan" as a badge of honor. Even President George W. Bush lauds our parents for "being willing to give up their children so that they could be free."[10]

Pedro Pan became such a clearly symbolic element of the exile experience that there was little need to question or reflect upon it. Until recently, few people outside the Cuban community knew of our exodus or questioned its meaning.[11] We, on the inside, had no real points of reference to understand how unusual it had been. The dramatic events of these family separations, confined in such a closed context, faded into a repressed collective memory, to be recalled only by a political rhetoric that resisted ambivalence or contradictions and portrayed our flight as a tale of heroism. Thus, while we could readily recount the factual episode of our early migration from Cuba, the emotional travails and complexities were now inaccessible—including mine.

In 1974, as a college student in Texas, I watched a story on the evening news about thousands of Vietnamese youngsters boarding planes, fleeing to the United States.[12] Images of my own flight on a plane filled with crying children came rushing back. This was the first stirring. But even then, the flashback had little meaning; it was just a memory, an event whose geography and smells were in a distant past that made little sense. I left it unexamined. Years later, the reactions I encountered when I recounted how I came to the United States should have been a clue that something about the trip was not quite normal. I remember, for example, a dinner party in Chicago at my mother-in-law's, when my story outraged one of the guests: "How could our government divide families in such a way?" she asked. The thought of separating children from parents tugs at some of our worst fears.

The context began to shift when I was in graduate school in Ann Arbor, where I started meeting Cuban students with similar experiences. I had always wanted to return to Cuba; many of them longed to return as well. In part we were idealists searching for an alternative politics, but most important, we were yearning to go home. The rupture of exile had left an ever-present void. We began searching for a way to return. I heard of publications such as *Areíto* and *Joven Cuba*, edited by radical Cubans in the United States. In 1978, I read about the Antonio Maceo Brigade, a group of young exiles who had successfully pressured the Cuban government for permission to return to the island for a visit. I made contact with the organizers; in 1979, they invited me to join the Brigade's National Committee. Many of the members were Pedro Pans.

My first trip back was in 1979. For years afterward, we organized other visits, all with the intent of recapturing for the Cuban nation the children who had been torn away. Still, my focus was not so much on the way we left Cuba as it was on our return.

In graduate school, I had begun to research U.S.-Cuban relations and to become involved in policy advocacy work. I supported lifting the U.S. embargo on Cuba. I wanted to help promote understanding between the two countries and dialogue between Cubans in exile and Cubans on the island. I felt we were all part of a single nation, and only needed more communication and engagement to bridge the division. My focus was on policy alternatives, not necessarily on understanding the historical context of the conflict. I still did not consider conducting research on Operation Pedro Pan.

Then, in February 1993, my first daughter celebrated her sixth birthday, the age I had been when my parents sent me to the United States. I tried to put myself in their place, but I couldn't. The separation was unimaginable: my daughter, on a plane alone, off to another country. Little by little, I began remembering how scared I had been and how lonely I had felt. My emotions resurfaced. I began to dig into my past.

For ten years, I have tried to reconstruct the context and the events that led to my departure from Cuba and to the mass exodus of Cuban children to the United States. I wanted to uncover as much as I could about our exodus. I felt that we had a right to know how and why we had been wrenched from our families and our homes. I thought that by understanding this past, we could somehow help other immigrants in other countries in turmoil, so that they would not be separated unnecessarily. What I did not realize was that a more layered exploration into this period would mean defying both the exile and island versions of our exodus.

Researching the Fault Lines

The Cold War has many fault lines. Research into the events that crossed these lines should not serve to perpetuate the chasm. Rather, the many voices from both sides of the fault lines must be heard in order to piece together the true story. I began with the hope that this project might be a bridge between those who left the island and those who stayed—that it could be an open reconstruction of history, in turn allowing individual memories to emerge without the constraints of the official story. This book is a research journey throughout which I have learned not only about events but also about how we come to know what we know. It is part of my intellectual quest to understand how diasporic communities are formed and how politics intersect with collective and personal reconstructions of the past. It is also an effort to understand the politics of memory and identity. And finally it's a quest to create room so that, we, the Pedro Pan children—"the most defenseless of refugees," as we were called at the time—have the space to explore and reexamine memories of events that changed the course of our personal histories.

I began by interviewing my mother, who was instrumental in making the decision to send me to the United States. By then I was living in Chicago, so I traveled to Miami, where they had moved after my father retired. I wanted to find out from her and later from other parents why and how they had obtained visa waivers for their children. I had assumed incorrectly that parents would be the best sources for these details. But in many cases parents had repressed the memories of these events. It wasn't until the last phase of the project, while interviewing the Pedro Pans, that I realized the children, now adults, were the best source. Many recalled their journeys in chilling detail. Some kept their travel documents neatly folded and stored away with the other mementos of their lives.

Interviewing my mother enabled me to understand something other than simply the procedures for obtaining the visa waiver necessary for travel. I had been afraid of this conversation. For years, I had had serious political differences with my parents. I had become a supporter of the revolutionary government and had seen my parents as "counterrevolutionaries." Now I was beginning to grasp the nuances of their politics. I knew of their involvement with the revolution. I learned how my mother abhorred the violence and corruption of the Batista regime. How she had dreamed of a sovereign and democratic Cuba. And I learned how her hopes for the revolution had been dashed as she saw the new government use violence to suppress its opponents, many of whom had fought in the revolutionary uprising. She had become fearful of the new regime. In the great divide of the Cold War, there was no room for those who had been supporters of the revolution but critical of Fidel. You were either a supporter or an opponent. I began to understand that the values she had fought for were not much different from my own. Maybe she would come to understand my politics as well.

My mother helped me understand the breadth of exile politics and the tragic fate of political reform in the era of polarization. Slowly, I began to question my views, and to reconsider the context in which decisions about our exodus were made.

Through interviews with other parents, I was able to locate other pieces of the puzzle. I tracked down individuals—many of them women—who had been at the heart of the underground opposition to Fidel Castro; part of their work had been to procure visa waivers for children. I interviewed many of them. Interestingly, most accounts of the opposition movement, both negative and positive, simply ignored the pivotal role women played. Yet, their stories fascinated me; their network led me to church and government officials, as well as to other members of the anti-Castro underground. In all, I interviewed over one hundred people related to the exodus: U.S. operatives, Cuban underground collaborators, parents and other family members in the thick of the drama, and the exiled children themselves.

But Pedro Pan was not only an exile phenomenon. It had left a mark on the island as well. In Cuba, there were young men and women whose brothers and sisters had been sent to Miami, and whose parents followed, but who, for one reason or another, had stayed behind. How did they view the exodus? There were Pedro Pan parents who remained on the island. Why had they opted to stay? I wanted to understand. And, of course, a very personal question loomed behind all this: What would my life have been like if we had stayed? Throughout the course of my Pedro Pan research, there were magical moments that transcended ideological and geographical borders. During one visit to the island, I ran into Natividad Revueltas. She was a family friend who had been swept up by the revolutionary movement. Nati fell in love with Fidel and gave birth to his daughter, Alina. When I saw her in 1993 in Havana, I told her about my project and shared with her what I had learned thus far: that Operation Pedro Pan originated with the director of Ruston, an American school in Havana.

"Neni," she responded, "that's Jim Baker. I know him very well; I graduated from Ruston before it was confiscated."

Nati invited me to her home in Nuevo Vedado the next day. We spent the afternoon rummaging through dusty boxes filled with old yearbooks. The musty smell of Cuban tropics penetrated the air.

"Did you know that his secretary, Noemi Booth, still lives in Cuba?" she asked. "Every year we receive a card from Mr. Baker." Nati, on the island, held a key to locating Jim Baker in Florida.

I had first heard of Baker's role in the Pedro Pan exodus from Elly Chovel, who at the time was president of the Operation Pedro Pan group, an association that has tried to reunite the now-grown children of the exodus. But it took both her contact with him and Nati's help to

reach him. Upon my return to the United States, I called to meet with
Baker, and since Elly had called to introduce me, he invited me to his
home. He lived with his wife, Sybil, in Ormand Beach, about a four-
hour drive from Miami. I would talk to Baker regularly over the next
few years until his death in the winter of 2001. Through Baker, I came
to understand the complex relationship between Americans who had
lived in Cuba and the Cubans who were fighting for democracy on the
island.

Reconsidering the Exile Community

I also began to spend a lot of time in Miami. As children, we lived in
Texas, and like many Cuban families who lived outside the exile community my family would visit Miami during summer vacations. Our
trips fascinated my sisters and me. We would eat Cuban food at Versailles and Lila's, listen to Cuban music at Los Violines, and if we were
lucky, catch a concert by Los Chavales de España at the auditorium.
South Beach was our favorite place to swim and trade family secrets
with our cousins who, being more fashion-conscious than we were,
shared their latest beauty tips. Two of my first cousins, also Pedro Pans,
had lived with us for two years during the early 1960s. They had ended
up in a camp in south Miami and later at a foster home in Albuquerque,
New Mexico. Eventually, they moved in with us until their parents were
able to leave Cuba through Spain in 1964.

With time, however, my sister's and my political values began to
clash with those of our relatives. When my sister Alicia and I decided to
return to Cuba with the Antonio Maceo Brigade, the relationship became strained. To my family, our return was an act of treason. Their reaction was simply an echo of what the larger exile community felt about
the Brigade. Those were extremely tense times. Extremists in the exile
community launched a campaign of terror against us. For me Miami
became a place of fear. Our names were broadcast repeatedly on the
city's infamous radio stations, provoking telephone death threats to
our workplaces and to my parents' home. We were often greeted with

pickets at the airport as we deplaned from Havana-Miami flights in the late 1970s, and we sometimes waited as the FBI inspected the plane, since we occasionally received bomb threats. As a consequence, even twenty years later, when the bombs and the threats had subsided, my trips to Miami were filled with fear and apprehension.

Elly Chovel and I had come to know each other through Yvonne Conde, another Pedro Pan, who was writing a book about the exiled children. I met Elly for the first time on my way to Cuba in 1993. Before I left, she had given me a note that said: "¡Qué alegría el haberte conocido! Que sepan nuestros contemporáneos en Cuba que aquí hay quienes los quieren y que desean lo mejor hacia ellos y nuestra querida y añorada patria" (I am so happy to have met you. Let our contemporaries in Cuba know that there are those here that wish the best for them and our beloved country we long for). Subsequently, Elly invited me to speak to her group, which met the last Saturday of each month at Versailles, the popular Cuban restaurant on Calle Ocho. Elly accepted my travels to Cuba, but this was still Miami, and to travel to the island, even for professional reasons, was, at the time, crossing a line in the exile community. I was scared as I drove up to the restaurant in the heart of what I thought of as enemy territory. I was apprehensive about the audience and about what to say. Elly hugged me and introduced me to the twenty Pedro Pans sitting around the tables in the mirrored room. I sipped my café con leche, took a deep breath, and began to talk.

I was honest about my travels to Cuba. They were curious and supportive. We engaged in a respectful debate about a Miami Herald article entitled "The Dark Side of Pedro Pan" that discussed the CIA's role in the operation. There are some who felt threatened by questions about the political motives of the exodus, since they want to believe that the operation was exclusively a humanitarian rescue mission, but many others wanted a fuller understanding, and were willing to entertain other viewpoints. That morning, I sensed important changes occurring in Miami—we could actually discuss such a sensitive issue as traveling to Cuba. I also sensed that something began shifting in me—I had found sympathy and support where I expected rejection. The Pe-

dro Pans in Miami made me begin to realize that, regardless of my es-
trangement from the exile community, I was part of it. The exodus had
marked an entire generation. While we had ended up in very different
places around the world, we shared that moment of separation from
our families and our birthplace. We had all expected to return home in
a few months. Now, some thirty odd years later, we sat around a Miami
restaurant trying to grasp how it had happened. It was the same desire
to understand that had led me back to the island.

There are many myths about the Pedro Pans—most notably that
we are driven and successful. Certainly, there is some truth to this: included among our numbers are corporate executives, general managers
of TV stations, doctors, university professors, artists, and writers. At
that meeting at Versailles there were bankers, real estate agents, secretaries, social workers, teachers, and even a leading expert on the history
of the Vikings. But what about all the others? We were, after all, a small
percentage of the over 14,000 children who left.

During the next few years, Elly became a bridge, sharing information and networking among the many Pedro Pans she met. But perhaps
her greatest contribution was to insist that we, as Pedro Pans, had the
right to explore our own stories and experiences, even if they challenged
the official exile version, which essentially casts the entire operation as
a pain-free and fully successful humanitarian rescue mission. In this
rendition, there was no room for the children who were mistreated,
abused, or who never saw their parents again. Furthermore, the thought
that maybe politics and not necessity shaped a program exclusively for
children could not be entertained. Elly understood that even though
these stories and perspectives were not part of the official narrative, we
needed to entertain them. But to open the political space to explore
these issues was to create the possibility that the official version of our
exodus could be challenged. And given the centrality of our exodus in
the narrative of the origins of the exile community itself, tugging at the
thread of our exodus could unravel the entire myth.

Nonetheless, Elly insisted that we exercise this right. In a certain
sense, we were at once the legacy of those who had resisted political po-

larization and still children whose lives contradicted the totalizing political illusions of an earlier era. In many ways, that conversation at Versailles marked the onset of an exploration into the memory of the exile community—of dormant memories opening complexities far beyond what the exile's political slogans suggested.

Other, more difficult Miami trips would come to provoke a more personal transformation. It was one thing to meet my contemporaries, youth of the 1960s raised in the United States, who could debate different points of view yet still understand my perspective. But my research was taking me to the heart of the opposition, or what had been called the *contrarevolución*. I would have to interview men and women from that sector in Miami that I thought applauded when bombs exploded against those who favored dialogue with Cuba. Still, I was reconstructing the story of our past in which they were actors, and regardless of what I felt about their politics, only they could answer many of my questions, describing for me how they saw that moment in history. I had to listen.

I was baffled by the secrecy of the operation—the propaganda and the misinformation I was uncovering from both the U.S. and Cuban governments. The men and women of the underground described to me how the rules of the games were different then, how laws were made and broken arbitrarily. How at any given hour one action could be legal, and minutes afterward Fidel could go on national television and declare it illegal. This helped me understand the context in which politics unfolded on the island in the early 1960s, and why people reacted the way they did. I began to understand their political values. How they, too, had fought for what they believed in, first against Batista and then against Castro. Their political views were diverse. They, too, like the grown children of Pedro Pan, were looking for a voice in the official stories of exile.

The conversations with my "enemies" forced me to reexamine not only my deeply held assumptions about them, but about history itself. I also had to confront myself, and ask why I had viewed their history through such ideological blinders. After considerable self-reflection, these men and women became important links in my search for a more complex understanding of our past.

My research journey has also included fights, especially with government officials. In Cuba, an attempt to establish a collaborative research project was politically manipulated. I did succeed in obtaining some Cuban government records. But there is no freedom of information act in Cuba. In the United States, I did make ample use of freedom of information laws. Three presidential libraries collaborated, as did many of the offices in the national archives. Still, one agency held out—the CIA—the agency in charge of the Cuba project during the early sixties. After numerous requests and appeals were denied, I filed a lawsuit to try to obtain their records. Through the course of the lawsuit I did receive some files, but practice and law protects the agency from too much openness.I was, however, able to obtain U.S. government records including documenting discussions about an important film made of the children in the camps. The film's title was *The Lost Apple*.

The Lost Apple

The Lost Apple opens with the arrival of a little boy to Florida City, one of the South Florida receiving camps. The music for the documentary is based on a nursery rhyme called "The Lost Apple," the lyrics of which appear at the beginning of the prologue of this book. Through the music and imagery, we feel the sense of loss and abandonment clearly palpable in the child's expressions. We need not wonder why this child's parents have sent him away. Father Cistierna, director of the camp, addresses the children after a talent night: "You are a constant reminder that there is something very wrong in the world. I would like you to be boys and girls with a great sense of responsibility, because the New Society, a New World, is waiting for you to rebuild your homeland. That New World can only be built with New Men. Cuba is waiting for you."[13]

It would take almost thirty-five years from the time the documentary was filmed to ask more complicated questions about our exodus. Movements of refugees from one nation-state to another usually involve politics at multiple locations, but in our case crossing the aquatic border between the United States and Cuba was forbidden for many years—our histories had to conform to the geography of the Cold War. This book presents a critical history of Operation Pedro Pan which examines the underlying political agendas of *both* Cuba and the United States. I have woven together interviews of political actors and church officials in both countries, and interviews with Pedro Pans and their parents with information I have gathered from an extensive review of government archives.

Government documents from the Department of State, Children's Bureau of the former Department of Health, Education, and Welfare, Department of Defense, Department of Justice, and U.S. Information Agency have been reviewed at the National Archives. White House records and National Security Council minutes have been made available at three presidential libraries: Eisenhower, Kennedy, and Johnson. In addition, the State Department of Public Affairs library has a collection of declassified cables. Some of these, and others, are referenced in the Department of State, Foreign Relations of the United States, volumes 9 (1958–1960) and 10 (1961–1963): Cuba (Washington, D.C.: U.S. Government Printing Office, 1997).

It is helpful to understand the chronology of Operation Pedro Pan in several periods. The first period is its inception in 1960 to the Bay of Pigs invasion in April 1961, a time during which the main concern of the organizers was the safety of the men and women in the underground. It begins with the issuance of two hundred student visas, which ultimately could not be processed because of the break in relations between the United States and Cuba. In an unprecedented move, the U.S. government then granted a Catholic priest in Miami permission to waive visas for children under sixteen. During this time, almost five hundred unaccompanied children came to the United States. The second period is framed by both the Bay of Pigs invasion in April 1961 and the October Missile Crisis in 1962. The number of children sent to the United States during those months surpasses 14,000. In Cuba, the period is characterized by the increased repression and radicalization of the revolution, including the government's takeover of private schools and the temporary closing of public ones. During this time, visa waivers for children became the most accessible way for Cubans to leave the island. The third period begins when the United States closed the immigration door in October 1962 and ends in 1965, when Fidel Castro announced that Miami relatives could come to pick up family at the Cuban port of Camarioca. Immediately following this incident, the United States reestablished flights between both countries. It is the same year in which the Cuban government declared that its goal was to create the "New Socialist Man," the same challenge presented years earlier to the child refugees in the Florida camps by a Catholic priest.

Kindergarten class, Havana, Cuba, 1960. María de los Angeles Torres, second row, third from right; Xavier Arruza, front row, second from left. Courtesy of the author.

As I reflected upon my research, I was still left with the lingering question of why? I wanted to understand this program in its philosophical context, for it was beyond its specific political details that an international ideological battle for the minds of children had unfolded.

Paradoxically, this story takes place between two states representing seemingly opposite systems of government. Both choose children as the means to wage their battles. Each government claimed that they could best protect the children's innocence; each promised a better future.

The Pedro Pan exodus thus becomes a window through which to understand how children's needs were defined, and indeed manipulated, in a moment when competing versions of the modernist project, communism and democracy, face off. It tells us about the place of children in modern societies and it suggests that the exodus was not a contest over protecting children but rather about competing state-building projects. But in order to understand this, we need to return to the beginning of Western thought to see how the concern about children's minds had evolved, and why the protection of one's innocence could take center stage in an international conflict. Thus, we will begin with political philosophy.

1

Children and the Destinies of Nations

Children have not always been a societal concern. This is not to imply that they have been uncared for by their parents and relatives, but that we have not always perceived them as a social group. Indeed, it could be argued that childhood, as a social category, emerged with the Renaissance, the period preceding the age of modernism.[1] The concern about children finds political expression in the modernist project of nation building. By the twentieth century, children and youth had acquired a central location in the collective imagination. They become a matter of public concern, particularly in regard to their education, since the rational project, the philosophical perspective that accompanied modernism, included the idea that the future could be constructed by remolding the present.

It is also in the twentieth century that the competition between democracy and communism, two versions of the rational modernist project, intensified, particularly in battles waged by nation-states formed by revolutions. In both versions, children were the key to building future societies. Consequently, children's care and development became an arena in which democracy and communism fought their battles. Children and their minds became the central battlegrounds in the Cold War. It is through this lens that I write about Operation Pedro Pan, for the larger ideological struggle to control the minds of Cuban children set the stage for this unprecedented exodus.

The Philosophical Roots of Operation Pedro Pan

The roots of the ideological paradigm that framed Operation Pedro Pan far predate modernist states and twentieth-century revolutions. In *The Republic,* Plato wrote about the social impact of children's education, particularly on those who would grow up to be future rulers. If educated the right way, he asserted, these rulers could change the nature of society. Plato advocated removing the children from their families and placing them under the tutelage of guardians. The just society could be constructed by carefully monitoring the would-be rulers.[2]

Despite Plato's early recognition of children's role in the future of societies, the notion of childhood itself took several centuries to form. In the Middle Ages, religious doctrines began to differentiate between a child's and an adult's capacity for rational action. Many religions set age thresholds to determine when children became responsible for their actions. There were public rituals to signal the moment the child became a responsible member of the adult community. These rituals were often religious in nature, which made the church the responsible authority in the guidance of the new adult's moral actions.

But in medieval society, the boundaries between adulthood and childhood were not clearly demarcated. There were few distinctions between child and adult clothes or games in that respect, as Pieter Brueghel's 1560 painting, *Children's Games,* portrays.[3] Brueghel's children often ascended to the throne; child brides were not uncommon. Most children began working early and made important contributions to the family's own well-being with their labor. Children were also important links in the inheritance chain.[4]

Childhood as a distinguishable social category emerged with the Renaissance. With the concept of childhood was born the nuclear family. Labor in the family was divided, and males were given the public sphere, women, the private. Children now had a safe place in which to exist.[5] Children would eventually become protagonists in literature, becoming heroes or victims. Indeed, Charles Dickens would become one of the greatest proponents of child welfare.

Two notions of childhood are prevalent during this period: children as innocent and as imperfect beings, who needed to be safeguarded and reformed. For instance, for Catholics, children were born with original sin. However, what prevailed in paintings was children as innocents, a notion that would last well into the twentieth century. The classic 1788 painting by Sir Joshua Reynolds of a young girl sitting outdoors, barefoot, with her two little hands at her chest is entitled, *The Age of Innocence*.[6] Innocent children have malleable minds, a critical component of the liberal and socialist projects that rely on transforming the future through them. Paradoxically, it is precisely this portrayal of children that makes them vulnerable and easy to manipulate. Their innocence makes them desirable political objects. Indeed, safeguarding children's innocence would become the reason for struggling to control their minds.

Breaking away from feudal notions of fate, modernism promised that individuals could influence the outcome of their lives through rational thought and action. With this came the rise of modern nation-states that opened their political processes to citizens and, as such, the preoccupation with developing the *good* citizen. Children were the keys to this social experiment. The modern child was bound by infancy and adolescence. Infancy was reserved almost exclusively for family care, but childhood and adolescence were ages in which the public began to intervene in the education of youth.[7]

The education of children emerged as a public concern which would not be solely relegated to either the church or the family.[8] As with nation building,[9] the ideas of childhood and public education had been aided by the creation of the printing press, which required a literate public at the same time that it allowed for a rethinking of how and what information could be presented to children.[10] Therefore, access to information became one of the boundaries between adults and children.

Two currents of thought helped frame the social views of childhood and education in the seventeenth and eighteenth centuries. One, expressed by John Locke, was that "children are like the fountains of rivers, which may be directed in various courses by a gentle application

of the hand."[11] Locke believed that a human being was born a tabula
rasa, and as such society was responsible for shaping young minds and
creating good citizens. For Jean-Jacques Rousseau, humans were closest to nature when they were children. Children possessed feelings and
thoughts, but needed to be protected from society, a corrupting influence. However, Rousseau was concerned solely with the private education of children.[12] In contrast, Immanuel Kant, one of Rousseau's
greatest disciples, was concerned with public education. "Man can only
become man by education," he believed.[13]

By the early 1900s, Sigmund Freud proposed a framework that took
into account both nature (instincts) and the need to control them. For
Freud, nothing less than civilization was at stake. Children, Freud believed, had instincts and emotions, but these needed to be repressed
(molded) in order for them to enter into civilization.[14] Families were
responsible for the first few years of their lives, but society needed to
be involved in molding children through education.[15] This paradigm
recognized the role of both the family and society in molding children
and consequently forming societies. What was to be fought over in
the twentieth century was how much control each would have in determining their education.

Children and Nation Building in the United States

Operation Pedro Pan would be conceived in a uniquely American context that had its own political history. Founders of the United States believed that nations are built in part by imagining a hopeful future. Hope
required the possession of language.[16] The Founders advocated for
strong educational institutions that would produce an educated citizenry. Thomas Jefferson's view that knowledge of history enabled the
individual to participate and defend democracy drew from Enlightenment ideals of human possibility enacted through reason, liberty,
equality, and communality. Benjamin Rush, a doctor and early propo-
nent of free education, advocated creating a system of education that
would teach reading, writing, and arithmetic. The schools, which would

include women as well, would ingrain students with republicanism, creating a national character and uniting the country.[17] Unlike other Enlightenment scholars who placed a premium on individual freedom, Rush thought that pupils should be taught that they did not belong to themselves, but rather that they were public property. "Let him be taught to love his family, but let him be taught at the same time that he must forsake and even forget them when the welfare of his country requires it." The goal was "to convert men into republican machines. This must be done if we expect them to perform their parts properly in the great machine of the government of the state."[18] American culture also carried a Calvinist view of children that advocated hard work and discipline for the redemption of children.

Education, then, was the key to building a democratic nation. In contrast to Europe, the American nationality would not be based on blood lineage or by the intermingling of nationalities, but on unity of institutions, social habits, and ideals. Children's education would be the most important step in achieving this goal.[19] Early advocates of public education included Horace Mann, who asked, "Knowing, as we do, that the foundations of national greatness can be laid only in the industry, the integrity, and the spiritual elevation of the people, are we equally sure that our schools are forming the character of the rising generation upon the everlasting principles of duty and humanity?"[20] In a democracy, everyone had the power to govern, therefore every child needed to be educated. "Above all, children of a republic must be fitted for society as well as themselves," Mann wrote.[21]

In the twentieth century, as the rational project found its fullest expression, education became a central concern of the public domain. But it was not only the intellect that needed molding—morality itself was of prime importance. John Dewey clearly articulated that democracy could only function if children's moral compass and intellect were developed.[22] The goal was the construction of moral individuals who could live in a pluralistic society and engage in organic communication on free and equal terms. The American identity was tied to the American project of democracy.[23] Jean Piaget contributed to this perspective by defining the cognitive stages, through which children's moral development occurred, thus making the teaching of morality appropriate subject matter for schools.[24] The state could encroach on the turf of organized religion, and at times even work hand in hand with it, despite the constitutional separation of church and state.

But much of the debate about public education also had a less loftier motive in the assimilation of "undesirables," which included immigrants, particularly from Catholic backgrounds, as well as other "outsiders," such as Native Americans.[25] From the mid-1800s to the turn of the century, the United States witnessed an explosion in the number of new immigrants, many of them unaccompanied minors. In addition, there were increasing numbers of homeless children, some orphaned, others left behind by parents heading west. These children were portrayed as dirty menaces to society, as an infestation.[26]

The plight of these children moved Charles Loring Brace to found the Children's Aid Society and to launch an unprecedented program to place children from the streets of New York into homes throughout the Midwest. From 1854 to 1929, over 250,000 children were sent west, many on trains, thus giving this program the name "Orphan Trains." Brace idealized country living, and the program promised to expose them to fresh air and farm work that would help inculcate a strong Protestant work ethic and create worthy citizens.[27] A Calvinist vision guided his efforts. Predictably, the outcomes were mixed; in many cases, children became a newer version of indentured slaves, while others found truly loving and supporting adoptive parents.[28]

Not all the children were orphans. Brace simply assumed that many parents were not fit to raise a family and championed social reengineering "by breaking up the immiserated family of origin in order to 'save' the children."[29] Catholic social workers protested, claiming that children were being stripped of their religion. Still, the most problematic legacy of the program may be that it became acceptable to intervene in the lives of the poor on the grounds of protecting their children.[30] It unleashed a politicized notion of the working-class child without ties to a family, thereby making it acceptable for outside institutions to take charge. In the end, the Orphan Trains set a precedent for using family separations to save the children in order to make them future redeemers of the American Republic.[31]

The territorial imperative of Manifest Destiny was accompanied by a plan to Americanize young Native Americans. Policymakers viewed the older generation as incapable of being civilized. One government report stated: "It is a mere waste of time to attempt to teach the average adult Indian the ways of the white man. He can be tamed, and that is about all."[32] Progressives, however, argued that culture was not biological but learned, therefore children could be civilized. Through the Bureau of Indian Affairs, the federal government embarked on an ambitious program to "civilize" Native American children. The explicit aim of education for Indians was to provide basic skills, introduce them to civilized branches of knowledge, and Christianize them. By the late 1870s, the boarding school was established on reservations. Administrators of the programs were alarmed because they claimed that the children would revert back to their customs when they returned home, therefore they established the off-reservation boarding schools.[33] (A similar program was promoted in Australia, which lasted until the 1970s. There, more than 100,000 Aboriginal children, known today as the "Stolen Generation," were taken from their families to protect them from a disappearing race. Many had white fathers or grandfathers. These children were thought to be salvageable because of their mixed ancestry. They were placed in religious schools and then placed with families as servants and workmen.)[34] The schools for Native Americans shared an assumption similar to the one proposed by Charles Loring Brace: Children could be saved from their families. Native American cultures were deemed primitive because they fostered attachment to the tribe rather than the Christian family or the nation. Schooling would change them forever.[35] Ideally, at the end of the process they would be individual members of society rather than members of a tribe. It was immaterial whether or not they learned to read or write—the goal was to make them good citizens through participation in the community and earning an honest living.[36]

With the onset of World War I, the nation's anxiety about its identity and particularly about the loyalty of new immigrants to the American nation increased. A nativist backlash that included political, ethnic, and religious discrimination influenced debates about education.[37] Public education became the vehicle to Americanize those whom society deemed were not ready to become citizens.[38] The "Americanization" movement included political reformers who had a broad definition of democracy and wanted to be inclusive of immigrants, but it also included nativists who wanted immigrants to conform to their cultural and political definition of "Americanism."[39] They advocated for uniformity in education, including private schools, and insisted that only English be taught in all elementary schools.[40] However, both movements shared a basic commitment to using education as the vehicle to socialize children. And indeed, the progressive education movement contributed to making education compulsory and thus taking children from the factories into the classrooms.

African-American children have been conspicuously absent from the attempts to "Americanize" children from "marginal communities." This is reflective of the racist assumptions, present at the birth of the nation, that African-Americans were not really human beings. Segregation led to the creation of separate schools for blacks, and not until the world wars did the federal government begin taking an interest in their education. Army recruitment requirements included literacy and competency tests. Blacks consistently failed these, and the need for recruits spurred the federal government into action.[41] Later, international pressure combined with local civil rights activism forced the federal government to become involved in the desegregation of public schools throughout the nation.[42]

Children in the 1930s and 1940s: Refugees and Patriotism

In the early part of the twentieth century, children were seen as the most vulnerable victims of war, and as such, specific rescue efforts to save children were organized. These efforts served not only to secure the immediate safety of children but also to bolster the politics of the various factions involved in their rescue. For instance, there were unprecedented evacuations of unaccompanied minors during the civil war in Spain. Many of the bombings by Franco forces occurred in the Basque country, the zone captured in Pablo Picasso's *Guernica,* thus many children from this area were evacuated. The rescues were organized along the factional lines of the opposition. Each political group had its own underground network for the children of their sympathizers and each had its children's programs in different countries: the anarchists in France, the Communists in the Soviet Union. Other children were sent to Great Britain and Mexico.[43]

During World War II, resistance fighters spearheaded efforts to rescue children. Great Britain came to the aid of Jewish children, creating an underground network known as the Kindertransport to move them from Germany to England.[44] During the escalation of the bombing raids of Great Britain, the government organized a massive relocation of British children to the countryside and abroad.[45] Children were also uprooted during the Greek civil war of 1948; many were sent to camps in the Soviet Union, and the parents who resisted were shot by firing squads.[46] The specter of communists stealing children from their parents began to take root.

The effects of the separation between these children and their parents became the subject of study for Anna Freud and some of her associates, who documented how children slowly began to withdraw into themselves after even short separations from their mothers. In a dramatic film documentary that has become a classic of psychology, the researchers showed how a small toddler, left in an institution during the week to protect him from bombing raids, was transformed from being outgoing and happy to becoming a withdrawn and extremely sad child. He would lie in his crib for hours, staring off into space. The psychologists strongly recommended that children should not be separated from their mothers because they could suffer deep and sometimes irreparable damage. The documentary provoked a debate in England and eventually led to a revision of British emergency plans.[47] The children's advocates also influenced the post-Pearl Harbor debate in the United States over whether to evacuate U.S. children to the countryside.[48] The evacuation plans eventually elaborated did not include separating children from their mothers.[49] Postwar studies commissioned by the U.S. Army reinforced the perspective that separating children from mothers during wartime had negative effects on a child's emotional development.[50]

The war itself would also change the way society viewed children. For Italian Fascists, youth became the symbol of a new emerging nation. Athletic young men and women and young children became "Italy's Little Soldiers."[51] For German Fascists, youth was a political means to the creation of the Aryan society. They were considered undamaged goods who, if trained properly, could be the seeds of a new society. The Fascist program focused intensely on mobilizing young people in the name of creating a new race. Members of the Hitler-Jugend were the soldiers of an idea.[52] Hitler's Brownshirt youths did volunteer labor, hunted down Jews, and at the end of the war were deployed in suicide missions into Allied-occupied zones.[53]

In contrast, the focus on youth in the United States was on developing the individual since a more open society demanded strong, articulate, and educated individuals. The United States' entry into World War II was accompanied by a surge of patriotic fervor. There was an overwhelming sense of purpose and a conviction that the country, defending democracy abroad, was on the right side of history. The education of children assumed a more patriotic tone. By 1948, forty-four states had enacted statutes requiring "instruction on the Constitution in grade school."[54] Classes began with the Pledge of Allegiance and flags were unfurled in classrooms. Through the schools, children were encouraged to participate in war-related efforts such as Victory gardens, scrap collections, and the sale of war bonds. Children became aware of their country and its place in the world through these efforts.[55] According to the Child Study Association of America, "Belief in our children is the essence of democracy, of what we call our way of life."[56]

In 1950, Erik Erikson published *Childhood and Society*, a comparative study of childhood in various cultures. He wrote: "It is human to have a childhood; it is civilized to have an even longer one."[57] Child-hood thus is recognized as an important part of social development. The emphasis on developing the individual contributed to the emergence of childhood experts and the proliferation of child-rearing books. The way in which children became politicized, and how this affected their emotional development, would emerge as a branch of political science in the 1960s.[58]

By this time, society's views of children, and who had authority over them, had undergone a radical transformation. The state had achieved equal footing with the family. The state also took on the role of protecting children. Education was compulsory and child labor laws had been enacted. In addition, the rise of the nuclear family contributed to configuring unique ways in which children were cared for. Legal and cultural practices in which the state protected children at the same time families were their primary caretakers contributed to cementing the concept of childhood as a social category. The well-being of the nation depended on the well-being of its children.

The Cold War

Like many liberal thinkers, Karl Marx believed in the possibilities of radically transforming human beings and their societies.[59] It would take revolutions to bring forth the idea of reconstructing societies by using children as building blocks of the future. Indeed, the place of children in society became a point of contention during the Russian Revolution. Leo Tolstoy had popularized the myth of the happy child in his book *Childhood*, in which Nikolai Irten'ev, the narrator, reflects on his past to understand where he is in the present. The happy children of the gentry came to embody the very notion of what it meant to be Russian. In the fervor of the revolution, writers continued to perpetuate the tale of the happy children, but debated whether they belonged strictly in the past or whether it required a revolution to create happy children. Referring to the past, Leon Trotsky concluded that only a few had experienced a happy childhood.[60] In revolutionary rhetoric, every child, not just those of the noble gentry, held promise in the new Soviet Union.[61] Vladimir Lenin proclaimed that the youth would be faced with the actual task of creating a communist society;[62] that would be the purpose of their lives.[63] As such, an objective of the revolution was to convert schools from an instrument of rule by the bourgeoisie into an instrument for the overthrow of that rule.[64]

The role of children as makers of the future was also central in the political thought of another communist revolutionary leader, Mao Tsetung, who wrote: "Children are the masters of the new society."[65] Since children were seen as keys to the future, the quest to shape the future would necessarily include a struggle over the control of their minds. At the heart of this idea was a new socialist conception of the development of societies. In contrast to the French Revolution's idea of generations, specifically youth, as a catalyst for political change,[66] socialist thinkers suggested that class struggle was the motor of social development. Generational conflicts within families did not necessarily produce social changes. As such, children were not inevitably linked exclusively to their families. The state, therefore, could interrupt this generational process by educating the young in ways different than their parents had been educated.[67]

The active role of the communist state in the education of children ended up creating one of the sharpest conflicts of the Cold War.[68] In 1937, Pope Pius XI issued the encyclical, "On Atheistic Communism" (*Divini Redemptoris*), in which he stated that communism was incompatible with Christianity essentially because it posited a materialist view of the world. "Communism is intrinsically evil," he warned, "and no one who would save Christian civilization may cooperate with it in any manner whatsoever."[69] In practice, the encyclical said, communism strips parents of their authority and destroys the family; it denies parents the right to educate children, "for it is conceived as the exclusive prerogative of the community."[70]

It was in the educational arena that the first battles between the communist state and the Church were waged. Throughout the 1900s, the Catholic Church built an extensive network of schools in Europe.

In Hungary, in 1945, teaching manuals and textbooks were prefaced by the declaration, "In the light of modern science, nothing miraculous exists in the universe anymore, nor is there a place for God in it."[71] Three years later, the state nationalized all schools. The outspoken Cardinal Mindszenty of Budapest denounced the action, equating it to fascism: "The Hitler State educated its youths as little pagans. They came home from their youth camps to laugh cynically at their parents when they knelt in prayer."[72] By the end of the year, Hungarian police had arrested the cardinal. After weeks in the hands of the secret police, he "confessed" to charges of corruption. His trial would become an example of the communists' ability to brainwash. And the cardinal would become a world symbol of the struggle to save the minds of youth.

In the United States, Cardinal Mindszenty's trial had an immediate effect on the programs of the newly created Central Intelligence Agency. The agency was already concerned about what could happen if the Communists captured and brainwashed their agents abroad. If someone as outspoken and strong as the cardinal could be made to sign his own confession, what might happen to U.S. agents arrested in Communist countries? The Office of Strategic Affairs,[73] the CIA's predecessor, had already begun experiments into ways that agents could be trained to combat hypnotic suggestions, and the Cardinal Mindszenty's trials added urgency to these mind-control endeavors.[74] A series of experiments were initiated that included hypnosis and even testing drugs such as LSD on unwitting American citizens. Allen Dulles, CIA director, approved one such program known as the MKULTRA.[75] The term "brainwashing" was first coined by Edward Hunter, an agent who worked for Frank Wisner, then director of the Office of Policy Coordination, a special department within the CIA. Sidney Gottlieb, who worked with Wisner, would go on to play an important role in the Cuba project. While the program operated in secret, the CIA's preoccupation with brainwashing became a staple in the political rhetoric of the times.[76]

The most vulnerable minds were those of children. As such, the concern about their education now had a new dimension: protecting them from Communist brainwashing. The mass hysteria about communist infiltration and its threat to America's freedom reached shrill proportions on the topic of children's minds. Fueled by the McCarthy hearings, Congress jumped on the bandwagon. Members of the House Committee on Un-American Activities published a pamphlet that outlined "110 Things You Should Know About Communism and Education." It began: "This is to tell you what the masterminds of Communism have planned for your child in the name of education." Parents were warned that their children would be plucked from their nurseries and put in uniforms. The Communist would put a flag with a hammer and sickle in one of their child's hands, and a gun in the other. They would be sent to conquer the world. Instruction manuals on how to combat communist influence in education were published, including one on how to revamp the American education system.[77] A national presidential commission was created "to nurture the free, rational, and responsible men and women without whom our kind of society cannot endure."[78]

One of the strongest allies of the U.S. government's fight against communism became the Catholic Church. Communism was seen as the antithesis of a Catholic way of life that valued family and private education. American Catholics naturally followed the Vatican's teachings.[79] However, their virulent anti-Communism can in part be explained by the position of the Catholic Church in U.S. society.[80] The Catholic Church had never quite been accepted as truly "American." It was viewed as a church of immigrants and an institution controlled by a "foreign power," Rome. Indeed, the infamous Orphan Trains of the late 1800s and early 1900s had been a way to take 150,000 poor, mainly Catholic immigrants' children out of urban areas, placing them in "American" homes where they could become acclimatized to a new culture.[81] Through its anti-Communist stance, the Catholic Church could show how American it truly was. Catholic schools joined in the hyperpatriotism of public schools. And through many of its charitable organizations, the church began to dedicate its energies to saving refugees of Communist countries.

The Cuban Insurrection and Youth

The Cuban Revolution occurred at the margins of the Cold War. Radical nationalism and social justice, not pro or anti-Communism, defined its political discourse at the start.[82] The revolution rallied youth, the activists, and appealed for support with allusions to the importance of children in a new Cuban society. Castro often evoked the nineteenth-century nationalist hero José Martí, perhaps best known throughout Latin America for his essays and the monthly children's magazine, *La Edad de Oro* (The Golden Age), he published. In its introductory issue, Martí had written: "We are working for children because they are the ones who know how to love, because they are the hope of the world."[83] Martí, a modernist, linked the formation of an independent sovereign nation to the education of its people: "The happiest country is the one which has best educated its sons, both in the instruction of thought and the direction of their feelings."[84]

Martí also advocated, as other modernists did, that in order to have democratic countries, its children had to be educated. "The best way to defend our rights is to know them well. A nation of educated men will always be a nation of free men."[85] Literacy and education was a means to hold government accountable. "When all men know how to read, all men will know how to vote . . . ignorance is the guarantee of political misconduct."[86] In addition, Martí was a strong advocate of a nationally based public education system.

Revolutionary leaders also promoted equal educational opportunities, particularly for the poor.[87] Again, references to Martí framed this debate. In his well-known speech, "History Will Absolve Me," Fidel Castro stated: "A revolutionary government would undertake the integral reform of the educational system . . . with the idea of educating those generations which will have the privilege of living in a happier land."[88]

Unlike the United States, in Cuba in the 1950s there were few social or political references to communism as a threat to education. Rather, the educational debate centered on the distribution of services and on the nationalist content of instruction. Although Cuba had an extensive public and private school system in urban areas, rural schools were often one-room huts with palm-thatched roofs and dirt floors. According to the 1953 census, only slightly more than 50 percent of school-age children attended school. In 1959, 65,000 students—mostly white and middle class—were enrolled in Catholic schools. The major universities included the private Universidad Católica de Santo Tomás de Villanueva, with an enrollment of 1,500, and three public institutions: Santiago, Santa Clara, and Havana, by far the largest, with 17,000 students.

While private schools were permitted to teach religious education, public education had a strictly lay character. Cuban education had been part of the nationalist project. The Constitution of 1940 stated: "All education, public or private, will be inspired in a spirit of Cubanness and human solidarity, helping form, in the conscience of the educated, love of fatherland, its democratic institutions and all those who have fought for them." The constitution stipulated that those who taught courses in Cuban literature, history, geography, civics, and the constitution, whether in public or private schools, had to be Cuban by birth, and texts had to be written by authors who were born in Cuba.[89]

Since the 1930s, students had played a critical role in the political life of the country. The insurrection against Batista was no exception. University students formed one of the leading revolutionary organizations, Directorio Estudiantil.[90] Many young people, particularly Catholics, enthusiastically supported the revolution. Unlike many in the past hierarchy of the Church who had closer links to Spain than to the island, the younger Catholics were calling for a renovation of their country and their church along more nationalist lines and in support of Christian social justice. Many Catholic organizations such as Federación de la Juventud Cubana, Hermanos de La Salle, Agrupación Católica Universitaria of the Jesuits, Juventud Acción Católica and its labor arm, Juventud Obrera Católica, actively joined in the underground struggle against Batista.[91]

Catholics had been part of the process of drafting the Constitution of 1940 with the hierarchy issuing a document outlining amendments they were interested in including in the final version.[92] They had successfully advocated invoking the name of God in the preamble of the document and in protecting the rights of parents to choose the kind of education they wanted for their children, thereby protecting the existence of Catholic schools. However, they failed to convince delegates to include a provision to teach religion in public schools, a plank they had lobbied for by arguing that studies in the United States showed that the majority of juvenile delinquents had not taken religion classes.[93] So certain were the Catholic supporters of the revolution of their legitimate claim to be part of the future of their country that they advocated amending the constitution to allow the teaching of religion in public schools.[94] After all, Fidel Castro was a graduate of Belén, the Jesuit school, and he had promised a supportive clergy to introduce religious education in public schools.[95]

Controlling Children's Education

After the triumph of the revolution, the new government embraced the goal of transforming society, even as the revolutionary rhetoric called for the restoration of democracy.[96] In order to accomplish this, the legacy of the past and its influence on the present and the future had to be minimized. The revolutionary leaders turned to repression as a way to deal with those representing the past. This took the form of summary trials of opponents, jailings, and executions and, more massively, the Committees to Defend the Revolution, the block organizations that served as the eyes and ears of the government. The principal functions of the committees were to watch and report "counterrevolutionary" activities. At school, children were encouraged to denounce their parents if they were involved in opposition activities.

In contrast, the education of the children would be the key to the future and the means for laying the groundwork for charting a new path.[97] Fidel Castro harped on this theme repeatedly: "We should think about our children. They are the society of tomorrow. We have to care for them, watch over them, for they are the pillars on which truly beautiful and worthwhile projects are built. I repeat, we have to think of them more than in our selves. The task of this generation is to create for the future."[98]

Unlike their parents, children had virgin minds.[99] Thus the view of childhood was defined within a patriarchal vision that ascribed sexuality to the activity of education and control. For if their minds are virgin, then it is the role of the state to penetrate and control. Educational institutions were critical to successfully mold children's minds. A social battle would be waged in order to set a new direction for education. Military barracks were turned into schools. Fidel Castro declared: "Why have we been able to turn barracks into schools? Because since the first of January, from the triumph of the revolution, each school has become a barrack of the revolution."[100] The guerrilla culture, forged in the armed struggle, would permeate everything. The labor force was organized in "brigades," as were solidarity movements outside the country.[101] It was, in fact, as if the armed struggle had never ended.

The struggle over control of education and knowledge took on a certain urgency, for these were the vehicles for reconstructing an entire society. Knowledge and who would be entitled to disseminate as well as acquire it became a question of political loyalty.[102] An individual's political position would in turn become increasingly important for social mobility. Even as children acquired a central location in the political symbolism of the revolution, their education became the key to success in the post-revolutionary society.

The Anti-Castro Opposition and Children: Fear of Communist Brainwashing

Castro's radicalization of the revolution and his attempts to centralize power were met with stiff opposition from many of those who had fought against Batista. Many started organizing to take back the revolution. Opposition forces claimed that Castro's purpose of converting military barracks into schools was to use children as shields against an invasion.[103] Their concerns came to include not only the physical safety of children but also their minds. Soon enough, the theme of saving the children from Communist brainwashing became central to the public discourse of opposition groups inside Cuba and of the U.S. government, which opposed Castro from the start. It was a theme familiar to then-CIA director Allen Dulles and other U.S. officials always in search of ammunition to fight "Communist-line indoctrination."[104]

As early as July 1959, Wayne Smith, who was assigned to the U.S. embassy in Havana, reported to Washington that "several schools for political indoctrination had started to operate. . . . Raúl Castro had commented that the schools would coordinate ideas and that good revolutionaries would all *think alike*." Smith warned that the establishment of the schools in which to mold the political thought of the nation smacked strongly of totalitarianism and did not inspire confidence in the future of freedom of thought in Cuba.[105] This theme also made great headlines. In March 1960, *U.S. News and World Report* published a spread of photographs of Cuban children in uniforms marching, practicing judo, and studying: "In class Luis is mindful of Castro's warning: Children who do not study are not good revolutionaries."[106] And on June 8, 1960, the *New York Times* reported, "The pattern of training is similar to that used by many totalitarian governments. It includes indoctrination in schools, on radio and in the press; military training from seven years of age; a hate campaign, this time directed against the United States; the organization of work brigades for boys 14–18; and meetings and fiestas, all with a political purpose."[107] At the end of the first year of the revolution, *Acción Cubana*, one of many opposition groups, which published a newspaper in Luxembourg, denounced what it claimed to be the state manipulation of children: "The Cuban Communists have gone beyond what the Spanish ones did. They have forced children to commit crimes by participating in their Roman circuses. They have forced them to testify in their parents' trials. And worse, they have put uniforms on them and given them arms and made them promise to give up their lives for the revolution."[108] Some of these allegations were true; children's organizations were being militarized.

Protecting the sanctity of the Church and parental rights over children became a key rallying point for many opposition groups that worked with the CIA. From early 1959, a group that had worked with the 26 of July Movement began organizing an opposition network. Manuel Artime, who would later play a central role in the Bay of Pigs invasion, was one of its leaders.[109] Artime, a handsome medical school graduate from Oriente, had joined the rebel army as a young man. He had been an active supporter of the revolution and, in fact, held various leadership positions in Agrupación Católica Universitaria, the Jesuit organization, including the presidency of its student group in Havana.[110] During the insurrection, he joined a small group called Liga de Acción Revolucionaria. A Jesuit priest urged him to join the 26 of July Movement, but he became disillusioned soon after the triumph of the rebels and began organizing an opposition group. On November 7, 1959, *Avance,* an opposition paper, announced that Artime was resigning from the rebel army. A few days later, Artime was taken to the American embassy and a gentleman called "William" helped him escape the country on a Honduran freighter.[111]

The CIA had bought into the strategy of promoting a young student leader to head the opposition to Castro.[112] According to Justo Carrillo, who was named to the executive committee of a CIA-organized group called Frente Democrático Revolucionario, Jesuit priests, including Avery Dulles, who was CIA director Allen Dulles's cousin, were instrumental in advocating for this strategy. By the beginning of 1960, Artime had become one of the CIA's most valuable assets; indeed, he became known as its Golden Boy.[113]

The United States was worried that a direct intervention in Cuba might produce a backlash in Latin America. This concern was outlined in a State Department and United States Information Agency directive sent on September 15, 1959, to all American diplomatic and consular corps: "It remains important, however, particularly at this stage, that any awakening public skepticism about Castro retain the appearance of being an indigenous Latin American reaction."[114] As to the Cuban opposition, steps to be taken included the formation of an "exile" opposition whose slogan might be "Restore the Revolution" that had been lost to a new dictatorship of Cuba subject to Sino-Soviet influence. While the political opposition was to include former politicians and Castro cabinet members, the CIA was particularly interested in promoting young people loyal to the ideals of the revolution. Former Batista supporters would be kept at bay. A coalition of organizations was brought together. Frente Democrático, as it became known, was organized under the directive of President Eisenhower, who on March 17, 1960, had ordered the CIA "to bring about the replacement of the Castro regime with one more devoted to the true interests of the Cuban people and more acceptable to the U.S. in such a manner as to avoid the appearance of U.S. intervention."[115] By the end of the year, the Movimiento de Recuperación Revolucionaria, an underground military group with close ties to the CIA, was organized and Artime had become its head.

One of the main focuses of Artime's group was Cuban youth. While the CIA wanted to encourage the men to fight, they wanted to establish a program "to convert every woman and child in exile into an active fighter for the battle of ideas."[116] An underground agent described as an "important leader of Manuel Artime's MRR-Resistencia Cívica" noted that recent stepping up of the drive to indoctrinate Cuban youths through the literacy campaign and the creation of pioneer groups was an indication that Castro thought his days were numbered and that he was concentrating on leaving behind a large number of our young people indoctrinated with the Communist line.[117] Another member of Artime's organization said, "We had our own plans . . . we were going to greatly influence Cuban youth."[118] According to the CIA's Bernard Baker, "Manolo spoke of having to start anew with the Cuban youth that had been indoctrinated with Fidel's communism. They had to be disintoxicated. He told me that his first priority [was] to change them into future citizens by schools, jobs, and patriotic organizations."[119] The education of youth would continue to be central to Artime's thinking. In 1964, he pleaded with the pope to support their underground movement against Castro so that parents once again could have the choice of educating their children in Catholic schools.[120] In the meantime, the CIA did set up a "university," a program to "prepare young democratic students to be leaders on their return to their country."[121]

As political opposition was organized—complete with military and propaganda arms—the control of the youth became a central theme. The draft platform of Artime's group began by asking Cubans: "Do you really love your country, your religion, your family, your liberty, and your human dignity?" It warned that under communism freedom of religion is lost.[122] And it raised fears about state control of the education process.

In June 1960, the CIA sponsored a speaking tour for Artime in various Latin American capitals.[123] He was to disseminate the platform throughout Latin America as a way of isolating Cuba from the hemisphere. Given that the revolutionary government had begun interfering in the activities of the student federation, a call for the elimination of government meddling in the development of the plans and activities of Cuban university students was among its major themes.[124] Traveling throughout Latin America, Artime emphasized the effects that the new regime was having on Cuban youth.[125] His message, reported to the press in Santiago de Chile in April 1960, warned that the Castro regime had created a children's militia in which the youngsters were educated in Marxism and marched in the streets cheering "*Uno-dos-tres-cuatro-viva Fidel Castro Ruz.*"[126]

The theme would not be lost to other organizations. In a Frente Revolucionario Democrático pamphlet entitled "Twenty Questions on the Truth About Cuba," parents were asked why should we be concerned about the education of our children. The answer was: "The children, from 6–15 will be educated by the state not their parents. Thus by taking advantage of the innocence of children they will inculcate the materialist and diabolical ideas of communism."[127] The protection of children's innocence would become one of the contested arenas for the next five decades. Radical changes in Cuba, combined with this U.S.-

backed propaganda campaign, would contribute to the spread of fear among Cuban parents and underground activists of what could happen to their children. In the fervor of the revolution and its aftermath, many had come to believe that their family and national destinies depended on the political education of their children.

2

The Military Origins of
Operation Pedro Pan

Throughout 1960, the situation on the island of Cuba deteriorated. Arrests and executions of opposition fighters increased as U.S.-backed groups escalated their campaign against the regime. The underground activists needed the ability to leave the island quickly, and many were afraid for their children. They feared that if they were imprisoned or killed they might suffer the fate of Spanish children who during the Civil War were sent to Russia.[1] Some approached James Baker, the director of Ruston Academy, an American school in Havana, for help.

The Bakers were part of a 5,000-member American colony in the capital. The colony, which had been steadily growing since the early 1900s, reflected the deep economic ties between Cuba and the United States.[2] Right before the revolution, U.S. investments on the island totaled about $800 million, and Cuba was largely dependent on the United States for its foreign trade. In fact, 60 percent of its exports (mostly sugar and tobacco) went to the United States and 75 percent of its imports originated in this country. Many Americans were owners of sugar refineries. Others, like the Bakers' good friends the Everharts, had tobacco ranches in Pinar del Río. And still others worked for U.S. corporations like Sears and Esso. Another 200,000 Americans visited the island every year.

Many of the Americans who lived in Havana were members of the Havana Yacht Club, which had whites-only rules that effectively barred black Cubans from admission. Unlike many American business owners, who were mostly interested in making a profit, the Bakers were educators with a mission to bring democracy to Cuba. In the 1950s, they were highly regarded by Cubans who were fighting against Batista.

"They knew that I was first of all for Cuba, against Batista, and that I was for the future of Cuba and the establishment of democracy," Baker recalled.[3]

Many years later, in his home in Ormond Beach, Florida, Baker remembered how tense it was right after the triumph of the revolution. One day, a parent, active in the underground opposition, visited him. The father had two sons at Ruston and was afraid that something would happen to them.[4] He was haunted by the memory of the Spanish civil war, in which children had been used as hostages. The same could happen in Cuba. Thus he could only continue fighting if he knew his sons were safe. Could Baker get them a scholarship in the United States?

An American Colony in Havana

Cuban parents chose Jim Baker partially because of who he was within the American colony of Havana. Baker was fond of telling everyone that he thought of himself as an American-Cuban, just as friends from the island would later refer to themselves as Cuban-Americans. Cuba had become his home. With his wife, Sybil, he had first moved to the island in 1930 to work as assistant director to Hiram Ruston, who had founded the academy to help Cubans gain entry into American colleges. With the outbreak of World War II in 1936, the Bakers returned to the United States. But in 1944, they moved back: Ruston's health was failing, and he wanted to leave the school in Baker's hands. When Ruston died a year later, Baker became director and turned the school into a not-for-profit educational foundation.

The academy grew into a school for the children of Havana's elite. About half of its students were Americans whose parents were the owners of Havana-based businesses or U.S. embassy employees. Some of those parents would become principal architects of U.S. policies toward Cuba, most notably David Atlee Phillips, who became the CIA's coordinator of anti-Castro propaganda in 1959. The other half of the student body was composed of Cuban children whose parents wanted them to learn English and later attend university in the United States.

James Baker, headmaster, Ruston Academy, 1960. From Ruston Academy
yearbook.

Mr. Baker, as his students called him, had a dream of bringing the United States and Cuba closer together by providing cross-cultural educational opportunities. "My first experiences teaching at Ruston Academy made me appreciate more fully the democratic traditions and helped me understand the profound ways in which the spirit of community cooperation and service had contributed to the development of our country," he said. "I saw that by sharing these values with Cubans, the school could contribute to the development of democracy in Cuba."[5]

In keeping with this vision, the school promoted open discussions for the public and for students. Every month Ruston sponsored talks on cutting-edge pedagogical and developmental questions. Lectures on such topics as "Independence in Adolescence" were held in English and Spanish. Parents and students were encouraged to think critically about family relations, their society, and its politics. Former students like Nati Revueltas remember an open political environment at Ruston.[6] There was an active debate team and even a course called "The Problems of Democracy," not a common subject in Cuban schools.

But while Ruston Academy was committed to teaching civic responsibility and democratic values, Baker found that it was difficult to discuss these publicly in Cuba during the late 1950s era of the Batista military regime. The search for democratic alternatives had become synonymous with support for *los rebeldes*, with whom Baker and many Cubans, including his students, sympathized. Batista represented the antithesis of democracy, and Baker increasingly became a support person to those fighting in the underground opposition against him. The Bakers felt strongly that the United States should not support Batista.

Paul Bethel, public relations spokesperson for the U.S. embassy in Cuba in the late 1950s and author of *The Losers*, a book published in 1969 that struck a chord among Cuban exiles and many American readers, described these Americans:

Upper and middle class, for the most part, they belonged to clubs frequented by Cubans of the same social and economic strata, and

joined their friends in attempts to oust Batista. American businessmen hid anti-Batista activists in their offices and in their homes,
and contributed money to buy arms and food for urban guerrillas.[7]

Bethel added an interesting observation, not noted by historians of
the revolution, that American women in particular were at the forefront
of the battle against Batista. Bethel mentioned specifically Maraida
Arensberg,[8] assistant to Jim Baker at Ruston Academy, who worked
closely with Elena Mederos, a civic leader and close friend of the Bakers. He also referred to Louise Smith, wife of Gilbert Smith, owners of
Harry Smith Travel Agency, who hid rebels in her home. The Smiths
lived next door to the Bethels in Miramar, an upscale neighborhood of
Havana. All would come to play key roles much later in the exodus of
the children.

Other Americans swept up in the romanticism of the underground
would also risk their lives in the anti-Batista movement.[9] William Morgan, a young American marine, became a commander of the rebel army,
and Gerry Patrick Hemming a sergeant. Both became disillusioned
and ended up fighting against Castro. Morgan was executed by a firing
squad; Hemming escaped and continued to organize armed raids from
Florida. He would also raise serious concerns to his American handlers
about the evacuation of children because he felt that Cuban intelligence
was using them as a way to trace the parents of the underground. His
view of the program was that it was a means for the CIA to control underground opposition.[10]

In March 1957, Victor Buehlman and Charles Ryan, age seventeen,
and Michael Garvey, fifteen, ran away from their families at the Guantánamo naval base to join the Cuban rebels fighting in the Sierra Maes-
tra. Buehlman's father was the commander of the base.[11] The Bishop of
Santiago, who was sympathetic to the rebels, finally helped bring them
home three months later. The boys were thoroughly impressed with the
rebeldes and reported that they had spent a lot of time with Castro. Despite Buehlman Sr.'s attempt to silence them at a press conference, they
told reporters in Santiago about their experiences in the mountains and

predicted that "the Cuban army won't get them because they don't like to shoot their own countrymen." A reporter summarized the incident, *clearly* stating: "The parents lost three young teenage boys in February. In May *propagand-* they had returned to them three thoroughly indoctrinated revolutionary spokespersons."[12]

CIA agent William Patterson and Oscar Guerra, the American consul in Santiago, were personally sympathetic to the rebels and advocated pulling support from Batista. In Havana, Richard Cushing, the public affairs officer of the American embassy, and Bill Bowdler, political analyst, hid some of Castro's underground leaders in their respective homes.[13] However, it should be understood that other American officials, like Bethel, were adamantly opposed to the *rebeldes*, and not all Americans sympathized with them. According to a 1958 Department of State report, harassment of American citizens and destruction of their property had increased, resulting in significant losses estimated at five million dollars. Also fueling criticism of the rebels was the dramatic kidnapping of forty-seven U.S. citizens and three Canadians living in Santiago in July 1958. The kidnapping was a result of a military order issued by Raúl Castro, Fidel Castro's brother, calling for the detention of "all North American male citizens in his zone." In addition, in August 1958, the rebels had begun levying taxes on sugar mills in the liberated zones in the eastern sections of the island.[14]

Yet Batista's brutal repression convinced many Americans that the rebel cause was just. Eventually, those sympathetic to the rebels succeeded in exerting tremendous anti-Batista pressure on the American embassy. They were relieved when, in 1959, Philip Bonsal replaced Earl Smith, the American ambassador who had actively supported Batista.[15] In contrast, Bonsal reached out to the *rebeldes*.

Unfulfilled Promises: Disaffection and Opposition

For the Bakers, as well as for millions of Cubans, the triumph of the revolution was a watershed in their lives—a moment filled with excitement and promise. There was a resurgence of national pride mixed with anticipation of the emergence of a new society. The editor of Ruston's 1959 yearbook wrote: "This has been our most glorious year. Cuba is free! If before we did not study hard enough, maybe it was because of the intranquility of spirit provoked by the Tyranny's action; now we understand that our supreme duty is to study to help our country and become useful professionals for her in the future."[16] Fidel Castro, the principal leader of the largest rebel groups, had promised that elections would be held in ninety days. The Bakers and many of their American friends now believed that they could live the rest of their lives in Cuba.

citation?

The first months of Castro's new government were chaotic. Elections were not held. And despite overtures from Ambassador Bonsal to the *rebeldes*, relations between Cuba and the United States quickly deteriorated. Jim Baker, however, recommended caution and patience. He understood the complexities of the situation. Castro had come to power with the help of many organizations that were deeply concerned about the direction that his government was taking. Baker realized that one of Castro's most serious defects was his tendency to blame others for situations created by his own mistakes. The United States should not react to his taunts, he believed. Don't give him a scapegoat, Baker urged friends in Congress. The Communists would be the first ones to pounce on the United States for actions such as lowering the sugar quota. "Above all other considerations," he wrote to Senator Wayne Morse, a family friend and Batista critic, "is the basic one that Cuba is important to us in our defense against communism in this hemisphere."[17]

Whatever civil institutions existed in 1959 Cuba were destroyed, among them the court system. Opponents of the revolutionary government were summarily sent to the firing squad. By January 13, 1959, only thirteen days after the inception of the new regime, an estimated two hundred persons had been tried, found guilty, and executed.[18] On February 16, 1959, Castro publicly stated that the military tribunals had executed more than three hundred people. Until then, the death penalty had been prohibited by the Cuban constitution. The Spanish had left behind a bitter history of governmental use of physical violence against the island, and Cubans abhorred the death penalty. On October 28, 1959, Article 174 of the new criminal code granted revolutionary tribunals jurisdiction over any crime, criminal or civil, committed by a person classified as "counterrevolutionary."[19] By October 1960, estimates of political prisoners ranged from 3,000 to 6,000.

Bill Bowdler, who worked at the American embassy as a political analyst, was a personal friend to many who had supported Castro. By 1960, he was aiding the anti-Castro opposition. In December of that year, he wrote:

> The decline in the unprecedented popularity of the Castro regime began as soon as he assumed power. The execution of close to 600 alleged "war criminals" during the first three months of his government earned the enmity of their families and raised the first big doubt in the minds of many Cubans regarding the nature of the regime.[20]

Bowdler had witnessed the moral and material support given to the revolution by a middle and upper class mainly interested in the restoration of the constitution and a return to democracy after Batista. But the anti-democratic turns taken by the new regime spread disaffection.

The supporters of the revolution were emotionally and intellectually dedicated to the proposition that Batista had to be overthrown in order to return to a state of constitutional normality and to usher in a period of political, economic, and social reform. A not inconsiderable portion also looked for a more independent Cuba politically, economically, and culturally, particularly in its relations with the United States. But they did not envisage the radical type of reforms, which had been instituted, or the divination into the Soviet bloc.[21]

Many Ruston teachers and parents had actively fought in the underground against Batista, interrupting their plush lifestyle and risking their lives for a chance to create a democratic government. The 1959 Ruston yearbook was dedicated to "all those who contributed to the triumph of the Cuban revolution." But the dedication went on to warn, "Let us not permit that the noble objectives that stimulated the struggle for a better Cuba be frustrated."[22]

The Bakers' close friend Elena Mederos was appointed to the first cabinet as Minister of Social Welfare. Early on, she began to sense that Castro did not have a commitment to a democratic society, yet persevered, hoping for a change. But by 1960, she and several other cabinet members decided to resign. Mederos was dismissed the day she was to announce her resignation. This event dashed the Bakers' hope that democratic change could still occur. Bethel, for his part, was not surprised. He noted what a strange twist history had taken as two former *rebelde* supporters, Mederos and Louise Smith, briefed a reporter of the *New York Times* on the horrors of the new regime.[23]

As repression on the island increased, many of those who had struggled against Batista began organizing against Castro. The United States was ready to support them, as were many of the Americans in Cuba. By the end of 1960, the *Times of Havana,* which had refused to take subsidies from Batista, took a stand against the Castro dictatorship.[24] Ruston parents once again, as they had during the revolutionary insurrection, approached the Bakers for help. This time, they wanted to send their children to the United States. Baker also knew of parents in the underground who were afraid that if they were jailed or executed their children would have no one to take care of them. Parents of older boys feared that their sons would become active in the opposition and that they would be jailed or sent to a firing squad.

By mid-1960, the American embassy was reporting that many minors were being condemned for so-called counterrevolutionary crimes simply for having anti-government pamphlets in their possession. The sentences were harsh. In one case, three youths, nineteen and twenty years old, were given sentences of ten to twelve years. There were rumors that a boy, allegedly twelve years of age and accused of being a counterrevolutionary, was shot to death by guards in Puerto Boniato prison. Bitón Navarro, a sixteen-year-old, was murdered by guards at La Cabaña.[25]

But Baker's fears were not only about the physical safety of the youngsters; he was also afraid of Communist indoctrination. The Cuban government had already announced a program to send Cuban students to the Soviet Union. Fidel's son, Fidelito, would join the group. Finally, in November 1960, Baker agreed to contact a friend at the embassy and fly to the United States in search of help.

Washington and Refugee Policy: National Security Needs

Jim Baker would find support for his efforts, since U.S. refugee policy at the time was sensitive to both the propaganda and military needs of the Cold War. The policy, based on President Truman's national security doctrine, placed most refugee matters squarely in the framework of the rivalry between the West and the Soviet Union, and made provision for both propaganda and military needs. The Displaced Persons Act allowed for the entrance of up to 15,000 escapees from the USSR, and the 1951 Mutual Security Act allocated funds for the program.

As a way to circumvent Congress's quotas, the CIA worked with private relief organizations. The agency would funnel monies to these organizations and they in turn would sponsor émigrés. Leo Cherne, of the International Rescue Committee, had been involved with CIA programs aimed at preventing re-defection of Soviets by providing extensive aid once they arrived in the United States.[26] The CIA again tapped the International Rescue Committee to help with Cuban refugees.[27] In the next year the IRC would not only help with defections and resettlement of refugees, they would be given the authority to waive visas as well. The other major recipients of government grants included the National Catholic Welfare Conference, which in 1960 was receiving 30 percent of all government contracts aimed at assisting refugees.[28] Refugee movements were an integral part of the Cold War, and Cuban refugees were certainly no exception. Almost all government officials active in refugee problems counted on the propaganda value of the escapees at some level. The Cuban Revolution, although not yet officially supported by Cuban Communists, was perceived nonetheless as a threat to U.S. hegemony in the Caribbean. In the context of the Cold War, any challenge to the United States would weaken its power in relation to the Soviet Union. U.S. foreign and refugee policy proceeded accordingly.

The refugee issue engendered a rich debate regarding what criteria should be used in implementing the policy. The CIA, the Psychological Strategy Board of the National Security Council, members of Congress, and the State and Justice Departments debated whether "refugee programs should be generous, or restricted to leaders who could aid the resistance, provide intelligence or otherwise discredit the USSR."[29] Frank Wisner of the CIA was especially adamant about the agency's need to have open immigration channels. In 1950, the CIA approached Congress for permission to bring in 15,000 people from Iron Curtain countries. But Congress reduced the number to 500, and defined admittees as persons who could aid the national interest. Thus, much concern centered on the information that potential refugees could provide.

High-level defections were also encouraged. Manolo Ray, who had been Castro's first Minister of Public Works, received tourist visas from the U.S. embassy for his wife, children, and nursemaid to come to the United States.[30] So did José Miró Cardona, whose departure from Cuba was reported to the Undersecretary of State by Ambassador Bonsal.[31] Both Ray and Miró Cardona later became members of the CIA's Revolutionary Council. Another example is the case of the former president of the Cuban Supreme Court, Emilio Menéndez, which was reported in a Department of State telegram on December 19, 1960: "Dr. Menéndez wishes to remain in the U.S. with family which reportedly is now there. Given his prominence and decision to break with the Castro regime for reasons specified in his letter of resignation, the embassy believes it is in our national interest to allow him stay in the U.S."[32]

Others, however, were worried about their families. For instance, in October 1960 the State Department sent a telegram drafted by Robert Stevenson, of the U.S. embassy in Havana, asking for help in evaluating Dr. Angel H. Poba's request for defection. Poba would only consider this if his wife and two children were safely out of the country. The telegram stated: "Seems to have useful intelligence information but difficult to evaluate without evaluation of man himself. Can embassy help?"[33] Officially, the State and Defense Departments were to be in charge of these persons, but in reality the CIA ran the Iron Curtain refugee program.

June Cobb, an American who worked in Fidel Castro's office, was informing the CIA about potential defectors. In a note scribbled on June 7, 1960, she wrote that Juan Orta, the chargé d'affaires of the office of the prime minister "had a very positive experience in Miami when he was exiled during the revolution. Wants to send his children to study in U.S."[34] The agency was bringing in Cubans who could provide intelligence and work on covert programs.

The "visa problem," as it was referred to in several unclassified State Department documents, was raised at another high-level government meeting. A Memorandum of Conversation dated November 29, 1960, entitled "Activities Against the Castro Regime" noted:

> Cuban refugees arriving in this country were most reluctant to issue strong denunciatory blasts against the Castro regime so long as their immediate families remained in Cuba. For this reason, it was frequently of great operational interest to expedite visas for family members, however it was usually very difficult if not impossible to arrange such matters. The standard answer received was that another office, another department or another agency of the United States had jurisdiction.[35]

In the same memo, a request is made to increase aid to the refugees so that they do not exhaust military supplies for their families:

> The latter are arriving without clothing or personal effects or funds. On humanitarian grounds they must be taken care of and the Frente Democrático Revolucionario frequently "stakes them." This represents a strain on its funds, however, and it should be

borne in mind that if other resources were available to care for the refugees it would help to ease the drain in FDR funds and allow them to be used in more productive ways.[36]

In addition, Cubans arriving in Miami on tourist visas had begun to worry about their legal status in the United States. This was suggested in a Department of State Memorandum of Conversation held March 23, 1960, between a group of Cubans (whose names are classified) and Charles Torrey, from the State Department's Office of Caribbean and Mexican Affairs. Among the various requests presented by the group was a plea to help "the great number of Cuban exiles in the U.S. on visitor's visas or illegally."[37]

By the end of 1960, more than 80,000 Cubans had left for the United States. Although facilitated by U.S. policy, the trips were undertaken initially with little fanfare. According to an analysis of the situation in Santiago de Cuba written by Wollam, a consulate official, the demand for visas was increasing for a variety of reasons:

> Some wish to get away from the possibility of another revolution, others . . . *in case.* Others think that the government is going to place further restrictions on travel, despite official denials. Still others are leaving because of the economic squeeze as a result of revolutionary laws. . . . Some persons are going to considerable length to make trips appear casual, e.g. splitting up families or going by different routes to the U.S. or other countries. This and leaving without publicity are attempted because they do not want to attract attention which they think might bring intervention or confiscation of their properties.[38]

Castro's regulations made it increasingly difficult to leave. Travelers had to have a military exit permit along with a U.S. visa, and the airline ticket had to be purchased in American dollars. Part of the process of obtaining an exit permit included a household inventory. A guard would come to the house and document all the belongings, from curtains to pianos. If any of it was gone on the day of departure, the exit permit was revoked. Very little money could be taken out of the country. These rules were constantly changing. On the other hand, U.S. immigration visas were almost impossible to obtain, since these required guarantees from a relative in the United States that the relative would take financial responsibility for the refugee. The application required proof of employment, financial status, income tax receipts, and other documentation.[39] People went to the embassy to secure tourist visas instead.

In November 1960, a *New York Times* reporter noted that almost a thousand Cubans were arriving at the embassy each week. So many minor government officials were fleeing that the Cuban government required them to obtain written permission from their superiors to leave the island "for a visit," since they could not say that they were emigrating.[40] According to Ambassador Bonsal, "During these months the most tangible opposition to Castro was the rush of Cubans to leave their homeland."[41] Bonsal wrote of the heavy burden on the services of the American Consulate General, which was called upon to handle tens of thousands of applications for admission to the United States. The U.S. policy was to make it as easy as possible for Cubans to gain entry. "The regulations were stretched as far as they would stretch. Yet Bonsal's assessment was that Castro, for his part, was not sorry to see these people go."[42] In fact, though Castro had always maintained that anyone wanting to leave Cuba could do so, he now saw that the exodus was creating a serious brain drain for Cuba, and authorities began turning back professional men and technicians at the airport.

In the United States, there was political pressure on President Eisenhower to aid Cuban refugees.[43] American business and civic leaders meeting with State Department representatives expressed their feelings that the government should not only act on humanitarian grounds when it came to the refugees but remember the potential consequences of giving them a poor welcome. Business leaders feared that if the refugees had a difficult time in the United States, they would return to Cuba with great bitterness in their hearts toward this country. "This would hurt us in our relations with Cubans in the future."[44] Congressional representatives shared this concern. Assistant Secretary of State William Macomber, in response to the Senate's inquiry about the treatment of refugees, explained: "The Department is naturally greatly interested in assuring that suitable action is taken in connection with Cuban refugees so as to reflect credit upon the United States in response to the needs of these victims from oppression by the Castro government."[45]

Days before the 1960 presidential elections, Under Secretary of State Douglas Dillon and John Hanes Jr. of the State Department, met with Tracy Voorhees, who had been in charge of the Hungarian refugee program. They sought to enlist his help with Cuban refugees. Dillon was clear about the government's interest: it was important from a foreign policy perspective that Cubans in the United States not fall into need or into a situation where they could be portrayed abroad as in difficult straits in the United States. It was critical for the U.S. position in Cuba and elsewhere that Cubans fleeing to the United States were adequately received and handled.[46] Leaving a socialist country as a vote in favor of freedom, and the care given to refugees would be a reflection of democracy.

Propaganda, however, was not the CIA's only concern. President Eisenhower had authorized the use of a wide range of covert and overt activities to reach this goal, including an armed invasion of the island. At the time, the CIA was organizing an invasion. Cuban exiles were being trained in the jungles of Guatemala, and the CIA was working closely with the underground opposition on the island. Creating an escape route for them and their family members would be part of the invasion support system. Baker's precise request had been that members of the underground, fighting with the help of the United States, needed a guaranteed exit out of the country for themselves and their families. The issuance of visa waivers was one escape route considered, but initially this option was discarded because the use of such extraordinary documents could tip Cuban intelligence.[47] Instead, student and tourist visas would be issued by the American embassy to those who did not have old visas on their passports to provide a quick exit if needed.

The Department of the Army had warned that Cubans who had joined the U.S. military efforts and still had relatives living in Cuba were a potential security threat since they could be exploited or recruited through coercion by Cuban intelligence.[48] Having the children of the underground served multiple purposes. For one, the parents could continue fighting in the underground without having the immediate pressure of having to tend to their children. Then there was the fear factor if they were caught—what would happen to their children? In addition, the CIA would have control over the children ensuring compliance on the part of Cubans.[49] At the time, CIA psychologists had warned that with Cuban operatives, "the biggest problem appears to be that of long-term loyalty and control. Essentially, the Cuban is only loyal to himself."[50]

Refugee policies had operational interest in a quick movement of people out of the island, but that movement had political, ideological, and propagandistic aspects as well. This included the children of the underground.

Unaccompanied Minors

On October 24, 1960, the White House held a meeting to discuss the Cuban refugee situation, 85 percent of whom were in Florida, mostly in Miami. The following week another meeting was held in Miami. The meeting report contains the first public government record to make a reference to the problem of unaccompanied minors:

> Apparently there are many unattached children in the group of 5,000 minors. It is reported that this problem is expected to become more serious as plans are now being developed by the Castro regime to make children wards of the state. Most of the unaccompanied children were sent to family friends in the United States. However, it is reported that some are roaming the streets in the Cuban community depending upon the sympathy of persons they meet on the streets for food and shelter.[51]

President Eisenhower ordered Tracy Voorhees to investigate and devise a plan to handle the increasing influx of Cuban refugees. In preparing his report, Voorhees sought information from Miami local officials. Joe Hall, Dade County Public Schools Superintendent, reported that 3,127 "non-immigrants" (defined as political exiles or visitors on student visa) had enrolled in three high schools in Miami for the fall of 1960.[52] Monsignor John J. Fitzpatrick, of the Centro Hispano Católico of the Diocese of Miami, noted, "Many of the younger people, as well as families, are forced to sleep in cars." The Diocese recommended foster home care for unaccompanied children.[53] The Welfare Planning Council was even more direct, recommending "foster care in institutions or family homes for children separated from their parents, who have been sent here to avoid coercive regimentation."[54] This recommendation became one of the resolutions adopted by the Cuban Refugee Committee in their report to the federal government.[55]

On December 2, 1960, President Eisenhower approved $1 million from the Mutual Security Program to assist Cuban refugees arriving in the United States. The Mutual Security Act, as amended, authorized relief programs to encourage the hopes and aspirations of people who have been "enslaved by Communism." The Cuban government had conclusively demonstrated that it was politically, economically, and ideologically aligned with the Sino-Soviet Bloc, the act noted, including the indoctrination of schoolchildren beginning with the earliest grades.[56] Eisenhower also named Voorhees to head a presidential commission on Cuban refugees.

During the next few weeks, Frances Davis, director of the Division of Child Welfare for the Florida State Department of Public Welfare, asked the Children's Bureau for assistance in discussing policies that might facilitate the care of children refugees. Katherine Oettinger, director of the Children's Bureau, convened a meeting. The case of two Cuban children left by their mother in Key West was discussed. While the courts had resolved the immediate care of these children, the problem could intensify. In this way, the Children's Bureau began to lay the groundwork for the impending arrival of unaccompanied children.[57]

Laying the Groundwork for the Evacuation
of the Children of the Underground

After a visit from one of the Ruston parents, Baker met with a friend at the American embassy.[58] Baker felt there was a need for a program to get children out of Cuba. There were parents who were willing to continue fighting in the underground as long as their children were safe, and there were adolescents fighting in the underground who had to leave quickly. Baker's contact agreed to inquire about getting student visas for up to 200 Cuban youths. But first, arrangements for their sponsorship in the States would have to be made.

Baker traveled to Miami in early December 1960, where he met with a group of American businessmen from the Havana-American Chamber of Commerce. As the economic and political situation on the island deteriorated, many American corporations had pulled out of Cuba and their representatives were waiting in Miami for what everyone assumed would be the quick overthrow of the Castro government. They were well aware of Eisenhower's plans of military action. They had no reason to believe that John F. Kennedy, who had just been elected president, would change the course of these plans. Kennedy's stance on Cuba had hardened over the course of the campaign.[59] So from the perspective of these businessmen, it was just a matter of months before they could return to Cuba.

Many of the corporations represented by the American Chamber of Commerce were already aiding in the government's efforts. The International Rescue Committee, which was working closely with the CIA on refugee matters, had already enlisted their help. In April 1960, IRC members Leo Cherne and John Richardson Jr. had met with CIA director Allen Dulles to discuss projects aimed at refugees from Cuba. The International Rescue Committee had provided the CIA with an extensive briefing on its trip to Cuba the year before. The committee had concluded that there was Communist infiltration.[60] Dulles requested a detailed budget and offered to return to the committee with funds.[61] As part of the plan, the IRC was to raise monies from corporations. The oil refineries Texaco and Esso Standard Oil, members of the Havana Chamber of Commerce, would be particularly generous.

Jim Baker was well known to the group. Many corporate leaders had enrolled their own children at Ruston Academy and almost all of them had bought advertisements in its 1959 yearbook. Esso Standard's, for example, read: "Education forms the cornerstone of a free world. Congratulations."[62] The U.S. embassy staff also sent their children to Ruston. The crisis on the island had interrupted their children's education, and they supported the idea of establishing a boarding school. This way, the children could resume their studies in Miami while their parents in the underground opposition could continue fighting. At the Chamber of Commerce meeting, one participant agreed to contact Monsignor Walsh, then director of the Catholic Welfare Bureau, another agency with ties to the intelligence community's refugee programs. He would set up a meeting for Baker with Walsh, so that Baker could discuss the care of the children.

3

The Plan to Save the Children from Communism

Father Bryan Walsh was born in 1930 and grew up in Limerick, Ireland, where he studied with the Jesuits. His father had been a British soldier. When he was twenty years old, he moved to the United States and was ordained a priest in 1954 in Florida. A year later, he was appointed to the Catholic Welfare Bureau.[1] His first assignment was aiding Hungarian freedom fighters who had sought refuge in the United States, including placing unaccompanied teenage boys with foster families. The bureau's program was organized through voluntary national relief organizations, though, not through licensed child welfare agencies. Father Walsh was keenly aware that many of the placements, including some in Miami, had failed.[2] Reforming how services for refugees, especially children, were organized would become a lifelong quest.

Walsh recalled being approached by members of the American Chamber of Commerce of Havana about taking care of the children of friends who were fighting in the Cuban underground. James Baker had come to Miami to find help to take care of approximately two hundred students whose parents had told him they would continue fighting only if their children were safe.[3] Since most of the children were Catholic, Baker thought it was logical to ask Walsh for assistance. He knew the young priest had been part of a local group that successfully pressured the White House to include services to unaccompanied minors in their refugee relief effort. At this initial meeting, Baker and Walsh found a mutual concern that transcended the safety of the children: a desire to help parents save their children from the danger of Communist indoctrination. Thus, ideological concerns began to frame the exodus of Cuban children.

According to Walsh, his first actual contact with one of these children occurred on November 15, 1960, when he met a fifteen-year-old boy named Pedro Menéndez who had been wandering the streets of Miami alone, going from home to home. Walsh helped him, understanding "that Pedro would be the first of many as the situation in Cuba got worse."[4] This led to discussions with the Welfare Planning Council; on November 22, 1960, the council's Cuban Refugee Executive Committee passed a resolution to include in their proposal to Voorhees the problem of unaccompanied children.[5] The word spread like wildfire, and the American Chamber of Commerce went to see Walsh.

There were questions of logistics: How to get the children out of Cuba? How to care for them in the United States? Baker, obviously in conjunction with U.S. authorities, had a plan to get the children out with student visas but had no concrete ideas on how they would be cared for in the United States. He also needed a local school to provide the request for the student visas. Walsh, on the other hand, had ideas about the provision of proper care. He told Baker that a boarding school would only be a partial solution. The job required a social service agency that could plan for the total care of the children, including legal questions of custody, since the parents would be in another country. He felt the younger children belonged in foster homes, not institutions. He was concerned that a decentralized effort would damage the cause. Baker agreed. Walsh later wrote: "Thus began the collaboration *Operation Pedro Pan*, our project to fly the children out of Cuba."[6]

The operation to bring the children to the United States would be conducted in secrecy in both countries, although the Cuban Children's Program, the component of the plan that would take care of the children in the United States, would be conducted overtly once the Department of Health, Education and Welfare began to fund it.[7] Despite the various components, Operation Pedro Pan was a wholly unified program, as Baker described the operation in a memo to Bonsal: "I organized a project for bringing to the United States a group of children whose parents wished to save them from the danger of communist indoctrination. They received student visas. A committee of the American Chamber of Commerce of Havana and a group of Cubans raised funds for their passage from Havana to Miami. The Catholic Welfare Bureau of Miami assumed the responsibility of caring for the children in foster or group homes."[8] Operation Pedro Pan was under way.

However, it seems that there were already other programs under way. In November 1960 *Bohemia* published an article, "Villanueva," which quoted a former student as saying that "Villanueva's yanqui connections, like other American counterrevolutionary sectors linked to American educational institutions, are taking some of their students to study in the United States. The State Department is providing the funds. They are even enticing students with the offer of a job in Puerto Rico or the United States."[9] In October 1960, a group of fifty Cuban girls had been transferred from their school in Havana to an Ursuline school in New Orleans. Eventually they would be sent to Father Walsh.[10] And the CIA was actively recruiting students for their "university" which prepared young democratic students to be leaders on their return to their respective countries.[11]

The First Arrivals

Baker returned to Cuba on December 13, 1960. The agreement was that all communication between Baker and Walsh would now be handled by U.S. diplomatic pouch. Chargé d'affaires Braddock in Havana and Culver Gidden of the State Department's Miami Reception Center would take care of this function. The exit program would work in the following manner: the U.S. embassy would be asked to grant a student visa. The Catholic Welfare Bureau would give Baker a letter accepting responsibility for the children and arrange to have U.S. Immigration Form I-20 completed by a school; Coral Gables High School was chosen for this.

On December 15, members of the American Chamber of Commerce (including Kenneth Campbell, Bob O'Farrell of Esso Standard, and Richard Colligan of Freeport Sulphur Company) brought a letter to Walsh with the first 125 names. Campbell raised the initial monies from members of the Chamber. Esso Standard and Shell Oil were especially generous. Later in the operation, according to Baker, the money would come from the U.S. government.[12] Indeed, a few months later, the State Department circulated a memo to all their embassies in Latin America stating that "the Department will defray costs of transporting about 20,000 Cubans who have visas or visa waivers. If queried, they were instructed to state that this was a humanitarian effort designed to reunite families."[13] In order to prevent the Cuban government from tracing the funds, the first donations were paid to the Catholic Welfare Bureau, which in turn issued checks to a series of American citizens residing in the Miami area. Those citizens then issued personal checks for airplane fares, which were transmitted to the Harris Smith Travel Agency.[14] The travel agency was owned and operated by Gilbert Smith, the executive secretary of the Chamber of Commerce, whose wife, Louise, once a supporter of the underground opposition to Batista, was now working against Fidel.

In Miami, Monsignor Walsh began looking for places to house the children. Temporary space was guaranteed at Assumption Academy and St. Joseph's Village. Maurice Ferre, a local businessman, who would later become mayor of Miami, donated a house that would be christened "Cuban Boys Home."

Since no one was quite sure how many—if any—children would arrive on any given flight from Cuba, Father Walsh began meeting every flight at the airport. At first, none came because none of the children had received the student visas. Breaking the security procedures they had agreed upon, Baker called Walsh to tell him that the embassy was holding up the issuance of visas, and that he should call Frank Aurbach at the State Department. Within hours, Aurbach called back to say that the department was willing to issue 250 student visas requested by Baker if a recognized and established organization in the United States assumed ultimate responsibility for the children. Walsh, aware of rumors circling Cuba that no children would be allowed to leave after January 1, accepted that responsibility. Thus, in late December 1960, under a special agreement with the Catholic Welfare Bureau and the State

Department, an extraordinary arrangement was made to issue up to 250 student visas for unaccompanied minors from Cuba.[15]

Father Walsh grew increasingly excited as the time drew near for the first flights. On December 26, 1960, the first children arrived. Two more came on the twenty-eighth, six on the thirtieth, and 12 on the thirty-first. Walsh recalled, "No longer were we simply a social service agency concerned about a community problem. We were now sharing the worries of families we did not even know, hundreds of miles away, in a life-and-death struggle in the Cold War."[16] However, not everyone shared Walsh's excitement. Some members of the anti-Castro opposition were alarmed when they heard of a program to send children of underground activists out of the country. They feared that Cuban intelligence could identify the activists by figuring out who was sending their children abroad.[17] In saving the children, the organizers of Operation Pedro Pan were inadvertently providing information to Cuban state security. How much they knew would continue to preoccupy Father Walsh until his death.[18]

Father Walsh. Courtesy of Operation Pedro Pan.

Diplomatic Break

On January 3, 1961, the future of the entire program was jeopardized when the Eisenhower administration broke diplomatic relations with the Cuban government. A month before, Secretary of State Christian Herter had ordered Ambassador Philip Bonsal to abandon his post, stating "the Cuban government has no intention of attempting to settle differences through diplomatic negotiations."[19] Tensions between the countries escalated when the United States increased its military support to the underground. This had the effect of increasing actions such as bombings in Havana and coastal raids along the island's northern coast. In response, Fidel Castro continued tightening the reigns of his newfound power by dismissing his cabinet, ignoring court decisions, reneging on promised elections, and using firing squads to squelch the growing opposition. A State Department intelligence report concluded that in less than two years' time, the Castro regime had consolidated its hold over Cuban society. The report warned that "the regime can also be expected to attempt to increase its already great authority and influence with Cuban youth through an extension of the authority and organization of the existing 'revolutionary' youth groups." Furthermore, it predicted, "Activities aimed at strengthening Castro's control over Cuba will probably include moves to reduce the influence of the church—particularly in the educational process."[20]

The Bakers decided that if the U.S. embassy closed, they, too, would leave Cuba.[21] The embassy had issued an alert to Americans living in Havana that it could no longer protect them. However, this warning was not made public, since the embassy thought that the suspense as to whether or not Americans would flee would unnerve Cuban officials.[22] The closing of the embassy meant that, in effect, all embassy work was suspended, including consular affairs. Some U.S. officials argued that it was to the United States' advantage to close the embassy and its visa operations; this way the refugee escape valve would be shut off and pressure inside the island would increase.[23]

Before closing, the U.S. embassy had issued student visas to only 22 of the 250 students on Jim Baker's list. Therefore a new plan to send youth out of Cuba had to be devised, and it would require cooperation from a country that still maintained diplomatic relations with Cuba. Great Britain's embassy, for example, could issue visas. One of Baker's former employees, Penny Powers, worked at the British embassy in its intelligence division and could help.

Powers was a natural. A small but energetic woman (who some would characterize as stubborn), she knew Cuba intimately. Powers was known for her bravery and her commitment to children as well. During World War II, she had assisted with the evacuation of Jewish children from Germany to England in what came to be called the Kindertransport. Wayne Smith had first told me that Penny Powers had been involved, and that she was living in Cuba. Though I had been unsuccessful in finding her while doing research, Elly Chovel in Miami spoke to Philip Grice, who worked in the British Tourist Office in Miami and had been assigned to the British embassy in Havana in the early 1960s. Although he refused to be interviewed, he did contact the British embassy in Havana and helped arrange my meeting with Powers.

When I met Powers in Cuba in 1993, she had suffered a stroke and was in a wheelchair.[24] She had trouble speaking but remembered the children and her friends from the underground, including Baker and Father Walsh. Before her assignment in Cuba, she had worked in China. For Powers, there was little difference between fascism and communism, but she doubted that U.S. policymakers understood this, nor was she convinced that the United States would really help save Cuban children from communism. (The U.S. government had disappointed her once before, during World War II, when Congress voted down legislation sponsored by Senator Lyndon Johnson to admit 30,000 German Jewish children into the country. Only after public outcry did the United States accept the Jewish children—all under age sixteen—who had fled Europe aboard the SS *Quanza*.)[25] She admitted that she did not trust the Catholic Church, either, but she was more fearful of communist regimes. She insisted "the children, the children needed to be saved."[26]

Powers stayed in Cuba, working for the British embassy, until her death in 1996. She opened the International School for children of diplomats, which would become one of the best in Havana. In 1982, she received the Order of the British Empire for her work with children and her struggle against oppressive regimes. The motto of the order is memorable: "For God and the empire."

In 1961, Baker and Powers conceived a plan: the British government would issue student visas to go to Jamaica or the Bahamas, both still British colonies at the time. Most children would board KLM's Havana-Miami-Kingston flight and simply stay in Miami when the plane landed there. Others could take direct flights to Kingston, spend a night, then receive a visa from the U.S. consulate and fly to Miami the following day. But the intricacies of this new scheme required coordination and cooperation, and this could only be done by organizing a tightly woven underground network.

JFK'S Open Door Policy

On January 20, 1961, John F. Kennedy became the twenty-third president of the United States. Kennedy had boxed himself into a get-tough policy with Cuba. He had learned of Eisenhower's covert operations to overthrow Castro's government and knew that Nixon was not free to speak about them publicly. He used this to his advantage during the first-ever televised presidential campaign debates; Kennedy criticized Nixon for allowing the communists to establish a beachhead only ninety miles from the United States. Now on record as being inflexible on communism, Kennedy had to deliver. Awaiting him in the bureaucratic wings of government was a plan to invade the island. But now, without an embassy in Havana, the coordination of support services for invasion plans and the movement of people was extremely difficult. This would complicate the exodus of children as well.

Talk of an invasion and the worsening political and economic situ-

Penny Powers, Havana, Cuba, 1993. Photograph by the author.

ation in Cuba was spurring a dramatic exodus from the island. Kennedy
was inclined to an open-door policy and committed to reforming immigration laws to make it easier for visitors and refugees to enter the
United States.[27] However, he was saddled by the Immigration and Na-

tionality Act of 1952, which featured not only a discriminatory national origin quota system but a provision requiring an extensive and cumbersome security check of all visa applications. Many Cubans had valid visas on their passports, but many more did not. As requests for entry into the United States increased, the administration scrambled to find a loophole.[28] The 1952 Immigration Act gave the attorney general discretionary authority to make exceptions to the law. After considerable discussion between the INS and the State Department, a decision was made to waive visa requirements for Cuban applicants. A waiver of nonimmigrant visas had been in effect in Cuba after World War II but was suspended in 1950 because too many Cubans were staying in the United States. In 1955, the United States tried to reinstate the waiver policy, but the Cuban government resisted. In 1959, the United States reintroduced it without consulting the Cuban government, but a U.S. immigration official would have to inspect a passenger with a waiver before boarding the plane,[29] and the Cuban government would not give permission for the United States to station its immigration officers at the airport. Therefore, a new twist was added to the visa waiver program: the attorney general could grant them a parole status, which eliminated the need for an airport inspection and permitted the refugees to work. The United States hoped that by waiving visa requirements, Cubans leaving the island would not be forced to apply for exit permits, which made underground fighters particularly vulnerable. This measure would drastically facilitate their departure, as Cuban exit permits not only tipped off the government as to who was leaving but also allowed confiscation of property for those who did not return to the island within sixty days.[30] The entire program was conceived as a temporary measure, for in a few months, they thought, an invasion would oust Castro from power.

Children's Visa Waivers

After Jim Baker left the island in early January 1961, he met again with Father Walsh, and the pair contacted the State Department to discuss the new plans.[31] Walsh had flown to Washington on Sunday, January 8, 1961. Frank Aurbach of the Bureau of Security and Consular Affairs instructed him to come around to the side door of the State Department. Walsh would later recall, "It was a bright, cold winter afternoon, and the streets around the department were completely deserted. Somehow the weather, the day, the time, the happenings of the past few weeks, all combined to create an atmosphere of intrigue and conspiracy."[32] He met with Robert Hale, the head of the visa office in the State Department and several other men,[33] including a representative from the British embassy.[34] One individual present may have been a representative of the Central Intelligence Agency.[35]

It was at this meeting that Walsh first heard of the notion of "visa waivers." The words, pronounced with a thick Spanish accent, would become part of the early exile vocabulary. Aurbach had suggested that the Catholic Welfare Bureau could petition the State Department to waive visa requirements for children coming directly from Cuba. Children there were in imminent danger of communist brainwashing, he argued, and this constituted an emergency that under the law could be the basis for granting this petition. With these waivers in effect, airlines would not be penalized for transporting passengers without proper visas.

Walsh soon received news that both visa plans were approved. The Jamaica plan was to run as conceived by Baker and Powers. The British consulate would issue a visa to travel to Jamaica, and thus give the minors a legal way of leaving the country. However, the implementation of this plan would prove cumbersome. The embassy in Kingston reported that the British embassy in Cuba was receiving more than 1,000 visa requests a week. The Jamaican cabinet in an emergency meeting decided that their island could not absorb so many people.[36] By February 17, over 850 Cuban refugees were in Jamaica awaiting visas into the United States. Seventy-five percent of them involved divided families. It was unclear to the British exactly what U.S. policy toward the refugees would be or, indeed, if aid for the refugees was forthcoming. Philip Bonsal, then stationed in Washington, wrote a memo to Robert Stevenson of the State Department urging him to expedite entrance to members of divided families, noting that "the continued exodus of Cubans from Castro's paradise is good propaganda for our side. It may force Castro to take measures to stop it."[37]

Given the difficulties with Jamaica, the U.S. visa waiver plan would become the preferred mode of exit. Technically, the waiver was issued in Washington, but Father Walsh had the authority to grant waivers to anyone under sixteen years of age. Other private organizations had authority to issue waivers to all individuals. These included Al Trout of the International Rescue Committee, who signed on behalf of a Department of Visa Waiver,[38] and Dr. Carlos Piad (later replaced by Wendell Rollason) representing the Cuban Revolutionary Council, the CIA's exile political organization. This is the way Baker described the program to Philip Bonsal: "A list of names would be filed in the immigration office at the Miami airport. A second confirmation was based on the list of names sent by the travel agency in Havana of children who were on their flights. INS would OK the name if the student was on the original list and he is under eighteen years of age. If it was an emergency situation, the minor had to be under sixteen years of age."[39] J. Edgar Hoover insisted on FBI approval of the seventeen- and eighteen-year-olds, but Father Walsh was given blanket authority to issue them to children age six to sixteen.

This last provision concerned Baker, who wrote Bonsal for help: "As our original plan was to obtain student visas, the list included some students over eighteen. The present plan does not allow us to bring those who have passed their eighteenth birthday. This limitation presents a problem, about which we are concerned." According to Baker, this policy had already had consequences since "a boy not allowed into the United States had been shot by a militiaman."[40] Baker was insistent. There had to be flexibility in the visa waiver program; after all, they were working with people who were risking their lives to fight communism. He asked for special consideration to allow them to substitute names of minors not on the list when they were in danger, even if they were over sixteen. The older ones were often in greatest danger.[41]

Furthermore, he wanted to expand the scope of the visa waiver measures. The State Department had approved another 250 names, but Baker thought this was not enough and continues in his letter to Bonsal:

The ever-widening program of Communist indoctrination makes countless parents increasingly anxious to get their children out of Cuba. These parents are fearful of the publicly announced program to send to Russia a group of 1,000 children eight to ten years of age on an "exchange" basis. The parents watch with deep concern the establishment of groups of adolescents that are being organized and sent out to the country to be trained as farmers, and the "volunteer" groups being sent out to cut cane. Now more than ever government attention seems to be focused upon organizing groups of children for "brainwashing" programs. Fidel announced about ten days ago that after Easter, secondary schools would be closed for the year so that the students could be sent into the country to help with literacy programs.[42]

Baker continued:

As the programs for turning more and more children into Communist robots are accelerated, we become more than ever eager to try to save more children. We wish to begin immediately to prepare a new list of unaccompanied children refugees. Priority of turns for leaving Havana was determined by the emergency of the individual cases and the danger in which the children were involved.[43]

Yet the FBI continued to insist that the names of the sixteen- to eighteen-year-olds be checked. The agency feared that these adolescents could potentially be communist spies sent by Castro. However, J. Edgar Hoover was on board with the program, and on January 27, 1961, he commented on a meeting with State Department officials, that "one good angle came out, the fact that there is a group of young Cubans who want to go to college here in this country and that is a wonderful opportunity. The communists always went after the youth first and we ought in this country to see if we can't place these young people into schools and indoctrinate them with democracy."[44]

On February 3, Kennedy charged HEW secretary Abraham Ribicoff with the administration of *overt* refugee programs for Cubans, including one to care and protect unaccompanied refugee children, whom he described as "the most defenseless and troubled group among the refugee population." But the visa waiver program for minors would remain classified.[45] Everything about the visa waivers and the transportation of the children would be done in secret. In a directive to all state welfare departments, Katherine Oettinger stated: "No publicity should be given to this program since it would inhibit the possibility of other Cuban children coming to this country. Any publicity might endanger families and relatives."[46]

Some were high-level officials in the Castro government, like Osvaldo Dorticós, who had a nephew among the Pedro Pans, others like the Cuban ambassador to the Netherlands was in the process of defecting and wanted his children in the United States.[47]

Baker's Secret Network

The Cuban portion of the operation was part of the infrastructure of the opposition to Castro. It can be imagined as two distinct time frames: before and after Bay of Pigs. The underground organizations and their roles differed pre- and post-invasion. Moreover, U.S. policy underwent dramatic restructuring after the failure of the Bay of Pigs invasion. Jim Baker's group was the first active organization on the island, although Father Walsh had his own contacts that would later play a more important role. Penny Powers, who worked for British embassy, was a constant throughout the program, especially as her embassy became a critical link in providing visas to children of the underground and in procuring safe mail services.

Baker's group consisted mainly of teachers and former students from Ruston Academy. Most were women who were deeply moved by the idea of saving children from communism. Many had left behind their canasta games to join the underground fight against Batista. They became the support structures for the urban insurrection, driving men around town, providing safe houses, raising money, and transporting arms and ammunitions. Herbert Matthews described one such woman as "from a well-to-do, upper-class Havana family, a fanatical member of the 26 of July Movement, typical of the young women who risked—and sometimes lost—their lives in the insurrection." He goes on to comment, "The extent to which the women of Cuba are caught up in the passion of the rebellion is extraordinary, for like all Latin women they were brought up to sheltered, nonpublic lives."[48] Therefore, when the new regime reneged on promises of democracy, many of these women felt personally betrayed. For many, their commitment to finish the promise of the revolution took priority over all else. Some sent their own children ahead to the United States and stayed in Havana to work. It was the women's job to collect the names of children who needed to leave the island from representatives of various underground organizations and Catholic schools, and then turn them over to the British embassy, which would pass them along to the travel agencies. They worked in a secret cell-like structure in which many did not know the others involved.

The leader of Baker's group in Cuba was Serafina Lastra de Giquel. Charismatic, witty, and intelligent, Sera, as her friends called her, had become a landscape architect as a way to support her hobby of importing exotic flowers from all over the world. Sera's brother was a renowned surgeon in Havana; her husband, Sergio Giquel, was a friend of the Bakers and a well-known orthodontist whose clients included the children of Havana's elite. From the very beginning, he helped by relaying messages between Miami and Havana. Travel documents were kept in his office before they were distributed to the parents. If caught, he could claim that they were dental records. Serafina's role was to gather names and distribute documents. Sera had no excuses to offer if she was caught.

During the 1950s, Sera had befriended Adelaida Everhart, one of the American Cubans of Baker's circle. They had become especially close through their work for Ruston Academy. Sera had been contracted to do the landscaping, and Everhart was then president of the PTA. Everhart, a graduate of Ruston Academy, lived in Cuba with her husband, Jack, who had been a teacher at Ruston and owned a ranch in Pinar del Río, Cuba's rich tobacco-growing land. Like the Bakers, she had helped friends who had fought against Batista. She, too, had believed in the revolution but had become disillusioned early on and had decided to leave Cuba in the summer of 1960. In Miami, she worked with Al Trout of the International Rescue Committee who, according to Adelaida, they all thought worked for the CIA. Indeed, connections between the refugee work and the CIA were so close that after Bay of Pigs, Trout asked Everhart to debrief those returning from the invasion and fill out questionnaires.[49]

At first, Everhart's disillusionment with the revolution caused a tremendous tension between the friends, but later Serafina, too, came around to a more critical view and joined the underground. Everhart became an important link for Serafina; she would receive requests from Serafina for visa waivers. The letters, written in code, also informed her when young passengers would arrive, and she would go out to the airport to meet them.

Everhart's work was not exclusively aimed at helping people escape; she was also a "mailbox" for messages from Cuba. Her work with Serafina, however, concerned her most. She knew that her friend in Cuba would be jailed, maybe even executed, if she was caught. Serafina was also gathering intelligence information and passing it on to Everhart, who in turn gave it to her husband and his contacts in the CIA. In fact, some of the first reports of the presence of Soviet missiles in Cuba came via a coded letter sent to Everhart by Serafina. Serafina eventually became a translator for the Unidad Revolucionaria, an umbrella group established by the CIA in Havana to try to unite the underground after the failure of Bay of Pigs. The women, Cuban and American alike, were grateful to the United States for its support of the underground. To show their gratitude, they sent, in early 1961, an amethyst for Jackie Kennedy.[50]

Berta de la Portilla Finlay, a Ruston teacher, and her sister, Ester de la Portilla, were involved with Baker's committee from the very beginning as well. They had both sent their children out. Portilla sent hers in early 1961 when she heard that the Cuban government would intervene in the Catholic schools. The Cuban government took control of the schools in May 1961. She worked closely with delegates from the Catholic Church, since priests and nuns were key in the identification of children who could come on the waiver program. In an interview in Miami, Portilla explained to me how each Catholic school had a delegate who would compile a list of children in need of visa waivers. The sisters would pass on the names to key contacts, collect the passports, obtain the visa waivers, and occasionally distribute the visa waivers themselves.[51] Most of the children she obtained visas for came through church contacts; some came from the underground movement as well.

Portilla's contact person was Ignacio Martínez, an employee of Pan-American airlines, which was committed to helping out. Indeed, Mario Montane, the station manager of Pan-American at Rancho Boyeros airport, had approached the embassy in September 1960 offering assistance with whatever was needed.[52] Portilla revealed that some of the people for whom she obtained visa waivers were *quemados,* meaning those who needed to get out quickly after being involved in an armed action. For instance, she obtained waivers for two students who had placed a bomb in the Almendares tunnel, the underground connection to the western section of Havana. It was a dramatic bombing that set off panic throughout the city. The two young students were hiding in a home in the Vedado neighborhood. She brought a box containing an undergarment and the visa waivers. A third student, who was over eighteen, left with a scholarship from the Italian embassy.

Pancho Finlay, Berta's husband, was the grandson of Carlos J. Finlay, the renowned Cuban physician who discovered the cause of yellow fever. He also was director of the Dutch airlines KLM in Havana, and therefore had contacts in the Dutch embassy. He helped to secure seats on the planes and to falsify affidavits stating that the children had visas waiting for them in Miami, which at one time had been a prerequisite for boarding a plane in Havana. Marie Boissevant, the wife of the Dutch ambassador, would fly from Havana to Miami to pick up bundles of visa waivers.

Another member of Baker's group was María Teresa Cuervo, an employee of Harris Smith Travel Agency, located at the stately Lonja del Comercio building in Old Havana.[53] While too timid to conduct clandestine work, Teté, as she was called, had plenty of savvy since her husband and father-in-law had both been in the underground against Batista. Batista, in fact, had her father-in-law killed, an action that galvanized the opposition against his dictatorship.[54]

Teté described other details of the elaborate operation. She was in charge of making reservations for the children who had visa waivers. Priests dressed in civilian clothes would bring the children needing visa waivers to her office. Gilbert Smith, the son of the original owner of the agency, arranged for the waivers with the American embassy. Special arrangements were made for those over eighteen to go through the Bahamas, where they would secure a visa from the U.S. consulate. KLM had two flights to Jamaica each day: one direct flight and one that stopped in Miami. Those on the direct flight were to spend the night in Jamaica, where they would be issued a visa to go to the United States. The children on the stopover flight would simply stay in Miami. At first, Teté secured six seats a day; later, the number increased.

The operation was financed by "donations" from businessmen in Miami received by Smith, or by the children's parents, although Smith also paid for some of their tickets himself. Teté said that the visa waivers had been available to the underground in 1960, but they feared that Cuban intelligence would detect underground cells through these rather unusual documents. Therefore, Cubans in the underground were told by the Americans that they would be using student visas, so parents could claim that their children were going to the United States to study.

Margarita Oteiza, a former Ruston student and later a teacher, who was another veteran of the underground fight against Batista, served as courier, delivering packages of documents from one person to another.[55] Oteiza's father was a minister in President Carlos Prios's cabinet at the time of the Batista coup d'état. Clandestine activities had become second nature to her. Oteiza's husband was already in training for the Bay of Pigs invasion, so she, too, left the island, early in January 1961. He was killed in action, and Oteiza volunteered at the camps that were eventually created in South Florida to house the young refugees.

Father Walsh began developing his own contacts in Cuba. He claimed to have worked with hundreds of people. At one point, through Maurice Ferrer (the millionaire who had given him one of his homes for the housing and care of the children in Miami) he met Sara del Toro de Odio, who worked with an opposition group on the island and had brought five of her own children to Miami.[56] Walsh needed to transport the visa waiver documents to the island, yet very few people were traveling between Miami and Havana at the time. Moreover, his Catholic contacts were already under suspicion. So, he asked Sara to smuggle them in. Walsh also had to devise a way to send money to Cuba. For a time, tickets had to be paid for in U.S. dollars, and since it was illegal for Cubans to possess American currency, these dollars had to come from the United States. There is some debate as to where the money came from. Baker claims it came from the government. Father Walsh says it came from Baker's business connections. Whatever its provenance, Father Walsh found another courier—the husband of Pola Grau, a woman who would come to play a pivotal role in the exodus of the children after the Bay of Pigs. Like the members of Baker's secret network, those working with Father Walsh were also involved in other clandestine activities, including intelligence gathering, military action, and other support activities. As Baker explained, "We had to protect the people who were working. We thought they were in danger."[57]

The Other Visa Waiver Network

Another way that visa waivers could be generated was through direct petitions by relatives in the United States. Wendell Rollason, an immigrants' rights community organizer who had started a group to defend the rights of Puerto Rican migrant workers, was in charge of this component of the program. Rollason was tapped by State Department officials to coordinate the gathering of applications in Miami and to process paperwork with Washington. On the island, according to Manolo Ray, each underground organization had one person in charge of securing visa waivers, and they needed someone to coordinate with their U.S. contact.[58] Rollason became the intermediary between them and the Frente Democrático Revolucionario (later known as the Council) early in July 1961.[59] Several years ago, with the help of Father Walsh, I tracked Rollason down at his home in Fort Myers. I was trying to determine why there was one program established expressly for children and another for the population in general—indeed, a program in which parents and children could come to the United States together.

Rollason had worked at the Dade County Port Authority, which operated the international airport, but was fired after he blew the whistle on the illegal traffic of Puerto Rican farmworkers.[60] This earned him a certain degree of notoriety as a concerned do-gooder interested in immigrant issues. He received a phone call from Frank Watterson, head of the State Department's Secret Service for the southeast U.S. region, and did not hesitate when asked to help in getting endangered Cubans off the island. Rollason knew that those Cubans who fought in the underground—or whose family members did—were living in oppressive conditions and, if left on the island, could be killed.[61]

According to Rollason, Watterson had two purposes: to achieve the maximum number of Cuban departures off the island, because Washington was interested in Cubans "voting with their feet," and to evacuate persons who were fighting in the underground and their families.

The greater the numbers, the less likely that Cuban authorities would detect the flight of the particular individuals they were pursuing.

Rollason maintained an office on Biscayne Boulevard in Miami with several full-time employees. Members of the Frente Revolucionario Democrático (FRD) would bring applications of relatives they wanted to get out of Cuba. One employee, Evora Arca, recalled that the applications were sent to Washington, and then a visa waiver was formally issued.[62] While there may have been a formal review process, in reality, Rollason effectively held the power to issue the waivers or deny them. On rare occasions visa waivers were denied. Rollason points to a letter from a student working for the Unidad Revolucionaria, a CIA umbrella group, who had traveled to Chile and needed reentry into the United States, but whose passport was not in order. The student had gone to the American embassy and was told by an embassy official that he would have to return to Cuba since there were too many *chivatos* (Castro spies) in Santiago.[63] Of course, had Rollason reviewed this particular case with officials in Washington, no documentation of this interaction would exist: he was under instructions to destroy all correspondence with the State Department.[64]

The State Department, specifically its Bureau of Security and Consular Affairs and the visa division, was the agency formally in charge of the visa waiver program. However, other federal agencies worked on immigration issues as well: the CIA initiated requests for visa waivers. The Immigration and Naturalization Service was in charge of airport operations. In fact, INS was not only tasked with guarding the borders but also with debriefing exiles as they came through the airport.

However, Rollason claimed that it was the CIA who paid his monthly check. He also said that though he was not the only person issuing visa waivers, he was told that 60 percent of them came through his office. Particularly after the Bay of Pigs, his operation grew.

The wait for child visa waivers averaged only four months, since children under sixteen did not require a security check. Their names were simply passed on to immigration officials in Miami, and upon their arrival their names were checked against the list at the airport. In contrast, the people whose visa waivers were requested by a relative living in the United States required at least the formality of a security check. The names of these applicants were checked against the Caribbean Index, a list of known criminals, Communists, and other "undesirables" compiled by the CIA. (Normally, a person wanting to emigrate to the United States would face a security check right at the U.S. embassy in their home country when they applied for a visa. Since the embassy in Havana had been closed, however, this process was conducted in Washington.) Bob Hale, a visa officer at the time, recalled that he and his colleagues sat around at the State Department with boxes and boxes of visa waiver applications. They would take them out of the boxes in piles, quickly skimming the names; very few applications were turned down.[65]

Some notable differences are apparent between Walsh's and Rollason's visa waiver programs. The Rollason waivers were requested in the United States by persons connected to the underground who still had relatives in Cuba. The Walsh waivers were requested in the island by people connected to the underground or the Church. Visa waivers through Walsh were apparently more readily available, since he had blanket authority to issue waivers to anyone under sixteen. Rollason's visa waivers, however, had to endure (at least in theory) a formal application process, including a security check in Washington; thus they took longer to process. In addition, Rollason's waivers required a signing relative on this end, while Pedro Pan visa waivers did not. As such, Walsh's visa waiver program emerged as the option for those without relatives in the United States. Indeed, it provided for the first relative (the child) to come to the United States. The child, once in the United States, could then apply for a visa waiver for his or her parents through the State Department. Children became classic immigration anchors for their families.

In essence, bureaucratic regulations about application procedures shaped the development of these programs. National security concerns were instrumental in shaping the distinctions as well: the children did not require the same kind of security checks that adults needed, even if the adult checks were conducted merely on a pro forma basis. Still, the fact that there was a separate program exclusively for children has added to the speculation that the purpose of the program was to use children in propaganda warfare against Cuba.

claim
↓
It was
easier to
get use
waivers
for children
because they
did not need
security clearance.

4

Children and the Bay of Pigs Invasion

Conceived as an evacuation plan for the children of underground combatants, Operation Pedro Pan had to be kept secret, or at least disguised as another type of initiative-student scholarships, for example—so Cuban authorities would not be tipped off. As the date for the planned invasion of Cuba grew closer, the CIA intensified its propaganda campaign. Children naturally became a central theme. The conflict created by the need to keep the operation secret and the use of children as a propaganda tool would create tension between those working directly with the children and the propaganda makers. Ultimately, the safety and emotional needs of the children would be overshadowed by politics.

The CIA's anti-Castro operations basically served three functions: political, propagandistic, and paramilitary. Propaganda was the domain of David Atlee Phillips—code-named "Knight," also called Maurice Bishop—a tall, almost theatrically handsome man, who had spent most of his CIA career undercover, had lived in Latin America, and spoke fluent Spanish.[2] He had been propaganda chief of what the CIA considered its most successful project to date: the overthrow of the Arbenz government in Guatemala in 1954. In the late 1950s, Phillips moved to Cuba, started a public relations firm, and became active in an amateur theater company. His children studied at Ruston Academy.

Phillips was in charge of all covert propaganda, that is, according to his description, propaganda not traceable to the United States.[3] By the end of 1960, Phillips had begun organizing Cuban students and women's groups. Children, family, and educational issues were key themes in the pre-Bay of Pigs propaganda offensive.[4] Two of Phillips's main recruits were Rufo López-Fresquet, who for the first fourteen months of the revolution was Minister of Finance, and Antonio Veciana, who worked at the National Bank and would become an important anti-Castro organizer.[5] (Four years later, Phillips would again employ similar themes in the CIA's campaign to defeat Salvador Allende in his 1964 bid for the Chilean presidency. In one CIA-paid tour to the country, Juana Castro, Fidel's sister, who had gone into exile, urged: "Chilean mothers, I am sure that you will not allow your small children to be taken from you and sent to the Communist bloc, such as happened in Cuba. . . . The enemy is stalking; it is at your doors. Remember your families; remember your children.")[6]

Patria Potestad: A Propaganda Campaign Unfolds

The propaganda campaign raised one particularly incendiary issue: who would have *patria potestad* over Cuban children? *Patria potestad* is a Roman legal concept regarding the authority to make decisions for children.[7] In Roman law the father had almost absolute authority over his children. This later evolved into parental rights. By the early twentieth century, it was well established that this authority, including how to educate children, fell on the parents. But throughout November 1960, Radio Swan, a CIA station beamed at Cuba, reported night after night that the Cuban government had plans to abolish parents' *patria potestad* and take children away from their mothers.[8] According to Cuban intelligence records, in October 1960 Radio Swan made its first reference to the theme:

> Cuban mothers, don't let them take your children away! The Revolutionary Government will take them away from you when they turn five and will keep them until they are eighteen. By that time they will be materialist monsters.[9]

> Several days later, another report was taped stating this would become law and that parents should go to their churches and receive instructions from their clergy.[10]

The first written record of this campaign is a denial from the Cuban government, published in a December 1, 1960, article in the newspaper *El Mundo:* "This *bola* (rumor) was obviously too stupid for anyone with common sense, for if adopted, such a measure would have no practical or revolutionary results; on the contrary, it would create insuperable material difficulties for the government, which would have to house and care for thousands of Cuban children."[11] Still, the government saw fit to deny it, "since this *bola* of children had some success."[12]

The fear that the government would control the children was persuasive. Cubans wanting help from the United States appealed to the embassy on this basis. In a conversation with an embassy official, a Cuban citizen looking for asylum described the situation as follows:

> The struggle in Cuba today is one between Christianity and freedom and the hammer and sickle and slavery of Russia. If the United States does not act forthrightly in Cuba with a more firm policy now tomorrow will be too late. There is a program today in Cuba, the object of which is to actively "brainwash" thousands of impressionable Cuban youths between the ages of 12 and 20. This program will in the near future result in these young people becoming devout members and supporters of the Communist Party and then Cuba will be forever lost.[13]

The embassy official observed: "He spoke with extreme emotion—tears rolled down his cheeks—when he made reference to the youth of Cuba turning to Communism."[14]

The CIA had identified target populations and themes from past effective propaganda efforts. Messages regarding women and the fatherland, with strong religious content, were thought to be extremely effective.[15] A Department of Defense memorandum had advocated calling global attention to Cuban refugees to make the world choose the anti-Castro side: "Emphasis in publicity should be on the victims of terrorism, children and the aged."[16]

In Cuba, the rumor regarding the government's intention to relinquish parental rights was disseminated through various mechanisms. In early November, underground groups working with the CIA were instructed to spread news that several laws were in the works that would adversely impact Cubans. One was the Ley Monetaria, a comprehensive proposal to restructure the value of Cuban currency; the other, a law that would take away parents' *patria potestad*. Arturo Villar, who was then head of intelligence for Unidad Revolucionaria (a CIA umbrella organization prepared to support the invasion), asked specifically whether passage of the *patria potestad* law was true.[17] He was told no, so he refused to disseminate it, arguing that "the truth was bad enough."[18] Yet others like Antonio Veciana continued to do so. Their success in spreading the false rumor of the impending Ley Monetaria persuaded them to push ahead with the *patria potestad* fabrication. "At the time we did many things that would be incomprehensible today, but our goal was to destabilize the regime," Veciana reflected years later.[19]

The CIA organized the dissemination of the rumor in Cuba and throughout Latin America. One objective of the propaganda campaign was to alienate Cuba from other Latin American countries as well as to spread fear of communism in countries, flirting with leftist regimes. In Latin America, the CIA continued to sponsor speaking tours spreading the same message.[20] This time they sent women. When asked by the press why they had left Cuba, they responded:

> Because among the many dangers besetting Cuba these days, there is one, which directly threatens our children. In the schools Communistic indoctrination is being intensified and students are being prepared for the most repulsive practices such as, for example, spying on and reporting their own parents. And they have just announced a new measure, which will permit the State to take over the tutelage of children from their own parents.[21]

On December 13, 1960, the local press announced the overnight visit of Señoras Mirta Fernández de Riverón and Isabel Bequer de León to the San José branch of the Frente Revolucionario Democrático (FRD). Riverón and León were returning from a tour of FRD units in Bogota, Quito, Guayaquil, and Panama.[22] The CIA paid for this whirlwind tour, stating in a report that "the women's organization has directed propaganda to the Cuban domestic population and has conducted propaganda campaigns with similar organizations in various countries."[23] The headquarters of their group, Cruzada Femenina Cubana, was purported to be Miami, Florida. Local FRD officials brought them to call upon the editors of various papers, all of whom accorded them publicity. The women stated that their mission was to awaken the conscience of mothers all over America to the threat of Castro-Communism. The U.S. embassy in San José reported that during their visit, the women announced that they had proof of the Cuban government's intent to implement the *patria potestad* law. Bequer de León stated:

> There is irrefutable evidence that the Cuban regime will very soon put into effect a legal project which will transfer *patria potestad* to the state. Already, schools teach children to denounce their parents if they show any signs of disagreement with government actions. Children in first grade are taught the alphabet with these phrases: *f* for *fusil* (rifle); *r* for *revolución* (revolution); and *p* for *paredón* (firing squad).[24]

The women confirmed that thousands of Cuban children had already arrived in Miami seeking refuge from such indoctrination.[25]

The Catholic Church in Cuba weighed in on the question of who had *patria potestad* over children. In a December 1960 article published in *La Quincena*, Damian Henández asks whether parents had the right to educate their children. He concludes that the family has the natural right of *patria potestad*. While all human beings eventually became members of a civic community, the family was the point of entry for new citizens, and as such the obligation and the right to educate children rested solely on the family.[25]

On December 21, 1960, the U.S. representative to the Organization of American States addressed the delegates on "The Problems of Cuban Refugees." He stated: "A recent and more serious problem is the entrance of unaccompanied children who are economically strapped. The tragedy of these children and the adults has been aggravated by new regulations imposed by the Cuban government on money exchanges and that they only let refugees leave with five dollars."[26]

The image of helpless children fleeing the island captured the imagination of anti-Communists throughout the world. In Argentina, a group of women formed La Cruzada Femenina Argentina pro Niños Refugiados de Cuba (the Argentinian Women's Crusade for Cuba's Refugee Children). They appealed to the French Union Internacionale de Protection de l'Enfance (International Union for the Protection of Children) for help. That organization, in turn, wrote to Katherine Oettinger, Chief of the Children's Bureau of the U.S. Department of Health, Education and Welfare, requesting information about Cuban refugee children. Its members had heard that there were many in Miami, New Orleans, and elsewhere in the United States.[27]

The Threatened Youth

The U.S. embassy in San José reported in January 1961 on the activities of a group called Comité de Vigilancia Democrática, which fanned the fear that Communism would take children away from their families. In one of their leaflets, Castro's soldiers are shown snatching a boy from his mother to carry him off to a Communist school. The text reads: "They come to your homes and they take away children from their mothers to take them to state-run schools where they are taught not to believe in God or family or their parents. There are cases of indoctrinated children who have even informed on their parents and have helped send them off to firing squads."[28]

A month before the Bay of Pigs invasion, the CIA's propaganda efforts increased. A report aimed at Latin American countries, "The Communist Totalitarian Government of Cuba," said:

Newspaper advertisement, January 1961: "Costa Ricans Alert! This is happening in Cuba . . . don't let it happen here!!"

The educational system has been converted into a vast apparatus for indoctrination, in the process of which the autonomy of the University of Havana has been abolished. Only doctrines and ideas which agree with "the Castro philosophy" and only teachers who are politically acceptable to the Castro regime can teach them. Textbooks have been altered to fit the propaganda line of the government, and teachers are given the choice of accepting the new orientation or being ousted. Fidel Castro announced that all new teachers would have to go to government-run normal schools in the mountains before they would be given certificates. Inspectors would be trained to oversee teaching and curriculum. The Castro regime is moving ahead with its plans to establish large communal school cities where thousands of children will be taken away from their home environment for concentrated education and indoctrination.[29]

Some of the parents' fears were exacerbated when, on January 23, 1961, Castro announced the formation of "youth farms" where children over ten would be fed, housed and instructed in agricultural methods. He indicated that Russia and Cuba would exchange 1,000 youths each to work on their respective cooperative farms.[30] A U.S. government report stated: "The government has mobilized large segments of the population through paramilitary organizations blanketing all age groups. For children there are the *patrullas juveniles* (juvenile patrols) under the control of the police. The teenage group is covered by the *Asociación de Jóvenes Rebeldes* (Association of Young Rebels) under the command of rebel army major José Iglesias."[31]

A CIA message sent on March 3, 1961, from "Bell" to JM WAVE states: "All colegios being closed April 15th . . . we must provoke either the intervention of the colegios by the Cuban Government prior April 15th or intensify campaign for student General strike." Alternatively, the message proceeded, "Call students to organize and await signal from the Directorio Revolucionario Estudiantil."[32] If children were to be saved, the youth need to be mobilized.

During the first week of April, several U.S. magazines carried stories on the children of Cuba. *Newsweek* warned about the "Children's Crusade" and how Castro's Year of Education was really the year of indoctrination.[33] And *America*, a monthly magazine published by the Organization of American States, carried an article entitled "Commies and Cub Scouts," announcing that the Cuban government planned to shut down schools and send all school-aged children from the cities out to the countryside to teach peasants to read and write. The article warned, "Anyone who knows the Communists realized that the teaching program is only a cover-up: the true objective is to indoctrinate the pre-teens of Cuba." It goes on to mention, "Parents in Cuba are horrified at this threat to their children. Every family that can afford it is getting its youngsters out of the island; hardly a plane reaches Miami or the nearby Latin American capitals these days without its cargo of unaccompanied boys and girls."[34]

Youth themes would continue to dominate CIA pre-invasion propaganda. On April 4, CIA headquarters sent five propaganda themes for the invasion to the director of JM WAVE, the CIA station in Miami. These themes, communicated in telegraphic language, read as follows:

Publicize Miró statement in Cuban exile White Paper (counterpart to Department of State White Paper) and announce Cuban government organized Unión de Pioneros Rebeldes on April 4 with aim of having children of tender ages 7 to 13 "investigate" opposition activities and take military training. Note identical word (Pioneer) and age range for Pre-Komsomol Kids in Soviet Union. Also comment that it is epitome of totalitarianism to regiment young children, teach to spy on elders, etc.[35]

Of utmost importance to the Kennedy administration was the message that Cuban exiles political leaders would give upon their return to Cuba once the invasion triumphed. Arthur Schlesinger Jr. was charged with reviewing the platform of the Cuban Revolutionary Council and asked the CIA's Tracy Barnes to send him the materials. The platform included the demand to reestablish the freedom of educational systems promoting the moral formation of children and youth. In addition, it promised to suppress all militarization and totalitarian indoctrination of children and youth.[36] Barnes and Schlesinger approved the statement, which was to be read the day of the invasion by José Miró Cardona, the spokesperson for the Cuban Revolutionary Council. On April 16, 1961, on the radio, Miró Cardona pronounced the following: "To the people of Cuba, the peoples of America, why we are flinging ourselves to the struggle . . . all the schools from primary to those on the university level have been converted into centers of Communist indoctrination in which must be learned how to hate, in which it is attempted to destroy the religious faith of the greatest majority."[37]

The Bay of Pigs

As the propaganda offensive increased, so did acts of anti-Castro sabotage throughout the island. In March 1961, the CIA reported that there were about 1,200 active guerrillas and another 1,000 individuals engaged in various acts of conspiracy and sabotage, including bombings, the tempo of which had been rising.[38] By April 12, the CIA reported that there were 7,000 insurgents under some degree of agency control with whom communications were active. About 3,000 of these men and women were in Havana, 2,000 in Oriente, and 700 in Las Villas.[39] The same day, in a televised press conference, Kennedy assured the American people that the administration had no plans to intervene in Cuba with U.S. armed forces. Further, the United States would try to prevent the involvement of its citizens in aiding Cuban freedom fighters, and it would not allow Cuban refugees to launch an invasion from U.S. ports.[40]

In reality, the administration had already approved an invasion of the island, although the CIA had been instructed to make it look "Cuban."[41] They had initiated support activities for military actions such as ensuring combatants safe passage out of the island. The internal opposition placed bombs in different public places in Havana and throughout the island. One bomb exploded in El Encanto, the most luxurious store in Havana, sparking the fire that razed it. Aerial bombing raids around Havana and other parts of the island also escalated, and on April 15 seven people were killed. At their funeral services the following day, Castro declared for the first time the socialist character of his program: "We will defend this socialist revolution with our guns."

The bombings were accompanied by terror campaigns, with tactics that included making phone calls to people's homes claiming bombs had been planted at neighborhood schools or stores. Many young people, particularly young Catholics, who had supported the revolution, had by now turned to the opposition. Raquelín Mendieta, then fifteen, joined an underground group and assumed the task of placing these phone calls from public telephones. Her younger sister, Ana, who was twelve at the time, kept watch nearby, ensuring no one was near enough to overhear the conversation. Their father, who was chief of an opposition group in their province, soon discovered that his daughters were involved in an underground cell and decided that they needed to leave the country quickly.[12]

In my own home, I remember my mother fearfully answering the phone, waiting to see if the caller was someone she recognized or yet another terror call. The threatening phone calls had been coming with some frequency. We did not know if we were targeted as potential defectors, because of my uncle's involvement in the revolution and subsequent opposition, or whether these were just random phone calls that we happened to get. Nonetheless, tensions were running high. My parents were now secretly aiding the opposition by offering our home as a safe house. Everyone lived in a state of panic. And everyone knew the invasion was coming.

Executions and Mass Arrests

The Cuban government responded with repression. Days before the invasion, it launched a series of mass arrests in which men and adolescent boys were picked up and detained in collective jails. It increased the crackdown on all suspected of involvement in underground activities.

In one of the most dramatic roundups, the police brought in a group of university students suspected of having guns. The group included a young man named Virgilio Campanería.

My mother had known the Campanería boys all their lives. Their mother, Nina, was an alumna of La Inmaculada, the same school my mother had attended. Nina often came to alumni gatherings on the Havana campus, where she would visit and set up a playpen for her baby, Virgilio. My mother and the other boarding school girls loved playing with the baby. Years later, while at the university, his older brother Albertico became a close friend of my father's. My parents knew of Virgilio's involvement in the anti-Batista movement and had helped him during that time. Like so many others who had dreamed of a democratic Cuba, Virgilio was quickly disappointed and joined the underground against the Castro regime. He became part of the Directorio Revolucionario Estudiantil (Revolutionary Student Directorate).

On April 17, 1961, in a summary trial that lasted twenty minutes, the entire student group was condemned to death, with the sole exception of Tomas Fernández-Travieso, a sixteen-year-old who was sentenced to thirty years in jail. The other eight young men, including Campanería, were executed. As he was led out to the firing squad, Campanería told Travieso, "*Voy a gritar un Viva Cristo Rey, Viva Cuba Libre, Viva el Directorio, que le va a traquetear.*"[43] ("I am going to yell a `Long Live Christ the King, Long Live Free Cuba and Long Live the Directorate,' that will shake them up.") These executions let Cubans know that Castro would not deal with his opposition leniently. My parents' disaffection was sealed, as was the disillusionment of many others. After all, these young men had not done anything that Fidel Castro himself had not done by engaging in armed rebellion against a government they opposed.

Robert Stevenson, of the U.S. State Department, recalled that around 200,000 people were arrested days before the invasion and held in baseball stadiums and theaters.[44] Antonio and Tony Bechily were among them. The Bechilys lived in Matanzas, the second largest city in Cuba. The family had three children, all active members of the Catholic Church. Like many other Cuban families, they had supported the revolution but grew disillusioned as the conflict between church and state escalated.

Tony Bechily was a boarding student at a Canadian priests' school in Colón, Matanzas, and was home for Easter vacation. He told his mother that he was going to a teacher's house a few blocks away. The teacher, a priest, was popular among many of Bechily's friends, and his home was the meeting place for a Catholic youth organization that he sponsored. When Bechily's father came home, his wife told him that their son had gone out. The streets had been filled with militiamen and Bechily grew scared. He ran out to find him.

The priest's house was crawling with militiamen, some poised on the rooftop with rifles aimed toward the street. The young men were being led into paddy wagons. The senior Bechily tried to intervene. As he began speaking, a militiaman poked him in the back with his machine gun and said, "You, too, are arrested." Concha Bechily, Tony's mother, recalled the panic she felt as she heard the news. "This was the beginning of our terror, the arrests of minors."

Sometime in the afternoon, a messenger came to tell Concha that her husband and son (and the others) had all been taken to the sports stadium. Later, she learned that they were moved to a chicken farm on the outskirts of Matanzas. She tried desperately to see them, but was not allowed near the compound. Finally, after more than a week, they were released. Tony was very ill. He had contracted typhoid fever from the filth of the chicken farm. The family realized that the repression wasn't going to go away. They, too, had heard the rumor that the government had plans to take away their *patria potestad*. In their case, however, the decision to send their children out of Cuba had more to do with Tony's arrest. They started making arrangements immediately.

Baker's Group Arrested: The Myth of the *Becas*

The Bay of Pigs invasion lasted two days. Of the 1,297 men who landed on April 17, 1961, 1,180 were captured. A triumphant Castro paraded the prisoners across the island and the country rallied behind him. The underground was in disarray. The popular uprising the CIA had counted on to help the invaders never materialized, in part because so many had been arrested in the days before. The arrests and summary trials escalated. Now more than ever, young people in the opposition needed to leave Cuba.

Most of the members of Baker's group had been arrested days before the invasion or shortly thereafter. Teté Cuervo was detained by a group of militiamen who came to the travel agency. This was not the first time. Once before she had been arrested, but the police officer in charge had vouched for her and said that she was not involved in sending children out of the country. She had assisted the man in sending his children to the United States. This time, however, she explained to me. "They wanted to take me down to the station to ask me a few questions about the kids I was sending out." She recalled that "they were very persistent and wanted to know why there were kids leaving by themselves. I told them that they knew nothing; that for years, the U.S. embassy had authorized a plan to give visas to Cuban students studying in the United States. And that they were part of that student program. That they returned home when they were finished with their studies."[45] They still took her in. As she was brought away, Cuervo asked someone in the office to call her house to tell her family what was happening.

She was taken to a makeshift prison at the Plaza of the Revolution where she was questioned directly by Manuel Piñeiro, head of the intelligence division of the 26 of July Movement, who was known as *Barba Roja* for his bright red hair.

"They put me in a small room that had a small sink and kept me incommunicado the whole time," Cuervo recalled years later. Piñeiro first admonished her for her husband's participation in the invasion—after all, he reminded her, her father-in-law had been brutally murdered by Batista's secret police. He then went on to question her about the children who were being sent out. He had lists of names and he wanted to know about the program. The parents of most of these children were fighting in the underground; Piñeiro's line of questioning suggested that Cuban intelligence knew this as well.[46] Cuervo reiterated what she had told the arresting officers: that the children were going to the United States on *becas* (scholarships) that had long been given to Cuban students.

"This was a cover story," she admitted, "so that Cuban intelligence would not stop the program. We assumed that the guards at the airport were new and they would not know what had happened before."[47] Nonetheless, the rumor spread that Cuban children could obtain *becas* to study in the United States. As time passed, Cuban parents trying to decide whether to send their children to the United States would come to believe—as they had believed rumors about *patria potestad*—that such a scholarship program existed, and that their children would be sent to study in good American schools. In reality, no such program was ever established.

After three days of questioning, Cuervo was released only to find that many in Baker's group had either fled or been arrested. She knew about Pancho Finlay because she had overheard the interrogation in the next room and recognized Finlay's voice. He had not been as lucky as she: he was sentenced to a jail term. Berta Finlay's sister, Ester, was also arrested after her cleaning lady turned her in to the security police for possession of a batch of passports. She was questioned about how the group was getting people out. She left for the United States in July 1961, shortly after her release, and moved to Denver, where her daughter had been sent to an orphanage.[48] Serafina Lastra de Giquel was not arrested immediately, but she did discontinue her work on behalf of the children. Instead, she concentrated on gathering information about government actions, including the deployment of weapons, that was then passed to U.S. officials and the CIA via her friend Adelaida Everhart. When her husband died, she was arrested and charged with conspiring with enemies of the state. During her interrogation, Serafina was asked about Adelaida Everhart. Her interrogators wanted to know details about her friend's activities in Cuba before the revolution and what she knew of her work in the United States. Years later, Father Walsh would help Serafina secure a placement in a church-run nursing home in Miami.

Concerns about the Child Refugees

claim

Despite the intense focus on children in the propaganda war, there was little attention paid to what was actually happening to them after they arrived in the United States. But there were concerns. In 1961, Congress held hearings about the refugees and officials were asked about the plight of the children. The congressmen were told, "We have been at great pains to assure that the personalities of the children will not be damaged by their trying experiences and that they will be restored to their families at the first possible moment."[49] In early spring of 1961, Penny Powers had visited Washington, D.C., with a message: Cuban parents were sacrificing their lives, but they wanted to make sure that their children would be safe. With the help of Ambassador Bonsal, she spoke with government officials. In an April 3 letter to Bonsal, Powers stated that since January, more than 600 children had been sent to the United States and another 700 were ready to go. But parents were raising criticisms of the program daily. As an example, she mentioned José Ignacio Álamo, two of whose children were at an orphanage in New York. "These children's letters are censored and they cannot telephone or receive calls. He also has two boys in St. Joseph's in New York who are extremely unhappy," she reported.[50] Álamo, who was working in the underground with Tony Varona, one of the members of the CIA's Revolutionary Council, was so concerned that he was thinking of taking his children back to the island.

Powers also spoke of a Mr. Maurino, who was fearful for his two children in the United States. Maurino had received a letter from his thirteen-year-old daughter, who was in one of the camps in Miami, saying she was afraid that she was going to be sent north and separated from her nine-year-old brother—as had become the practice with siblings of different sexes. The parents had not heard from either child and did not know where they were. Powers was concerned that these children had also been sent to some institution up north, and that their letters, too, had been censored.

There were other cases of parents who did not know whether their children had arrived in the United States because they had not heard from them, nor were their names on the list of those who were supposed to arrive in Miami. Thirteen-year-old Francisco Gómez Valdez, for example, who was sent by Father Mauro of Maristas College could not be traced.[51] "This should be an opportunity for the children to see American life at its best form," Powers urged, "so that they would realize that Communism has nothing to offer them in comparison with democracy."[52] Frank Craft, the state director of Florida's Department of Public Welfare was upset about Power's letter and responded: "We are not sure what can be done to help Miss Powers understand better and accept the plans being made for unaccompanied children."[53]

Still, Penny persisted. In a letter to W. L. Mitchell of HEW, Powers outlined her criticisms of the program:

1. The present program, which keeps the children in an isolated orphanage atmosphere, does not do anything to further future Cuban-American relationship nor does it give the children an idea of a democratic way of life.
2. The atmosphere in these institutions is not comparable to what they were accustomed to in their homes in Cuba.
3. In this type of institution there can be no intensive preparation of our participation in a democratic process when they return to Cuba.
4. The separation of brothers and sisters, regardless of whether they are fairly young which is insisted upon intensifies unnecessarily the breakup of family life.
5. The above four points add to the already desperate situation of the parents in Cuba, who were given to understand that everything was going to be done to keep the children of a family together. As the children are mostly in orphanages spread out all over the United States, it gives parents a feeling of complete hopelessness and also makes them feel it as forgone conclusion that their children are thought of as orphans.[54]

After meeting with parents who were fighting in the underground and had sent their children out of Cuba, Powers insisted that the program not be exclusively Catholic. She was leery of the intentions of these institutions and strongly felt that a plan to educate children in democratic ways should entail a clear separation between church and state.[55] She also urged placing the children in boarding schools so that they would develop a sense of community and not feel like orphans. The curriculum could include English classes so that they could understand what was happening around them. To expose children to American ways, sponsors could be arranged to take children home for the weekend. There should be intensive courses on democracy. This was most important to Powers. After all, her idea of the program was that the children were being prepared to return to Cuba after Castro's ouster.[56] "If a program could be worked out directly with H.E.W . . . it would benefit greatly the children who are in search of something better than the Communism of their own country," she wrote.[3]

But Power's criticisms and suggestions were lost on a bureaucracy that was preoccupied with military objectives. By the end of April 1961, HEW reported the presence of 657 children: 402 boys and 255 girls. The future of these children—or, for that matter, of the entire program—was unclear to the organizers of their exodus. The program they knew was put in place to evacuate the children of those fighting in the underground and the youth who were risking their lives in opposition to the Cuban government. Would such a program continue if U.S. military plans failed? Repression was at an all-time high in Cuba, and the pressure to leave Cuba was only increasing.

Children's needs were ignored because the bureaucracy was preoccupied with military objectives.

5

Parents and the Decision to Send the Children

One of my sisters and I spent the night of April 16, 1961, in the bathtub of our home in the Havana neighborhood of La Víbora. The government had issued warnings and outlined safety measures in the event of bombing raids, and it advised that bathrooms have the strongest foundations. In Havana, such exercises had become routine since aerial bombings had been on the increase. My family initially supported the revolutionary government. We even had personal links with Fidel Castro: His first wife, Mirta Díaz-Balart, was my aunt's cousin. In 1953, it was my grandfather who sent money to Fidel's family when Fidel was arrested after the Moncada attack. After getting out of prison, Fidel continued organizing a rebel force. In the next few years, the *rebeldes* practiced shooting on my uncle's dairy farm near Jaruco, a small town on the outskirts of Havana.

My father, a doctor, had joined the revolutionary army, accepting the new government's offer of a commission in exchange for services. At the psychiatric hospital, he worked alongside Bernabé Ordaz, a medical school colleague who had risen to the rank of commander while fighting in the mountains. We spent Sundays at the hospital, where the two men, both passionate amateur musicians, organized a music program that would become a showcase of revolutionary medical health care.

Before long, my parents began to look on in horror at Castro's arbitrary use of power, particularly his dismissal of any semblance of the rule of law and his failure to hold promised elections. Moreover, the professional reforms they expected from the revolution never materialized. My mother, a chemistry professor, saw corruption at the university worsen. Armando Hart, Castro's Minister of Education (and later Minister of Culture), personally asked her to award unearned credits to students who had fought in the guerrilla war. But the one act that sealed my parents' decision to leave was the execution, by firing squad, of young Virgilio Campanería. (His mother would join a group of women who helped other youths leave Cuba with visa waivers.) Our home, once a safe house for the revolutionaries, became a site of opposition.

My father sought an exchange opportunity with a medical school abroad. We obtained passport photos at the Port Authority, in Old Havana, where the Health Department established a makeshift clinic to accommodate the thousands of people preparing to leave. I remember that day at the Port Authority vividly. We stood in a long line awaiting our smallpox inoculations as soldiers hurried the crowd along with their rifle tips. One pushed my younger sister by pointing a rifle to her head. As we elbowed our way through the crowd, my mother hailed a taxi. After we piled in, she dug out a couple of lemon wedges from her purse and squeezed them on our shots to minimize the scarring.

It's hard to reconstruct these memories of my last weeks in Cuba, they come in rapid sequence—everything was changing, but I do remember that these were anxious and fearful days.[1] I asked my parents what life was like for them, and what provoked their decision to leave. Years of conversation, of piecing together different peoples' accounts of our flight, of entering old memories tied up in pain and political slogans, have given me a partial story.

The situation was becoming more desperate. The neighbors on our block talked about sending their children away. My mother recalled whispered discussions with the women at the park at the end of our block. As they sat together and watched their children play, they spoke in hushed tones about ways of sending the kids out of Cuba. She also heard from friends at church, who also contemplated sending their children away. My parents put out feelers with friends in Miami about getting visa waivers for the entire family. Then they heard from José Antonio Arruza, a family friend whose sons attended my school and who was distributing visa waivers. He was also involved in an espionage ring, obtaining information and sending it in code to the CIA.[2]

The Arruza boys were traveling to Miami alone; they could send me with them. The oldest boy was already involved in anti-Castro activities and if arrested he too could face a firing squad. Still, the prospect of sending me alone frightened my parents. I was not yet six. They waited. The days after the Bay of Pigs, the schools were closed. Rumors persisted that all those who could read and write would be sent out to the countryside to teach literacy to peasants. Parents of teenage boys were afraid that they would be caught up in the opposition and arrested and possibly executed. Everyone was talking about the government's plans to take over *patria potestad*. My parents finally decided to send me.

Control Over Educational Institutions

If one singular government action can be pinpointed as the catalyst for massiveness of the Pedro Pan exodus, it would be the closing down of the schools. On September 26, 1960, Castro announced before the United Nations that the following year Cuba would launch an all-out offensive to eradicate illiteracy. "Death to illiteracy," he proclaimed, "would be the number one goal in 1961."[3] He went on to declare 1961 to be the year of education, and added that in April all schools would be closed for eight months so that the country could launch a literacy campaign.[4] "We shall be able to proclaim to the entire world that in our country there remains not one person who is unable to read and write. . . . We shall terminate the school year early and mobilize all the students from sixth grade and up. We shall organize an army of teachers and send them to every corner of the country."[5]

Imagine, for a moment, the panic that would ensue in the United States if the federal government decreed a closing of all schools. The CIA was counting on that panic as they organized a student strike to coincide with the invasion, hoping to have the Cuban government confiscate the schools before April 15.[6] The decision about where to educate

one's children had been a parental right throughout Cuba's history. The
Church protested. Parents predictably panicked. And the state's action
added credence to the rumor that parents would soon lose their *patria
potestad.*

One of the first clashes between the revolutionary government and
the Catholic Church had been over education. On January 13, 1959, the
new government issued Law 11 (*Ley Once*), which invalidated the de-
grees granted by the Catholic Villanueva University from November
1956 to January 1959. During this time, the Batista government had
closed down the public universities as a means of trying to stem the
growing tide of student support for the revolution. Villanueva, whose
American rector had walked an ambiguous line between the government and his university, had remained open despite the fact that Batista
had killed several of its students who were suspected of being revolutionaries. Now the university was to be punished for what was perceived
as a lack of support for the revolution.

On February 13, in response to the new measure, the Archbishop of
Santiago, Enrique Pérez Serantes, who had been a vocal opponent of
Batista—and a friend of Fidel Castro—issued the first pastoral letter
entitled "On Private Education," criticizing the new government:[7] "The
war is, then, against religious education in the public schools; the
war is against all Catholic schools, even the most prestigious, which is
Villanueva University. Can they say that being a student at a Catholic
school automatically constitutes a danger for society?" Serantes went
on to state that it was Masons, communists, and the people who favor
laicism who were denying people the freedom of educational choice by
not allowing religion to be taught in public schools. "To state things
clearly, the enemy they are combating is one, the only one that world
communism fears. Catholicism, that is their enemy.[8]

On February 18, a pastoral letter was circulated expanding on the
themes, stating that parents should have a choice of educating their
children where they saw fit, whether public or private schools, but that
all should have religious education. The bishops said they based their
demand on the fact that 95 percent of the Cuban population was

Catholic.[9] They drew parallels between Cuba and Hungary. Barely six weeks into the revolutionary government, lines were being drawn between Catholicism and communism.[10] The battle would be won by whomever controlled the education of children.

Two days later, on February 20, 1959, the government issued Law No. 76, which called for restructuring the educational system, giving each province and municipality its own department.[11] However, the Ministry of Education would centralize the planning and regulation of curricula and courses as well as the selection of textbooks. Private schools were still permitted to exist, and the teaching of religion was allowed, although their classes were subject to inspection by the government.[12] This fell short of what the Catholic Church had advocated. By October 1959, Article 149 was added to the Cuban constitution taking away the ability of private schools to set their own curricula.

The battles between the state and the Church dampened the ardor of young Catholics who had wholeheartedly supported the revolution. Emilio Cueto was fourteen when the revolution triumphed. He remembers volunteering gladly when two priests came to his school to recruit students to teach soldiers to read and write. Night after night, he and some classmates went out to the Manugua barracks in Havana. With a government-issued instruction booklet they taught the rebel soldiers: "*F* is for Fidel and *fusil*" (rifle). Cueto and his group were enthusiastic and very committed to social justice. Yet by April 1959, Juan Almeida, the commander in charge of the program, had dismissed the Catholic volunteers because he did not want the Catholic influence upon the rebel army. "I clearly remember the day Almeida showed up and told us that we could no longer be part of the Literacy Campaign because they did not want any Catholic influence. Imagine how we felt being told that we could not be part of the nation because of our religious beliefs."[13] Catholic youth organizations were also excluded from attending a Latin American Youth Congress that occurred in Havana.[14]

By mid-1960, the government had established the Instituto Superior de Educación. Among its tasks was to train teachers in a curriculum that included instructions on Marxism-Leninism.[15] The next year,

the government would also initiate the Schools of Revolutionary Instruction dedicated to "the ideological formation of revolutionaries,
and then, by means of the revolutionaries, the ideological formation of
the rest of the people," as Fidel Castro explained to a crowd of cheering
young people.[16]

In May 1960, the army's educational department organized the Association of Rebel Youth, which would later become the Union of Young
Communists, a select membership organization for youths ages fourteen to twenty-seven. By the end of the year, schools would implement
a new system of tracking students' academic and ideological records, *la
ficha escolar acumulativa* (the cumulative school record), that according to *Revolución*, the Cuban government's official paper, "was to put in
teachers' hands an instrument capable of orienting students' present
and future lives."[17] It was a detailed permanent record of a student's
scholastic, behavioral, and ideological development.

More alarming was the Union of Rebel Pioneers for grade-school
children. Children wore special uniforms, maroon with a blue scarf,
and were encouraged to participate in government-sponsored community service drives.[18] However, the level of organization and discipline
expected reflected the government's drive to militarize not only society
but in this case youth organizations.[19]

— Burden of proof.

The United States, the Church, and Children's Education

Initially, the United States tried to accommodate itself to the new regime, but relations quickly deteriorated.[20] The United States interpreted the Cuban revolution's radical nationalism as a challenge to its
position in Latin America. It saw the pamphlets distributed by the 26 of
July Movement as Communist-line indoctrination materials.[21] As such,
U.S. policymakers started to view the Cuba "problem" through the lens
of the Cold War. Communist influence on youth had been, for some
time, a U.S. concern and Castro's outreach to the youth in Cuba and in
Latin America was being closely monitored.

In August 1960, the U.S. embassy in Costa Rica reported: "During the past week the Cuban exile organization Revolutionary Democratic Front of Cuba (FRD) published a series of full or double-page advertisements attacking the Castro regime on various points, including the dispatching of Cuban youths to Communist governments for indoctrination and Communist training."[22] From Havana, José Miró Cardona, who had resigned as prime minister in 1959, echoed the same theme. In outlining the reasons for his opposition to the regime, he cited "the transformation of the primary school system, turning the children against Christian principles to give them a militia uniform and arms."[23] In November, the Frente presented a statement to the Organization of American States that asked, "What was next? . . . The Communist indoctrination of youth through the state monopolization of education and the imposition of a single history text?"[24]

The Frente condemned the persecution of the Catholic Church, particularly the forced-armed entry into various churches in Havana during the reading of a pastoral letter signed by all the bishops, condemning the communist nature of the regime. Rafael Ravelo, whose parents would eventually send him to the United States, remembers going to church one Sunday and watching as a gang of youths ran into the church and started screaming during the homily. "It was getting pretty scary . . . we didn't know if we were going to be a target of the people that would come to the churches and all of the sudden would stand up and become aggressive. They would go to the churches and when the priest began the homily they would become violent, go toward the altar."[25]

The U.S. government found an ally in the Catholic Church, which it had earlier perceived as soft on communism.[26] Wayne Smith, the U.S. embassy's liaison with the church, wrote in May 1960:

> It would seem that the Church has been overly cautious in not playing a more active role in orienting its members against the Communist menace implicit in the Castro regime. . . . For the present, then, there seems to be no probability that the Church will draw clear-cut lines of opposition before the Castro regime and its trend toward Communism . . . an agreement on a Pastoral Letter needs to

be reached before it is too late. Too, it is to be hoped that the appearance on the scene of Monsignor Eduardo Boza Masvidal and Monsignor José M. Domínguez as auxiliary Bishops of Havana may act as a strong stimulant in bringing about a more aggressive posture. Both were ordained May 15, 1960, are liberal, respected leaders, and strongly anti-Communist.[27]

Days later, on May 17, Archbishop Serantes issued a long-awaited pastoral letter entitled "For God and for Cuba." Not only did he openly criticize the establishment of commercial ties between Cuba and socialist countries, but he also strongly denounced communism and materialism. He warned Cubans that the danger was now within the country as well as outside its borders. He called on Cuban Catholics to combat communism within their own ranks and praised the United States for its outlay of funds to fight communism. "No one can be deceived, the cards are on the table. The struggle is not between Washington and Moscow, the two formidable military powers that are face to face grasping such deadly weapons as the world has ever seen," he wrote. Ideology was the definitive struggle. The battle was between Christianity and communism. "We condemn communism because it unnecessarily subordinates family life to the state, encouraging women to leave the home, and educates children as the state wishes, without considering parent's wishes."[28]

But this was not enough for the United States. On June 8, Wayne Smith again wrote: "In spite of the spirited attitude of Monsignor Boza Masvidal and the well-conceived strategy of Monsignor Martín Villaverde, the position of the Church will leave much to be desired in so far as a sharply drawn stand against Communism in Cuba is concerned until a clearly stated general pastoral letter is issued."[29] Nonetheless, the strains between the church in Havana and the Cuban government had continued to grow, the fissures occurring along old and new issues. Catholic schools were viewed as nests for conspirators, allies of threatening foreign powers.[30] The issue of the control of education solidified the Church in the fight against the government.

The tensions escalated. By midsummer, Smith was detecting a more hard-line stance on the part of the Church: "Recent discussions with Catholic clergymen and laymen have indicated that the attitude of the Church is hardening and that the more energetic members of the hierarchy can probably be expected to speak out with increasing vigor in the months ahead . . . have come to an agreement on the matter and are said to be considering the issuance of a letter at some unspecified date in the future." He went on to report that Monsignor Boza Masvidal, in an address delivered at the University of Villanueva on June 1, expounded at length on the attitude of the church vis-à-vis private property, the role of the state, nationalism, the class struggle, education, and confiscation and expropriation of property.[31] The Cuban government did not sit by and watch. It mobilized anti-Church protesters almost immediately, sending youths into churches to disrupt services. *Revolución*, the government's newspaper, began its attack with a headline that read: "What the Archbishop Forgot to Denounce: The True Enemy of 6,000,000 Cubans."

The American embassy was keenly interested in the ongoing developments. In fact, Smith recommended that: "If the 26 of July Movement, whose name is almost synonymous with the Revolutionary Government, launches a polemic with the Cuban Catholic Church, it may open its guard for a body blow on the psychological front in Latin America at large." He would keep the United States Information Agency up to date with any events that they could use in their propaganda programs.[32]

By July the government-sponsored protest against the church had spread to Havana. This time, Smith's tone was more optimistic: the government was attacking the church again. The discussion had moved to whether or not the new government was communist, and this, Smith thought, was important for the United States in order to build anti-communist sympathies with other Latin American countries.[33]

In August 1960, as the Church was still trying to reclaim its place in the nationalist struggle, another pastoral letter was circulated stating that "no one should ask Catholics in the name of misconceived unity to remain silent against communist doctrines that not only went against their faith, but against the faith of the majority of Cubans."[34] Particularly influenced by the civil war in Spain, the bishop's main fear was communism, and they saw the confrontation in Cuba as part of the international struggle of the Cold War. September 25, 1960 was Catholic Youth Day and more than five thousand young people gathered at Colegio Belén, Fidel Castro's alma mater, for a special mass. After the services the crowd broke into a chant of "Cuba Sí! Russia No!" a few shouted "Down with Castro." Increasingly, Catholic youth were becoming more outspoken against the government. In turn, the government began to monitor closely their activities, setting up vigilance of the Young Catholic Workers organization in Havana.[35]

The schism between the Church and the revolutionary government by now was unbridgeable. The embassy reported that the Catholic bishops had publicly addressed Fidel Castro with the strongest and most effective document that had been issued by the Cuban Church to date. The embassy recommended that "the fullest possible use of the letter be made and promoted by the U.S. government, and that consideration be given to: (1) its use in USIA output, particularly in Latin America; and (2) radio broadcast to Cuba of verbatim extracts by Radio Swan and others."[36] Wayne Smith concluded, "Though the role of the Church in bringing the destruction of the Castro regime should not be overemphasized, it does stand as a united block dedicated to the thesis that the Castro regime is an evil which must be destroyed. [It] can use its moral weight in the struggle and can deal the regime some psychological blows."[37] Clearly, the United States was well positioned to join in an ideological offensive.

The Literacy Campaign

Preparations for the literacy campaign that Castro had announced at the United Nations in September 1960 began in November of that year with a government census to identify illiterates in need of instruction. On May 1, 1961, Castro declared: "The state considers it within its duty, the revolution considers it within its duty, to organize and establish the principle of free education to all the citizens of the country. And the people consider it within their duty to mold future generations with a spirit of love for the fatherland, love of neighbor, love of justice, and love of the revolution."[38]

More than one-quarter of a million people were mobilized: literate men, women, and youths, supplied with three million books and more than 100,000 paraffin lamps, went into the countryside in buses. There was a sense of urgency and enthusiasm in the *brigadistas*, which is what literacy workers were called in keeping with the government's militaristic theme. By the end of the year, the government declared that the official literacy rate of 21 percent had plummeted to 3.9 percent.[39] The literacy test involved reading one or two paragraphs from a primer entitled *Venceremos*, reciting the slogan of the 26 of July Movement, taking simple dictation, and writing a letter to Castro. The government declared the campaign fundamental to the task of building a new society. For the opposition, however, the literacy campaign was a thinly veiled plan to take young people from their families to be brainwashed by the government and reeducate teachers in preparation of when schools reopened under government control.[40]

Aware of the growing fears of parents, the Cuban government launched a counteroffensive. On April 16, it ran a two-page advertisement in *Bohemia* inviting parents to meet with a group of *brigadistas* who had just returned from the countryside. They wanted parents to question the *brigadistas* directly. The ad closed with an appeal to parental responsibility and patriotism: "Don't deny your child this opportunity to serve the Fatherland."[41] The literacy campaign was presented as the idealization of the essential principles of the revolution itself: an egalitarian effort to make those previously denied the basic right to read and write literate. The disparity in education between the island's rural and urban areas were to be remedied by taking resources—young literacy workers from the city—to the countryside to teach their brethren. In addition, the division between manual and intellectual labor would be obliterated as city dwellers learned about agriculture and farms. In the government's view, this program not only embodied the core ideas of revolution, but integrated Martí's views about education as well.[42]

Beyond the revolutionary fanfare, the government was moving in the direction of resetting the ideological course for the nation by creating a series of schools aimed at training an elite ideological cadre. Unlike the public display accompanying the literacy campaign, the *escuelas de instrucción revolucionaria* (schools of revolutionary instruction) were born in secrecy. Their task was to form revolutionaries who would then educate the rest of the citizenry.[43] Enrollment was highly selective. In January of 1961, twelve provincial schools were opened in addition to the national school in Havana named Ñico López. They were full-time boarding schools, with courses lasting three months. Half the students came from the ranks of the Partido Socialista Popular (Cuba's pro-Moscow Communist Party) and the other half were from the 26 of July Movement. A few also came from the Directorio Revolucionario Estudiantil, the urban organization that was the counterpart to Fidel's army in the mountains.[44] Most of the teachers were from the party, and instruction materials came from the Soviet Union. Clearly, the ideological orientation of the schools—and indeed of the revolution—was moving in the direction of Marxism-Leninism.[45]

It would not be until 1962 that an extensive system of government *internados* (boarding schools) would be established.[46] But the discussions around their establishment and the actual emergence of the schools would give further impetus to many parents' decisions to send their children abroad. In 1961, the government started rewarding *brigadistas* with the *becas* (scholarships) that had been promised during the literacy campaign. Recipients were chosen according to their families' loyalty to the revolution. The boarding schools began in Havana, in houses left behind by Miami-bound Cubans.[47] "Their surroundings," noted a sympathetic observer, "are generally better than those of most Cuban families, since the scholarship schools are located in the mansions of those who left Cuba."[48] But plans also included sending children from Havana out to schools in the countryside. Parents feared that the plan to send their children away gave the government the opportunity to influence their upbringing and discipline, socialization and ideology. And years later a scholar would observe that by "rewarding ideological conformity, rather than intelligence alone, the Castro leadership succeeded in strengthening its grip on Cuban society."[49] By 1962, 70,000 children had attended the boarding schools.

Decisions to Send the Children Ahead

The closure of the schools also served the regime in its battle against the Catholic Church, as it minimized the Church's influence over the island's young people. Teaching was the main mission of many of the religious orders on the island, and without schools, these orders would have nothing to do. Moreover, with the schools closed, they could no longer collect tuition fees, so they could not support themselves. Ultimately, the Cuban government began expelling priests and nuns, starting with the Spanish-born, so many of the schools made plans to reopen abroad and take students with them. In a telegram to the State Department, the British ambassador asked the Swiss ambassador to arrange visa waivers for forty Carmelite nuns desiring to go to Puerto Rico, via Miami. The United States facilitated the issuance of visas for the clergy.[50] Finally, on September 17, 1961, the government expelled 130 priests and other religious workers sending them to Spain on a steamer named *Covadonga*.[51]

It was at this time that the vast majority of parents who would send their children to Miami via Operation Pedro Pan made their decision. It was not easy, because once parents sent their children, even if they were not involved in the opposition, they would be fingered as discontents.[52] There was a certain kind of mass hysteria when the schools were ordered shut, recalled Rafael Ravelo, who was thirteen at the time.[53] "I was in Havana in school at the Brothers of La Salle," he told me. "The panic started because people truly loved the priests and nuns—after all, these were their children's teachers." In addition, there was increased harassment of people going to church. "I remember being in mass and a group standing up and starting to yell revolutionary slogans in the middle of the ceremony." The division between those who supported the Church and those who supported the government was also seen as a rift between those who supported family unity versus those who did not. The government had a plan to send the youth out to the countryside, many believed. The children would be brainwashed, and when they returned they would belong to the government, not their families. Ravelo's parents made arrangements to send him abroad. First they had to sign a notarized consent form giving their son permission to travel abroad.[54]

"In my home," Ravelo recalls, "the discussion [about leaving for the United States] always assumed that it would only be temporary. Everyone on the block and kids from school were talking about leaving. This coincided with the literacy campaign. I left in May, weeks after the school closed, and, my parents were expecting me back that September, when they thought the school would reopen." It would be twenty-one years before Ravelo saw his parents again.

A report submitted to the CIA about the life of an ordinary Cuban echoes the fears expressed by Rafael Ravelo's parents. The father (unnamed in the report) was trying to decide whether to stay and fight or flee the country. His primary concern, however, was his daughter, who had studied with the Dominican nuns. After the closing of the Catholic schools, she enrolled in a technical school but was told she could only study if she participated in the student militia. The daughter, according to the father, was a good Catholic and therefore anti-Communist. His only alternative was to send her out of the country.[55]

Valentín Díaz had to make the decision about sending his two daughters to the United States very quickly: "My oldest daughter arrived from school saying that they were going to send her to the countryside. It was something I did not accept, most of all because of her age. She was fourteen."[56]

According to Jim Baker, who was by then back in the United States, there were stories going around about young women coming back pregnant. Reflecting upon the origins of the program almost forty years later, he wrote:

> One of the very special aspects of Cuban culture was the strength of family ties. Castro set out early to destroy any threat to his control. He separated teenagers from their parents and sent those from Havana into the interior where they were subjected to intense indoctrination under the guise of preparing them to participate in the program of reducing illiteracy in rural areas. Girls who had been carefully chaperoned all their lives were taught that sex was a natural need, which should be satisfied, as was hunger for food. As a result of this campaign to break down the family values, so many teenage girls returned to Havana pregnant that a special abortion clinic had to be established to cover up this catastrophe.[57]

There is no way of establishing whether or not these perceptions were correct. But there is no doubt that the fear parents felt for their children was real.

Thus, for Díaz the decision was simple: to have his daughters leave the country as soon as possible. He went to a friend who put him in contact with Teté Cuervo at the Lonja del Comercio in Old Havana. At the travel agency, Díaz was given instructions of what he needed to do: obtain an affidavit, signed by him and his wife and notarized, giving his daughters permission to travel since they were underage. "They told me to go with her to the Port Authority to get shots," he recalled. "Then I could not do anything else; I called this lady again. There was fear, because the children would travel through Jamaica and then to the United States. But it was the first avenue open to us."[58]

The plan that Díaz had so carefully arranged immediately before Bay of Pigs was delayed because of the invasion. After the invasion, everything became much more complicated, but Díaz did eventually manage to obtain papers for his daughters.

Emilio Cueto almost didn't get out either. His mother had watched with alarm as her son escalated his activities in Agrupación Católica

(Catholic Union) at the Universidad de Villanueva and began looking for ways to send him out of the country. Spain was a possibility, but the cost of a plane ticket to Madrid was prohibitive. As they searched for an exit, the young Cueto ran into a family friend who had just sent her children to the United States. When he told the woman of his predicament, she offered to help. Cueto was to get his passport to her as soon as possible and wait. On April 14 he received a call from a Jesuit priest who told him he had to meet with him right away. He went to meet the priest at the school where he taught and was given his passport with a visa to Jamaica. He went home to prepare for his trip, which was scheduled for Monday, April 17.

Cueto, too, had been told to see Teté Cuervo at a travel agency at la Lonja del Comercio. There he would pay twenty-five dollars and receive his airline ticket. When he arrived, Teté was very nervous: a bomb had exploded the night before at El Encanto, and aerial bombings had increased. She gave Cueto his ticket and told him he would not be able to leave on Monday because the invasion was on its way—her husband (a fighter in the underground) was coming. Cueto should check with the airport to see when his flight would be rescheduled, she advised. He returned home, and called his university friends to find out what was going on. All of them had been arrested. His mother decided that they should leave the house in case the police came for him. For the next four days, he hid at his grandmother's house. Finally his flight was rescheduled for April 26. Although his ticket was to Jamaica, he had been instructed to get off the plane on its Miami stopover. Teté gave him a coded message for Father Walsh and Jim Baker, which he wrote on page 121 of the French textbook he took with him. Emilio spent two months in a Miami camp and then was sent to Burlington, Vermont, to study English. In September he enrolled at Catholic University in Washington.[59] After a few days in Miami, Rafael was sent to Costa Rica to study in a seminary. Emilio, like Rafael, would not see his mother for twenty years.

6

Rescate de la Niñez:
The Aftermath of the Invasion

The failure of the Bay of Pigs invasion left the underground movement in disarray. Those who were still in Cuba faced a grim choice: prison or exile. Over one hundred thousand Cubans had fled to the United States after the revolution, and hundreds of thousands more now wanted to leave Cuba. For the United States, this was a problem, since there was already an anti-refugee backlash from the American public. U.S. government bureaucrats, however, turned their energies primarily to covering the mistakes that had contributed to the invasion's failure.

In Washington, the administration scrambled, first to deny involvement in the Bay of Pigs offensive and then to manage the fallout. On April 22, 1961, the National Security Council met. The president ordered that "there should be no further discussion outside of government of the meaning of recent landings in Cuba, since the object was now to move forward." For the time being, he did not want to *expand* support for guerrillas in Cuba, except where there was a moral obligation or to assist in survival or evacuation.[1] However, on November 3, 1961, Kennedy authorized the development of a new program designed to undermine the Castro government.[2] His brother, Robert, would head the efforts, code-named Operation Mongoose and General Edward Lansdale (the model for the principal character in the novel *The Ugly American*[3] and Graham Greene's *The Quiet American*) would be in charge of the daily operations.

The Kennedy brothers were deeply distrustful of the CIA and the Bay of Pigs invasion convinced them that they needed to move Cuban operations out of the CIA. Lansdale was the perfect choice; not only was he friendly with the director of the CIA, he was also an air force colonel. In addition, Lansdale was a master in psychological operations as he had demonstrated in his war against Communists in the Philippines. Most important, this would give Robert Kennedy control of the anti-Castro operations.[4]

Many of the policies and programs that had been put in place for the invasion were still operative. The immigration mechanisms that had been established for the military evacuation of agents and their families—the visa waiver program—would now provide channels of departure for the increasing numbers of civilian people wanting to flee the island.[5]

The question of what to do with Cuban refugees was a critical item on the president's agenda. It was reported that many Cubans were in the United States with visitor's visas, and "a lot of them are Castro agents."[6] In a memo addressed to the director of the CIA and the secretary of HEW, national security advisor McGeorge Bundy explained that Kennedy wanted to know how much money was being spent on the refugees and wanted a report on what could be done to help them settle in the United States.[7] The president assigned HEW the role of ensuring that exiles could begin to adapt to their lives in the United States. Both HEW and the CIA were tasked with drawing up a report on the refugees.

The Department of Defense would deal with the military end of the refugee problem. This included assessing the military risk of having a large number of refugees angry at the United States government for failing to support them during the invasion, concentrated in one geographic location, namely Miami. The Department would go on to advocate that "given the continued existence of the Castro regime, our only realistic policy in regard to the Cuban exiles is to scatter them throughout the United States and integrate them within the USA society in the shortest possible time so that they do not constitute a refugee problem."[8] In the eventuality of a possible collapse of the Castro government, it urged that the U.S. government have a group of Cuban exiles ready to assume leadership roles on the island, so they recommended that a small group be trained to run the military and civilian sectors of society. The CIA had already started doing this with their "university."

James Baker, who was now in Miami assisting Father Walsh, concurred. In the summer of 1961, he sent Congress a proposal that stated:

> The presence in the United States of a very large group of leaders from all areas of Cuban life provides the United States an unusual opportunity to help these refugees prepare themselves for service to Cuba in the post-Castro period. These leaders can benefit much from a study of the philosophy and propaganda methods of Communism. They need to know more about democracy; about community organizations and their function; about the benefits that a group of citizens can produce by working together to improve their city or nation.[9]

On behalf of the Truth about Cuba Committee, a group mainly composed of Americans who had lived in Cuba, including Jack Everhart, Baker proposed a plan to Congress to retrain teachers and leaders in an effort to counteract Communist indoctrination. He wanted to establish a two-pronged research project to combat the effects of Communist brainwashing on Cuban children and to develop in these students a comprehensive understanding of and belief in democracy.[10]

By the summer of 1961 there were 116,700 Cuban exiles in the United States.[11]

Table 6.1: Cuban Exiles in the United States

	Nation	Florida
Immigrants	65,000	26,000
Visitors, Students	29,500	20,000
Refugees	22,200	13,600
Total	116,700	96,000

Kennedy expressed his desire that aid to the refugees should be given openly and not just through covert operations. The president named a Cuban refugee coordinator who ran the program from offices located in downtown Miami. Eventually these offices were moved to a building that came to be known as the Freedom Tower. Refugees were required to register. This way they could be monitored. In turn, they were eligible for aid that consisted of food and cash allowances and relocation monies. This action would at least show that the U.S government did care about the refugees. Visa requirements were relaxed; Cubans would no longer be expected to have valid passports when applying for visas. "It is believed that these procedures now amply meet the humanitarian and public relations demands of the situation," a State Department cable said.[12] The Cuban Revolutionary Council was told by representatives of various federal departments that "obtaining waivers of visas for members of the underground who for their own safety need to get out of Cuba and were otherwise not qualified to obtain them . . . was not an insurmountable problem."[13] As a practical matter, of course, it would have been difficult to continue to spend so much money covertly.

For the Pedro Pan program, the effect of the president's directive would be this: the distribution of visas in Cuba would remain a covert activity while the unaccompanied children's program in the United States would be conducted openly. This included housing the children. HEW's revised plan for Cuban refugees asked for the adoption of an open-ended budget for any unaccompanied Cuban refugee child who came to their attention regardless of where they were or how they got to the United States. HEW estimated that this could go up to $700,000 for 1962.[14] Still, a National Security Council memorandum written at the time defined as "classified" the unaccompanied children's program within the United States, involving between 600 and 700 refugee children in foster homes and under group care.[15] Another memo identified the source responsible for the referral of the children. As of April 1961, forty-seven percent had come from Penny Powers.

Table 6.2: Unaccompanied Cuban Children by Sex and Referral Sources[16]

	Boys	Girls	Total
Children Under Direct Care	204 / 31%	107 / 16%	311 / 47%
Through Miss Powers	198 / 30%	148 / 23%	346 / 53%
Through Others	402 / 61%	255 / 39%	657 / 100%

The mention that the children's program was classified suggests that federal officials and activists were under orders to keep the program out of public awareness. Covert programs were run under strict secrecy codes. The reason Pedro Pan was ordered classified when thousands of children were openly boarding planes and coming to the United States reflects the secret origins of the program. Organizers had been afraid that the children's parents, many in the underground, would suffer repercussions. If the Cuban government was aware of which children had been sent alone to the United States, then they could easily trace their parents. This is precisely why on May 8, 1961, Mildred Arnold of the Children's Bureau, the agency in charge of the unaccompanied children's program for the federal government, declined an invitation from Carlyle Onsrud, executive director of the Public Welfare Board of North Dakota, to speak at a conference. The conference, he explained, would tell the human story behind the headlines of welfare work.[17] But Arnold responded that the government was "attempting to keep details of the care of unaccompanied children confidential because of possible recrimination for the parents."[18]

There were other concerns as well. For instance, the FBI worried that the Cuban government could use this program to infiltrate spies into the United States. They questioned visa procedures that would facilitate the airlift of 20,000 people from Havana to the United States in 1961. The State Department responded that although the U.S. government would subsidize these flights, the Cubans who would be coming already had visas or visa waivers, which needed to be checked. To qualify for a visa waiver, an individual had to be checked against State Department records; waivers would be granted to hardship cases based on reunification of families with members already in this country, or to children to attend schools in the United States.[19]

In reality, though, the president's directive that the evacuation should be continued meant that Father Walsh would still hold unabated power to issue visa waivers for children under eighteen, with the caveat that that those between sixteen and eighteen years old must have a security clearance.[20] However, a new network would have to be established in Havana since most of the members of Baker's group had been arrested. A parallel program for the underground was expanded through which over 600,000 visa waivers would be issued. Through that program, parents could travel with their children.

Youth in the Underground

The CIA had operational interests in getting young people out of Cuba. Thousands had been detained days following the Bay of Pigs, and the fragments of the underground that were still able to function were deeply divided. The story of my cousin Francisco (Pancho) León is but one example.[21] On July 24, 1961, the CIA office in Miami, code named JM WAVE, sent a telegram to the CIA director in Washington requesting assistance in securing a visa waiver for Francisco León Delgado, who was then nineteen. The purpose of León's trip would be to help reorganize the Movimiento Revolucionario del Pueblo (The People's Revolutionary Movement), an underground group that was suffering an internal political rift. León was part of the faction that opposed the leadership of Manolo Ray, who had resigned his post as public works minister in early 1961 and had left for the United States. Agents at JM WAVE were leery of the entire group, but especially of Ray whom they called "Fidelista sin Fidel," meaning that although he had broken with Castro, he still sympathized with many of the revolution's ideals. This group was more nationalist and independent than other exile organizations and the CIA was trying to control it.

Pancho León was on the National Committee of the Movimiento.

He was sixteen when he joined his older brother in the underground to fight against Batista, and eventually became coordinator of the 26 of July Movement in his coastal hometown of Caibarién. He had also been a member of the Juventud Universitaria Católica (University Catholic Youths). JM WAVE agents wanted Washington's help in expediting León's departure from Cuba. He needed documents to travel, and the only ones that could be obtained were visa waivers, since there was no U.S. embassy to secure a regular visa. A telegram of August 3, 1961, read: "Local [blacked out] not in position to issue waiver locally. León Delgado and Father Batarrica both members of MRP (Movimiento Revolucionario del Pueblo) National Committee. They are opposed to the Ray leadership. [blacked out]has made arrangements to house León Delgado and keep him isolated from MRP and other Cuban extremists."[22]

Why Pancho's visa waiver could not be issued on the island is unclear. Internal politics within the Movimiento may have been a factor. Yet, time was of the essence. The Cuban government was likely to be keeping tabs on Pancho León: he was intelligent, articulate, and a persuasive leader. Days before the Bay of Pigs, the secret police came to visit his family. The two boys were in hiding so the police took their father, Oscar, and told his wife, Masita, that he would be held until the boys surrendered. On August 10, another telegram was sent to Washington informing officials there that Pancho had reserved a seat on the Havana–Palm Beach Ferry, but that all services had been suspended: "[blacked out]had notified Wave that subject recently wrote his fiancée living in Miami that Havana Pan Am assured him of accommodations three days after receipt of visa waiver."[23] As it turned out, Pancho did not have time to wait for the visa. His father was arrested and so was his older brother. His mother helped him seek asylum in the Argentine embassy. At the time, she also made arrangements to send her youngest son, Tommy, through Operation Pedro Pan, for she feared that he, too, would become a target.[24] Tommy's visa waiver came through the family's church contacts.

Parents' concerns about their adolescent boys continued to fuel the mass exodus of Pedro Pans. The oldest of the Arruza boys, Pepe, was involved in a Catholic Jesuit youth organization. As Catholics became targets of the government, the youths went underground with their activities. Sometime in the spring of 1961, José, the father, found out that his son was involved in these activities and decided to send him and his brothers out of Cuba. He and his wife were involved in providing safe housing for activists, but the thought that his boys could be arrested made him decide that they needed to be out of the country. The three oldest sons left first to stay with an uncle in Miami.[25] A month later, Xavier, his brother, was sent as well.

The Visa Waiver Network after Bay of Pigs

The demand for visa waivers was increasing. Without Baker's committee to distribute them, Father Walsh enlisted the help of Polita Grau, one of the island leaders of Rescate, a CIA-supported- anti-Castro organization headed by Miami-based Antonio de Varona, a politician who was in Miami. Grau's uncle, Dr. Ramón Grau San Martín, had twice been president of Cuba. As youths, she and her brother Ramón, or "Mongo," had been involved in the fight against the dictator Gerardo Machado. Mongo's code name was "Pimpernel," after the hero of *The Scarlet Pimpernel*, who rescued French aristocrats from the jaws of the guillotine. In a document I received from the CIA, "Pimpy" is scribbled next to his name.[26] As members of the Cuban political aristocracy, the Graus had an extensive network of friends throughout the island, including many in the diplomatic corps. They would prove integral to the success of the visa waiver program after the Bay of Pigs, until the United States suspended it in 1962. The Graus continued with other underground activities until they were arrested in 1965.

Mongo and Pola's initiation into conspiratorial politics predates the Cuban revolution.[27] Because of his close working relationship with his uncle, Mongo had participated in Cuban politics since he was a young boy, even going into exile when his uncle fled the country under Batista. During his uncle's presidency in the 1940s, Mongo was involved in many meetings and late night discussions. As such, he had access to and personal relationships with many of the embassies. Yet his connections to the United States were mainly through the Catholic Church. Grau told me that he had once met Cardinal Spellman in the mid-1950s at a dinner with his uncle, then the president of Cuba. Spellman would play a critical role with Cuban refugees.

I was curious to meet Mongo. José Arruza, the person who procured my visa waiver, worked in his organization. When I met with Mongo during the course of my research, he lived in a tiny efficiency apartment in Miami. Its walls were covered with photographs of Mongo with his uncle and with leaders of the exile community, and with plaques of appreciation from numerous exile organizations. Mongo was the person who produced the visa waivers for my family. A friend, Sergio López-Miró, had quoted Mongo in the *Miami Herald* saying that "Operation Pedro Pan was unleashed by Washington not for humanitarian reasons, but as a means of spreading false rumors that could hurt Fidel Castro."[28] He, unlike others who had been involved in the operation, did not seem to want to remain secretive. I was curious to meet him and his sister.

At the time I started this research in the early 1990s, Mongo Grau was at the center of a controversy raging in Miami about who had really been in charge of Operation Pedro Pan. Radio talk shows hosted by exile personalities would open their microphones and invite the public to call in. The secrecy shrouding the nuts and bolts of the operation not only made for good drama but also allowed those involved, in one way or another, to say whatever they wanted to about their role. Mongo claimed that he had organized the program on the island and that Father Walsh was the contact in the United States. Indeed, upon his release from Cuban prison, Mongo contended that his masterminding of the "smuggling" of more than 14,000 children out of Cuba was what landed him in jail.[29] The charges on his arrest record, however, say "counterrevolutionary activities and espionage"; there is no mention of visa waivers or of a children's program.[30] At the time of his arrest in 1965, Operation Pedro Pan had been suspended for three years. Upon his release from prison, he was vilified in an article in *Granma*, the official newspaper of the Cuban Communist Party. Entitled "Glorification of a Crime," the article names Mongo as the person responsible for sending away 15,000 Cuban children from their homeland."[31]

The accounts of how Mongo became involved in the visa waiver program are contradictory. Walsh says that Polita had been active from the very beginning; this would date her involvement to 1960. But at that time her role, like others reporting directly to Walsh, may have been peripheral to the extent that it was her husband who was taking money from Miami to Havana for the purchase of air tickets for the children. Walsh, after all, had his own contacts in the Cuban underground like Sara del Toro de Odio and with island Church officials.[32] But Polita's organization—the women's section of Rescate and her brother Mongo—appear to have become main players in the visa waiver program only after Baker's group was dismantled.

Mongo started working against Castro sometime in early 1961, when he sent his son and wife out of the country. His son had become involved in actions against the Russian embassy and thus was at risk. With his family safely gone, he said, he could work in peace. His involvement with Pedro Pan (which he told me was known originally as Operation Exodus) began when he received a letter from a bishop in Miami immediately after the Bay of Pigs invasion asking him to run the Catholic Bureau in Havana. The letter, he said, was followed by a visit from twelve women, whom he named Las Apóstoles (The Apostles), representing the Catholic Bureau in Havana. One of the women had a box of passports that needed processing.

When his work on the visa waivers began sometime during the summer of 1961, his liaison with the Church was Penny Powers at the British embassy.[33] Mongo called her "Quilito," a Cuban translation for a penny, a name she remembered when I met with her in Havana three decades later.[34] After the closing of the U.S. embassy in 1961, Mongo maintained direct contact with the State Department and the CIA through the British embassy. He also could communicate with the CIA by radio. He claimed that he kept asking about the children and was then sent fifty visa waivers as a trial test. After this, he said, the program spread like "wildfire."

I asked him why all this was conducted in secret if it was not illegal to leave the country. Mongo explained that there were adolescents in the underground whose lives were in danger because they were *quemado* (they had been detected by Cuban authorities), and the Pedro Pan visa waiver program provided a cover through which to send them out of the country quickly. For Mongo, the priority for visas, or doctored passports or visa waivers, were for those who needed to flee the country for their anti-government activities. In effect, the increased number of departing children whose parents were not active in the underground would provide a cover to protect those at risk.

Mongo not only distributed the visa waivers signed by Walsh; he also gave the parents money orders with which they bought seats for their children on either a KLM or Pan American flight. The travel agencies and airlines maintained a series of seats for the children by waitlisting false names. Just like Walsh, Mongo was authorized to give visa waivers to children under age sixteen, whose names were passed on to INS for authorization. In the case of sixteen- to eighteen-year-olds, however, the FBI had to grant approval before they could enter the United States. He called these older youth "king-size" when he spoke in code to his "mailbox" in Miami (a family friend named Margarita Carrillo, whose husband was a friend of Mongo's uncle).

Others in Grau's organization had the authority to sign visa waivers for children. Among them was Tony Comellas, one of the people in charge of Pan American Airlines in Cuba.[35] Just like Walsh's visa waiver, these were for children under sixteen. Children ages sixteen to eighteen also needed clearance from the Miami INS office. The airlines telexed the list of names to Miami INS. Comellas was told to accept the visa waivers signed by Walsh as well as sign his own. His understanding was that the visa waivers were put in place because airlines would be charged a $1,000 fine if they brought someone in without documentation. In addition, the waivers fulfilled the Cuban government's exit visa requirements which stipulated that the applicant show proof of approval to enter another country.

Comellas told me that he had worked directly with the CIA without receiving payment. He was trained in security procedures by professionals in the United States. He, too, was under instructions from the INS, whose director in Miami at that time was Bill Moriarte, to give visa waivers to anyone eighteen or younger.[36] He would send the INS a list of children who were to travel on each flight, a list that he normally received from Penny Powers.

At this time, a black market of false visas began to thrive. When young travelers holding these visas arrived at the Miami airport, they were separated from the group and interviewed by U.S. government officials, who wanted to determine how they had obtained their visas.

For some time, Comellas distributed the seats on the flights, until the Cuban government tightened its control of the airlines. After this, travelers also needed to obtain an exit permit from the Cuban government. The exit permit was delivered to travelers' homes by telegram, usually by a messenger on a bicycle. The delivery boy would yell, "Telegrama de —," and everyone in the neighborhood would know that the person was leaving.

Around the time of the Bay of Pigs invasion, the Cuban government established a policy mandating that any child traveling was to have a notarized letter signed by both parents authorizing the child's departure. Comellas saw this measure as an attempt by the Cuban government to stem the tide of children leaving. It worked; before its enactment, he remembers, each flight had about thirty to forty children; afterward the numbers decreased temporarily.

Rescate de la Niñez: Women's Network[37]

Like her brother Mongo, Polita Grau recalled her life as one marked by politics and conspiracy. In 1958, she had gone into exile from the Batista government. She returned to Cuba in May of 1959. However, her worst

Pola and Ramon Grau. Courtesy of Operation Pedro Pan, Inc.

fears about Communist influence in the new government were soon realized, and several months later she joined the opposition to Castro.

Polita directed a group of women of Rescate (Rescue). The women
of her network provided the CIA with information on Soviet missiles
and were entrusted with the safe conduct of men and women fighting
in the underground out of the country; they were also involved in spying. In addition, along with her brother, Polita was involved in two unsuccessful attempts on the life of Fidel Castro. When Mongo sought
her involvement in Operation Pedro Pan (which she remembers being
called *Rescate de la Niñez* at that time), she enlisted the entire women's
group in the effort. Most had sent their children out of the country en-
trusting them to the care of the Catholic Church. They also trusted the
U.S. government. Polita claims that their activities were carried out under the direction of the CIA.

Polita and her brother organized a complex secret network to carry
on their underground activities. They constructed a public facade of a
socially active family to hide the traffic of people coming in and out of
their home. Polita recalled that people would come to the Grau home in

Miramar, across the street from the offices of the security police, where the Graus had established a counterfeiting operation. The visitors were first interviewed in the foyer of the house. Those who passed this interview were then led to an interior patio and placed in either of two queues: for passports or for visas or visa waivers. Those in the passport line would receive a false passport fabricated in conjunction with the Panamanian embassy. Those with valid passports but outdated visas could have the date on the visa changed by an artist working with Polita. Those with valid passports and without visas could have one stamped with the official embassy stamp that had been given to the Graus through their CIA contacts. U.S. visas were valid for up to four years.

Each of the women specialized in a certain task, such as doctoring the visas and making the passports. One of the principal operatives was Albertina O'Farrill, a direct descendant of the noble Irish O'Farrill family and a lady of Havana high society.[38] Like many wealthy Havana children, she went to high school in the United States, first to Florida and later to New York. She told me that she had been sympathetic to the children who were being sent alone to the United States because her own boarding school experience had been difficult for her. Yet she was committed to the fight against Castro, to the point that she was willing to send her own children ahead so she could work in the underground without worrying about them. She, too, had contacts and friends in the diplomatic corps, since her husband had been ambassador to Portugal. Through them she developed a network, including the wife of the Dutch ambassador, who would help the organization transmit messages from Havana to the United States. Her best friend, Nenita Carrames, was also involved in distributing visa waivers.[39] Alicia Thomas, who had a talent for painting, took over the falsification of the visas with materials supplied by their American contacts.[40] Many of the women had sent their children ahead as well. Nenita's oldest daughter stayed in Cuba. In 1965, the Cuban government arrested and sentenced to prison those who were still in the country. Security officers would tell Nenita that her daughter had joined the Young Communists and was being sent to Russia. She had no way of knowing that this was not true.

The Graus organization extended across the island and involved women outside of Havana. In Matanzas, Concha Bechily, who had sent her children to the United States right after the Bay of Pigs invasion, distributed visas. Bechily would drive into Havana and pick up the visa waivers signed by Father Walsh from Judge Oscar Piña, code-named Otelo, and his wife, Petite, who in turn were in contact with Mongo Grau.

The women of Polita Grau's organization were moved by a desire to save the children from Communism. Although they were involved in numerous other activities, the campaign to save the children became their primary motivating force. It also fit squarely into one of Operation Mongoose's objectives, which was "to enlist the cooperation of the Church to bring the women of Cuba into actions which will undermine the Communist control system."[41]

Patria Potestad: Once Again

In addition to the visa waiver program, Rescate was also involved in an intensive propaganda campaign aimed at disaffecting the middle class from the revolution. Working closely with other CIA-backed activities like Radio Swan, Rescate mimeographed and distributed leaflets with anti-government messages. One activity in particular was to spread the rumor that the Cuban government was about to take away legal parental authority. This *patria potestad* rumor, which had already circulated in late 1960, was back in the summer of 1961, only this time the women of Rescate were the main sources of the campaign. They traveled throughout the island distributing mimeographed copies of the supposed law in bulk to churches and other centers. They also embarked on a telephone campaign, calling people and discussing the law in detail. Soon panic ensued.

The U.S. press picked up the theme, just at it had in 1960. In September, *Time* magazine reported that Castro had announced that another 1,672 Cuban youth would be sent to be educated behind the Iron Curtain.[42] A month later, it reported that fifty mothers in the Cuban city of

Bayamo had signed a pact to kill their children rather than hand them over to Castro.[43]

The Rescate women knew they were spreading disinformation: Nenita Carrames acknowledged that Mongo Grau told her that threats of the legal proposal of *patria potestad* were not true, but that it was necessary to spread the rumor in order to instill terror in the country.[44] (Grau conceded this to *Miami Herald* columnist Sergio López-Miró as well.)

In June of 1961, state security in Cuba arrested members of the Directorio Estudiantil Revolucionario in Cienfuegos for counterrevolutionary activities, accusing them of spreading false rumors about a supposed legal project to take away parental rights. According to the arrest records, Carmen Diez Rodríguez and José Bello Ferré, both in their early twenties, were caught making copies of the supposed *patria potestad* law with a mimeograph machine. Diez was sentenced for six years, and Bello for ten.[45] Others in the group were accused of distributing copies of the false law and were sentenced to three to six years in jail. For some unexplained reason, the Graus escaped arrest until 1965.

In early September, Fidel Castro gave a long speech on television in which he vehemently denied that the government would propose a *patria potestad* law: "And now they have had the shamelessness of scaring Cuban mothers," he said, referring to the underground. "These people don't even know what our law-making process is. Laws are not down in my office; they come from the ministries. They had the gall to fabricate an entire law, with articles, conditions and whereas, some of the copies even have dates." Castro went on to criticize the moral bankruptcy of the counterrevolution.[46] The denunciation was followed by a blitz of positive propaganda in the Cuban press about all that the revolution was doing for children. Magazines were full of photographs of smiling children playing together in preschools.

The arrests continued as part of a counter-operation that state security called "*Caso Imprenta*" (the Case of the Printing Press). In September 1961, the Cuban government arrested another group, this time in Havana, for allegedly printing copies of the false legal proposal.

Indeed, *"Caso Imprenta"* resulted in numerous other arrests, particularly of women. For example, Carmen Rosa Lora Ángeles, a member of Juventud Acción Católica, was arrested in November for coordinating one of the chains of distribution. Her arrest record notes that she had also typed and mimeographed copies of the supposed legal project. She is a counterrevolutionary element, the record concluded.

The *patria potestad* campaign coincided with the CIA targeting youth on the island. Sherman Kent, chair of the CIA's Board of National Estimates, had written to Director Allen Dulles expressing concern about a youth group called Association of Rebel Youth, who terrorized their parents, their schoolmates, and the general public. The group was in charge of indoctrination within the schools.[47] The CIA responded with a new plan, which included preparation and distribution of pamphlets, and speaking tours to Latin America by women and students. It also increased support for anti-Castro radio programs on sixty Latin American stations and three in Florida, as well as the CIA's Radio Swan.[48] On November 15, 1961, the Cuba Daily Summary reported that *Avance*, an exile publication, had a story on the Castro government's attempts to take more than three million Cuban children through the abolition of *patria potestad*. The publication had reprinted information from the government's newspaper *Revolución* showing that there were already 2,090 Cuban students behind the Iron Curtain.[49]

Table 6.3: Cuban Students Behind the Iron Curtain

	Students in Advanced Grades	Specialists and Technicians	Laborers	Total
East Germany	90	45	180	315
Bulgaria	20		100	120
Red China		100	100	200
Hungary	30	40	80	150
Poland	60	15	180	255
Rumania	85	15	150	250
USSR	300	100	400	800

The U.S. Reaction

It had begun simply as a way to bring 250 children of the underground to the United States in preparation for a U.S.-backed invasion, but by the end of 1961, Operation Pedro Pan had expanded uncontrollably. In Cuba the opposition saw the visa waiver program as a bridge to safety and freedom, but in the United States the children's arrival was met with ambivalence.

In December 1961, at a hearing called by the U.S. Senate, a parade of South Florida community and political officials decried the influx: they supported the fight against Communism, yes, but did not want Cuban refugees dumped in their community. For instance, Dade County commissioner Arthur Patten testified:

> You have got the complexion of the city of Miami changing, and changing rapidly. I think that we should be aware of and at least cognizant of the fact that it is possible that the Cuban people who are now in the Miami area are being prevailed upon by certain extremist groups of one type or another to be used, welded together into some type of political organization, which might even possibly go so far as to promise them American citizenship immediately, with the right to vote, or anything of an extremist nature of that type, which might cause a lot of these people to want to remain in the United States instead of possibly going back to Cuba, and fighting Castro or resettling in their own nation.
>
> I know that many of our local citizens view this with alarm and fear the possibility that the Cuban population in the next several years can become American citizens in the Miami area and get the right to vote, and of course politically outvote our permanent residents . . . In Miami itself, on Saturday afternoon, you can walk up and down the streets and hear twice as much Spanish spoken as you do English.[50]

Ralph Renick, news director for WTVJ in Miami, reading from transcripts of a program aired by his station during the fall of 1961, quoted several Miamians:

> I, personally, of my own opinion, think the Cuban people are wonderful and should be encouraged to resettle in different parts of the United States for one reason. In Miami we do not have enough jobs for our own people let alone the Cuban people. . . . I don't think we should be giving them the money we are giving them and they should be back in their country where they belong.
>
> In my opinion—this is not my opinion only, of course—a good many people with whom I have talked, we resent them very much. We consider them arrogant, belligerent, noisy, and I think they are a detriment to our city. We hope that they soon will be relocated or returned to Cuba.
>
> I think the Cubans are going to take over Miami, the city of Miami, just like they took over—the Puerto Ricans took over New York City. It will be just slums some day and I'm sure everybody doesn't want that to happen. They should distribute them around the United States.[51]

The senators were also concerned, and wanted to know how many children had entered the country under the visa waiver program. Father Walsh shared the number with them, but pleaded that it be kept off the record.[52] Wendell Rollason, who was in charge of the main visa waiver distribution program for the underground, made an emotional appeal, claiming that the program was the lifeline for the ordinary Cuban wanting to be free. He was particularly passionate about the children's program:

> The special program and the rule-bending done to bring the children of Cuba into the United States, to educate them, to house them and to feed them surely must have the blessing of every American taxpayer. Each of us should swell up in pride that here, above all

else, our dollar was well spent. To be a small but vital part in the drama of taking from the grasp of Communism but one little child is a stirring accomplishment. This has been done by the thousands, here are thousands of little minds that cannot be warped by Communist indoctrination, that cannot be taught that there is no God, that cannot be taught to spy on their parents. . . . [He sounded the alarm bells.] Let me tell you a few things here that people I think in the United States should know about what the Communists in Cuba are doing with these children. They are taking the children of the underground members who have been caught and either jailed or shot. And to punish the families, these kids are being sent deliberately, being picked and sent to Russia as a way of retaliation, as a way of threats to other families of what is going to happen to their own children if they do not knuckle under. Children are paraded in front of their fathers in prison as a means of extorting confessions. They use the child in every hideous means known to man as a lever, as a means to force obedience.[53]

Rollason appealed for the expansion of the program. "So our recommendation is to provide the Department of HEW with sufficient funds to continue without abatement this program which opens the United States for any child who is a refugee from communism."[54]

Only one person raised concerns about the welfare of the children already in the United States, a Mr. Johnson, who is identified as the committee's staff director. He advocated prioritizing the visas of the parents so the families could be reunited quickly. But Miami's Bishop Carroll, who had been called to the hearing, seemed hesitant:

MR. JOHNSON: Just one question, Bishop Carroll. You have recommended that we abandon the concept of granting visa waivers only to those who have a husband, wife, or child in the United States and to grant them on a first-come, first-served basis, or in effect, let whoever has the price of a ticket get on the plane. In recent years, however, we have stressed increasingly in our immigration concepts the reuniting of families. Now, inasmuch as the number of visa waivers and the number of plane seats available each week are about 1,500 or 1,600, and therefore definitely limited, would not this be running contrary to the concept of the reuniting of families?

BISHOP CARROLL: In general, I do not believe that it would. I think that there are people—I think it would be a fairer approach. If I were in Cuba trying to get out and had no relatives in Dade County, I could not—there is no chance in the world for me to get out.

MR. JOHNSON: Well, I mean, for example, many of the unaccompanied children who arrive—

BISHOP CARROLL: Yes.

MR. JOHNSON: Whose parents send them on in advance so they will not become indoctrinated in Communist teachings. Now, I presume that many of these parents will hope some day to join their children.[55]

But the Bishop's sense of fairness led him to recommend against giving priority to the parents of Pedro Pans. Perhaps it was that the Pedro Pan program, at this point, had become one of the largest revenue sources for the Catholic Church's refugee programs. Or perhaps this clergy did not understand the importance of family and the need for children to be with their parents. At the time, children were awaiting their parents' arrivals—many in institutions unfriendly to the plight of Spanish-speaking children, others in orphanages that had become homes for delinquent children, still others with abusive foster parents. Even those who had found loving families to live with were suffering the trauma of separation from their own families.

7

The Children

Silence would shroud my trip to the United States. I was to tell no one that I would be going alone. As far as my extended family knew, my parents would be leaving with their children. We weren't really lying to our relatives when we traveled to Yaguajay to say farewell—my parents were working to obtain travel documents for the entire family. But my visa waiver was the only one they actually had in hand.

María de los Angeles Torres (far left) next to her Xavier Arruza at the José Martí Airport in Havana, July 30, 1961. Courtesy of the author.

I knew that I would be flying in a plane, and that I would travel with my best friend, Xavier Arruza. Americusa, my kindergarten teacher, who had gone to Miami after her school was shut down, would pick me up at the airport. My parents told me she would take me to Sally and Joey's house, the children of Nenita and Pucho Greer, who were family friends.

We began to fill a suitcase with clothes, towels, and handkerchiefs. I would take a gray and red vinyl backpack, and my doll, Isabelita, on-board. On the morning of July 30, just before sunrise, we loaded the car. The sky was just beginning to turn an orange pink as we drove to the airport. Today, I look at a photograph taken by Xavier's father at the airport: five of us, standing, slips of paper bearing names and phone numbers of contact persons in Miami pinned to our clothes. I cannot remember posing for the picture. I am standing next to Xavier, with a worried look on my face. Yet I do remember the airport, my mother leaning down and hugging me, her last words: "*Báñate todos los días, que los americanos no tienen esa costumbre.*" (Take a bath every day, Americans do not have that habit.)

As I walked out to the runway, a guard stopped me, searched my backpack, and demanded that I turn over my doll to him. In those days, the government wouldn't allow people to take anything of value out of the country, so many parents stuffed jewelry inside children's dolls. The guard let me keep my doll after he shook it and could hear that it was empty. On the plane, I sat next to Xavier. As we took off I looked out the window, excited to be up in the air for the first time in my life. Some of the kids began to cry. As hard as I try, I cannot recall whether I did, too. The next thing I remember is landing, stepping out of the plane, down the stairs, and into the airport. Xavier was pulled aside; I never saw him again. However, I did find him, forty-two years later, and was able to talk to him and one of his brothers by phone. He remembers nothing of our trip. A way perhaps of forgetting his experiences after arriving, which he and his brother shared with me. Theirs the most difficult stories for me to hear.

At the airport, I was scared. I couldn't see above the many adults who started to surround us. I couldn't see Americusa. I didn't know what I'd do if she wasn't there. Some time passed, it seemed forever. Finally I saw her coming toward me.

Here my own memory goes blank. What I recall next are fragments of the Greers' house. A few years ago, a friend asked me about my foster home experience. I told him that I had won the Pedro Pan lottery: the Greers were welcoming and very concerned about my emotional state. Nenita recalled that I was afraid and withdrawn for quite a while and shy—a reversal of what I had been like before the trip. Nenita sensed my loneliness and did everything she could to alleviate it. I remember that she gave me a box of chocolates, which I hid under the bed and the ants got to it. She remembers that when she asked me about it, I told her that I was saving it for my parents who would arrive any day. I was going through a difficult time. I slept in a bunk bed with her daughter Sally. Nenita even set up a small table for us to eat so that I could relate to the children and not be overwhelmed by the adults. I learned to blow bubble gum and started practicing English words. Sally was protective and Joey was playful. But I was sad, and at night I would cry softly so that no one would hear me. It was the uncertainty: no one could say when my mother and father would come. When they called, or we got through to them, I found it hard to talk to them. Their voices were a painful reminder that I was not with them. I was barely six years old.[1]

About two months after I arrived, Nenita started a difficult pregnancy. The doctor ordered bed rest, and she made plans to send me somewhere else. My mother had a cousin, Frances, who had seven kids and whose husband, Islay, had served in the U.S. Army. I was taken to her house. Pucho Greer occasionally came to visit and brought presents—a stuffed poodle, or candies. For the next two months, I was lost in the hustle and bustle of a home with so many kids. I started first grade in a public school in our neighborhood, which would later become known as Little Havana.

Finally, my parents received notice that their visa waivers had been approved. We weren't exactly sure when they could get a flight, but we knew it would be soon. I waited anxiously. On the day they were to arrive, I was not taken to the airport. When I got home from school, I found my mother and my two sisters at my aunt's house. My father, however, was not there. He had been pulled from the plane at the last minute. During the summer, the government had issued a regulation that no doctor could leave the island. A friend pulled strings and a few weeks later he was allowed to leave, but what I had hoped would be a joyous event was instead filled with sadness and anxiety. These emotions would come to define the way we would relate to all things Cuban, for there were still many relatives left on the island.

Throughout the years, I have often wondered why my parents were able to come relatively soon after me; why I was not taken to one of the camps, and my cousins, who left unaccompanied several months after I did, ended up first in the camps, and then spread out to foster homes in Albuquerque and orphanages in St. Louis. Why did some children never see their parents again? I knew that each family, indeed each child of the exodus, had a different story and that some of the differences concerned the choices their parents made. But I also suspected that some of the stories were about what choices were available to the parents. And these, of course, had to do with governmental policies.

We can't know what the experiences were like for each of the over 14,000 Pedro Pan children. We have only anecdotes.[2] The paper trail on Pedro Pan children is scattered across numerous federal agencies. Most of the files I found that made direct reference to the children were in the National Archives Central Files of the Children's Bureau of the Department of Health, Education and Welfare in Washington. The actual operations files would have been kept elsewhere. The Catholic Welfare Bureau files, which are considered private, have been donated to Barry University in Florida and are only now being processed. Individuals can ask to view their own files, but the public cannot. The state of Florida has not made their files public nor did they respond to my request to review them either. There are other problems: once adolescents turned nineteen, they were technically out of the system, hence we have no records of where they ended up. Also, no records were kept of those of us who ended up in friends' and relatives' homes even though at one point the Children's Bureau recognized that there could be serious problems in these placements and had stated that these homes should be studied.[3] Unlike foster families sponsored by Catholic Charities, many received no payments from the federal government. The documentation has many holes; indeed, some of our names are not even counted among the slightly over 14,000 calculated by Father Walsh's airport log.[4]

Therefore, this narrative relies on information retrieved from the National Archives and from a special collection of letters at the University of Miami. It is also based on extensive interviews of several Pedro Pans. Many are people I have known a long time; others I met while researching this book. Xavier and his brother I found as I was finishing this book. Unlike me, these children and adolescents ended up in foster homes or institutions; one even joined a religious order. The length of separation from their parents varied: one girl's family came within two years, another eventually was able to see his parents during a brief visit to the island after a twenty-one-year separation.

I don't claim that these stories are representative of the overall Pedro Pan experience. I have chosen stories through which we can understand governmental policies and their impact on the lives of children and their families. My focus is not on the emotional impact of the separation; this I can only imagine. What I can contribute is an understanding of how politics and ideology shaped the choices parents were presented with when making decisions about our futures. Others have studied the impact that the separations had on our emotional development. Others have begun to tell their own stories. Many others will I hope continue doing research on this extraordinary event. I am interested in understanding and what this says about how children were viewed.

Care of the Children: Emergency Welfare

Of the more than 14,000 children who came to the United States from Cuba, friends or relatives looked after approximately 6,000. Four voluntary agencies and the Florida State Department of Public Welfare, along with 137 children agencies throughout the country, cared for the remaining children as they were shipped to institutions, and group or foster homes in 40 states, the District of Columbia, and Puerto Rico. A total of $138,619,000 of overt monies would be spent on the unaccompanied children's program. By 1967, the U.S. government's Children's Bureau was reporting that 8,331 Cuban children had been cared for in foster homes and institutions.[5]

Table 7.1: Organizational Distribution of Cuban Children in Exile

Catholic Welfare Bureau	7,041	84.50%
Children's Service Bureau	365	4%
Jewish Family and Children's Services	176	4%
Florida State Department of Public Welfare	780	4%

President Kennedy charged the Department of Health, Education and Welfare with the children's care while they awaited their eventual return to Cuba. After it became obvious that the Castro government was not going to fall immediately, the focus shifted to providing care until the children's parents arrived in the United States. HEW's Children's Bureau assumed primary responsibility for the Pedro Pans' well-being. They were also in charge of coordinating and disseminating information about the program.[6]

The Children's Bureau worked directly with the Florida Department of Public Welfare, contracting its services and disbursing monies. The Department of Public Welfare in turn contracted out to various social service agencies. The contracts stipulated that federal funds would be reimbursed to the agency providing foster care: $6.50 per child per day in group care and $5.50 for those in individual homes. The contracts also allowed for reimbursement of incidental expenses, as well as travel, if needed, including travel back to Cuba. The contract between the Catholic Welfare Bureau and the state of Florida also included two provisions intended to protect the children:

> Children will receive care only in licensed or state-approved facilities and will have casework services available to them . . . ;

> The Catholic Welfare Bureau may request foster care from agencies and institutions outside of the Miami area but it will be responsible for central record-keeping and for assuring itself that the child is receiving proper care.[7]

The contract made no mention of scholarships to schools, as many of the parents had been misled to believe; rather, provisions were for care in institutions and in foster homes. The unaccompanied children's program was not an educational project but a child welfare program.

The agencies entrusted with the children's care were defined as emergency aid providers. These included the Catholic Welfare Bureau for Catholic children, the Jewish Family and Children's Services for Jewish children, and the Children's Service Bureau in Miami for Protestant children.[8] Nine out of ten children were Catholic. By March 1962, the Catholic Welfare Bureau's staff had grown to three hundred, including priests, social workers, doctors, and other support personnel.[9] There were concerns that some of their employees might be agents of the Cuban government, and Father Walsh asked the Federal Bureau of Investigation to run routine security checks on them.[10]

Religious denomination was considered to be an important defining cultural attribute at this time, and thus was to be respected in placing children, following the three-faith approach that had been the organizational principle during World War II. There was a well-established relationship between voluntary religious agencies and the foreign policy establishment that dealt with questions of refugees.[11] In a memo to Katherine Oettinger, director of the Children's Bureau, an HEW official urged the bureau to be most sensitive to the long-standing and ongoing role of the national voluntary agencies in the reception and resettlement of refugees and immigrants.[12]

Before the Bay of Pigs, Katherine Oettinger had issued strict guidelines about keeping the program low profile.[13] Maintaining secrecy was a high priority. But this secrecy is what made it difficult for the public to monitor the program. Administrators and organizers repeatedly asked Congress and the press not to scrutinize the program. Thus, while the policy of secrecy may have served the interests of future child émigrés, it proved traumatic for many of the children who had already been placed in the United States.

Nonetheless, secrecy would not be maintained for long. In late February 1962, Father Walsh received a call from Steven Van Beeler, a reporter for the *Cleveland Plain Dealer,* who had noticed Cuban children living in his neighborhood. He had tried to obtain information from the federal government and was referred to Walsh. As he had already done with other journalists, Walsh asked him to refrain from reporting the matter, as any publicity about the program could bring recriminations to their parents in Cuba. But Van Beeler insisted, and Walsh consulted HEW secretary Abraham Ribicoff. Together they decided to go to the press. Walsh called Erwin Potts of the *Miami Herald* and gave him the story. On March 8, the *Herald* headlined, "In 'Operation Exodus' 8,000 Cuban Children Saved From Castro's Brainwashing . . . Nearly 8,000 Cuban children sent away by parents to save them from communist indoctrination have been funneled into foster homes throughout the United States in a semi-secret 'passage to freedom.' "[14] The next day, another article appeared mentioning the name of Operation Pedro Pan.[15] Ribicoff then publicly appealed for help, asking American families to provide foster homes for the children.

Patria Potestad in the United States

Ironically, the issue of *patria potestad* that had fueled the children's exodus from Cuba emerged in the United States as well. Initially, the U.S.

courts assumed the right to make decisions for the children. One early case in a Miami juvenile court served as the basis for placing children in private homes.[16] On occasion, juvenile courts in Miami gave foster families limited custody in emergencies since only parents or legal guardians could make decisions about children's medical care. The juvenile court in Key West also issued rulings on behalf of children.[17] As a broader measure, the Children's Bureau asked the Catholic Welfare Bureau to develop a consent form that parents in Cuba could sign and send along with their children, thereby turning over certain legal authority to the bureau.[18]

In New York, the eighth district court heard a case that addressed the question of who was authorized to give consent for surgery and medical care for "Cuban orphans" under sixteen years of age.[19] The case progressed to the state supreme court.

Then there were the instances where families placed children in the program temporarily but then found it difficult to regain custody. For example, on December 20, 1963, Mrs. Earl Michelle wrote to President Lyndon Johnson on behalf of a Pedro Pan child living in a foster home and her aunt, who wanted the child to live with her:

> Since last April we have been trying to obtain the release of Clara Rodríguez from the Catholic Welfare Bureau. The aunt meant [the placement] to be only a temporary arrangement, until she could become established in Milwaukee. All necessary documents from Clara's father [in Cuba] have been secured. And all investigations by the local Catholic welfare have been made, they are positive. . . . It is against federal law to continue to hold Clara there against the wishes of her parents, relatives and herself, she is sixteen years old. . . . They refuse to release her before the school year ends.[20]

Eligibility for Assistance

Despite President Kennedy's public rhetoric about the "most defenseless of refugees," not all newly arrived children were accepted in the unaccompanied children's program. All sorts of bureaucratic procedures kept many children out. For instance, Jewish children who had not been born in Cuba but rather brought to the island by their parents were referred to as "stateless" and initially were not admitted to the program.[21] In addition, program eligibility required that the child be registered in Miami with one of the volunteer agencies. Often, however, a child would not be registered because he or she entered the United States under the care of a relative and did not require agency assistance. But if circumstances changed and the relative could no longer care for the child, that child would not be admitted into the program. The case of Ana Sarracén, then eleven, is illustrative. Described by a social worker in Chicago as a "part Negro foundling who had lived in a Salvation Army shelter in Cuba since ten days of age, [Ana] entered the United States as a Cuban tourist with a couple who posed as her parents, lived with a family in Arizona, then was taken to a woman in Chicago who wishes to keep her, but needs financial help to do so. Lutheran child placing agency in Chicago would cooperate with Children's Services Bureau of Miami if child is eligible as an unaccompanied child. Placement of a Negro child in Florida would be difficult."[22] The only way the youngster could be enlisted in the program was to return to Miami. Therefore, she was found ineligible since she did not live in Miami. The same bureaucratic requirements kept other children from receiving assistance.[23]

Other technicalities affected eligibility for the program. For example, once unaccompanied minors reached nineteen years of age, they were dropped from the program. At first the payments to foster families were cut off on the birthday. but this proved an administrative nightmare, so the Children's Bureau changed the deadline to the end of the month in which the teenager turned nineteen.[24] Several years into the program, it was determined that nineteen-year-olds should be automatically transferred to the Cuban Refugee Center so as to continue giving them support.[25]

Another problem involved keeping track of the children. At first the Department of Public Welfare was in charge of this responsibility, but the director of the Cuban Refugee Center wanted to have the list of chil-

dren in his agency. This is where parents had to register when they arrived in the United States and it was important to inform them immediately as to their children's whereabouts. A problem related to record
keeping had to do with children initially placed with a friend and relative and later switched to other homes without notifying the Department of Public Welfare.

There were other requirements that affected payments to foster
parents. On April 17, the same day the Cuban government defeated
the U.S.-backed exile forces at the Bay of Pigs, Frank Craft, director of
Florida's Department of Public Welfare, sent an urgent letter to Mildred
Arnold, director of the Children's Bureau's Division of Social Services:

> We need to clear with you a question in relation to the immigration
> status of unaccompanied Cuban refugee children as related to our
> payment for foster care. To be eligible for financial assistance, peo-
> ple are required to have refugee status. We are most anxious not to
> have to raise any question about immigration status in relation to
> unaccompanied children. If it were necessary that they have refugee
> status with immigration, it would be upsetting to the parents
> and could bring possible reprisals. No one would want to change a
> child's visa status without clearance with his parents, and in many
> cases this would be impossible and would only create confusion
> and danger.[26]

Arrival and Transfer Centers

Every unaccompanied Cuban child who arrived at Miami's International Airport, whether he or she went home with relatives or stayed
with the Catholic Bureau, was given a card with the name of a social
worker. Those who had relatives or friends waiting for them, like myself, left with them.[27] The children without relatives or family friends
were met by a man they only knew as "George." He would drive them to
one of several makeshift overcrowded camps throughout the Miami
area.[28]

Elena García Wagner, who arrived in the United States in May of 1962, described her journey in a poem, "Over American Waters."[29] These are some excerpts:

We land, and people hurry off with purpose.
All, seeming to know where they are headed,
as I remain silently behind
left to wander aimlessly . . .
I am seven years old and I feel lost . . .
I am so very alone. . . .

My senses are assaulted with the unfamiliar.
I am left there to listen to the sounds,
of words that I do not understand, . . .

Everywhere I turn I see strange faces.
I long to connect with those that I do not know,
and who in turn, do not know me. . . .

Time passes, and everything that I am goes with it.
I am startlingly aware that not one soul knows me,
that I stand out,
and that I matter to no one.
With this, I begin to feel smaller,
like an alien in my own skin. . . .

I resign then,
to go with them
in their shiny white van
over concrete streets.
an anxious little girl,
I sit alone, looking out
over my new gray world

which mirrors the wall,
recently built
around my young heart.

The children would stay until they could be placed in a foster home or sent to other facilities across the country. These facilities changed as the numbers and needs of the program changed.[30] The first children stayed at St Joseph's Villa since it was the only child care facility operated by the Catholic Welfare Bureau. The Sisters of St. Joseph staffed it. It had twenty-six beds and cared for dependent children under the age of twelve. Others in Miami included a home donated by Maurice Ferre, which came to be known as Casa Carrión, after the house parents who ran it for forty teenage boys. Another was the Saint Raphael Home, a two-building complex of apartments one-half block off Biscayne Boulevard in Miami, ran by the Jesuit Brothers, which housed seventy-four boys. Father Walsh eventually moved in, too.

Kendall's Children's Home was opened for Cuban refugee children on January 7, 1961. Previously it had been the county's home for African-American children. The previous summer, the county had desegregated its children's facilities. Kendall was located in southwest Dade County; the Welfare Department loaned Catholic Welfare three buildings that could accommodate up to 140 boys and girls between the ages of thirteen and seventeen. At first it was run by lay parents and by the Ursuline Sisters, followed by the Piarist Priests and then the Marist Brothers.

In July 1961, as Kendall became crowded, teenage boys twelve to fifteen were moved to Matecumbe. It was also located south of Miami; it had been a summer retreat for priests and served as a summer camp for Catholic youths. Now it was turned into a receiving home and school for 350 teenage boys. Its capacity was augmented temporarily by adding tents. The Brothers of La Salle ran a high school, although priests from other orders participated in the teaching as well. In 1962, Father Walsh was ordered by Archbishop Coleman Carroll to consolidate the camps and move the kids to Opalocka in what had been a military station. Despite attempts to make it a welcoming place, the facilities were stark and conducive to being run as what they had been—a military barracks.

As the number of children entering the United States increased, more receiving centers were added. In October 1961, Florida City, the largest shelter, was opened. It was licensed to care for seven hundred children and was located about 35 miles south of Miami near Homestead. Girls of all ages and boys under twelve were housed in three rows of garden apartments; meals were served in three shifts and classes were held at an elementary school run by Sisters of St. Philip Neri from Cuba.

The experiences at the camps were mixed. On the one hand, the kids were together and, in comparison to those isolated in foster homes, they had camaraderie. But the facilities at Camp Matecumbe were stark; Alfred Schwartz, a former army commander described it as follows in a letter to HEW secretary Ribicoff:

> I wish to inform you of a situation, which is inhumane and unless corrected immediately, will further lower the prestige of the United States among those we desire to help. Obviously no U.S. government inspection [team] has ever seen this camp. It "houses" over 400 boys in wooden shacks and tents. They sleep in three high bunks and each boy has a living and sleeping area of about 150 cubic feet. There are SIX (6) toilets and TWELVE (12) showers . . . there's practically no protection from the cold and heat. The camp is located in an isolated area which abounds in coral and rattle snakes, clouds of mosquitoes . . . instruction is poor and almost non-existing. . . . Many of the boys are ill. . . . It's surprising they do not ask what side the United States is on. . . . As a former Air Force officer and base commander, I was horrified by what I saw at Camp Matecumbe.[31]

Father Walsh tried to make the camps more like home for the children, hiring Cuban staff and bringing in many of the Cuban priests who had left the island. But others like social worker Joan Gross saw it differently, observing, "Teenagers are the hardest hit by homesickness. They are old enough to realize that a reunion with their parents is not guaranteed. The best anecdote to homesickness is rapid orientation to American ways."[32]

Many Pedro Pan children I interviewed remembered those camps as lonely and terrifying places. Margarita Oteiza had worked in Kendall for a while after helping transport the children from the airport to the camps for several months. She told me that her heart could not take it. The children would climb all over her asking for their mothers. "They were so little," she recalled.[33] She then signed up to work at Matecumbe.

Brothers and sisters were split by age and gender—a separation that would haunt even those who were eventually reunited in foster homes, for in the camps older siblings in effect became surrogate parents for the younger ones. The importance of this relationship was underscored in a letter sent to Jacqueline Kennedy by a young man who was sent to live with his uncle, while his brother went to the camps. The brothers were eventually reunited when his brother was old enough to care for Luis. But a new fear set in because now his brother was also old enough to be inducted into the army. Luis wrote to the First Lady: "I am writing to you this letter because I'm in great need. My parents are in Cuba, and I live with my brother, he is the only one around me who really likes me and takes care of me. What am I going to do without him?"[34]

Friends and relatives also complained they were restricted from visiting the children in the camps. Mireya Robles wrote to President Kennedy asking for permission to see her best friend's children. A Children's Bureau staff analyzed the problem for the White House:

> On September 10 three children, Yolanda, María del Carmen, and José Casimiro, six, seven, and nine, arrived at Refugee Center Kendall. She [Mireya Robles] has been visiting them every day; she is a friend of the family. The mother superior has requested that she limit her visits to once a week. The writer wants the president to intervene and to insure that the children remain in Miami until their parents who are awaiting a visa waiver arrive in Miami.

Rafael Ravelo, May 1961, days after he left Cuba. Courtesy of Rafael Ravelo.

The children's education was another issue of concern. Many Cubans had sent their children to the United States thinking that they would receive *becas* to school in this country. Many were disappointed to learn that there were no scholarships and that they would not attend boarding schools. Several adolescents from the Matecumbe camp wrote the U.S. government about this. Miguel de la Torre, Gerardo Ameijeiras, and Antonio Valdés Medina actually reached the president with their appeal for help in finding scholarships. They had left Cuba, they noted, to escape communism and study in the United States.[35] Alfredo Lanier, today a member of the *Chicago Tribune* editorial board, remembered that his parents' instructions before he left had been to study so that he could return to Cuba well educated. "I was very disappointed because we thought that I would be getting a scholarship to study in a school. And Matecumbe was like military barracks. In reality, there were no scholarships. That's what my parents had been told."[36]

A Second Displacement

As the number of arriving children grew, the Miami Catholic Welfare Bureau pushed to move the children in the receiving camps out. Therefore the children often went from family to family before a final home was assigned. For example, Carlos Erie, today a professor at Yale University, and his brother were separated upon their arrival in the United States. Carlos was sent to Florida City, his brother to Kendall. After about two and a half weeks, the brothers were sent to two different families; the families happened to know each other, so the brothers were able to stay in contact. But when the families realized that the boys were expected to be with them for more than a brief stay, they returned them to Catholic Welfare. Carlos recalls:

> We were kicked out. Then the real nightmare began. We were sent to a group home run by a Cuban family that had no children. Their name was Amador. It was near the stadium on 7th and 20th. There may have been eight or ten kids. The number kept changing. We did receive and send letters, but they were so slow. We could not call, though. We were only given one meal a day. I have a curvature of the spine that has been linked to malnutrition during my teen years. I was never hit, but my brother was, because his drawer was not as neat as the man thought it should be. We used to make a little money on the side by selling the magazine *ZigZag* door to door. There was little supervision and we used to roam the streets a lot. I did go to school during this time. We finally got out. I am not sure

how. My brother says he is the one who contacted an uncle in Illinois and he was able to take us in. My mother tried to come out of Cuba but she was not allowed into the United States until 1965.[37]

Alfredo Lanier was first taken to Matecumbe. Later he ended up being bounced around from relatives to foster care:

My parents decided to send me when the schools were closed. I went to a Catholic school, Los Maristas. My parents thought that this was going to be just a brief thing. They had to get the kids out of Cuba because they were in imminent danger of being abducted by the Soviet Union, or taken away from the parents. So there was a big rush, a big panic to get me out of Cuba. There was also a very firm conviction that it was only a temporary thing. That it was only three or four months, you would learn English or whatever and then come back to Cuba and resume life happily ever after. Of course, that didn't happen because I came here in February of 1962. Then the whole thing was shut down in October '62 with the Missile Crisis. And my parents didn't come here until '65. I really don't remember at all. It must be all in the back of my head somewhere. I don't remember getting to Miami. I know I went to Matecumbe. I had just turned fourteen.

After a three-month stay in Matecumbe, Alfredo himself made arrangements to go to a relative's home:

I tracked down an uncle who had been living in the United States for many years. He was like our mythical uncle who had made it in the United States. Finally I managed to get to New York. Well, the reality was that he and his wife and daughter were living in an efficiency apartment. I stayed there for two years, but it was horrible. It didn't work out, they finally kicked me out of their home. And through the International Rescue Committee and the help of one of my teachers they found another home for me. But that didn't turn out to be much better. It was a single guy, who used me as his personal maid. His parents and brother came from Cuba and then again I was kicked out. And after that I got a scholarship to go to a prep school. Another teacher helped me find another foster home, this one with an Irish-American family who put me to sleep in the basement of their home, but they treated me very well. I started working part-time at the library and one of the librarians, Mr. Al Linsky, one of the most important persons in my life, claimed my parents for me. By the time they came, three years had passed.[38]

The priests in Rafael Ravelo's school in Cuba were certain that he had a calling for the priesthood. They had persuaded his parents to send him to the seminary. When schools were shut down in Cuba, the order made plans to move their schools abroad and asked the parents of promising seminarians to let their children go abroad with them. Everyone thought that it would be for only three months. Rafael remembered:

I was thirteen years old and a sort of panic set in when the schools are closed in May 1961. My parents' decision was made very quickly. Never, never, did we conceive the separation to be more than just a few months. I'd leave by the end of May, and I would be back in school in the new fall term. You see, for me it was that the LaSalle Brothers who ran our school were going to reopen the school outside of Cuba until they could return. The brothers were also trying to recruit me into their order so they came to talk to my parents and they were the ones who convinced them to send me out. They were going to open up a school in Costa Rica.

Even though the flight of the children was supposed to be a secret operation, the expulsion of the priests and nuns from Cuba occurred with tremendous fanfare. On May 25, 1961, 110 priests arrived in Miami. As they got off the plane, they began chanting a hymn, "God, Fatherland, and Home." They were greeted by the press. The next day head-lines read, "Priests Fly to Miami, Fleeing Religious Prosecution."[39] Rafael was on this flight.

> But first we were going to meet up in Miami. About 110 brothers went out with us. There was a huge welcoming when we got to Mi-ami. Father Walsh was there to receive us. The press was every-where. That's when I started to think that maybe the separation would be longer. There was some problem in Costa Rica so we ended up waiting several days in Miami. Finally they called a meet-ing and there was a petition to keep the brothers in Miami [and] open up a school. But a group of us was sent to Costa Rica. The first six months were very difficult, the language was the same, but cul-turally it's very different. I could only communicate with my par-ents by mail and a letter took over a month. After some time, the brothers tried to reunite all the novices in one place, and we were shipped to Santo Domingo. Another adjustment. There I finished high school and got sent to Colombia. For now, a return to Cuba could not even be contemplated.[40]

Institutional Placements

Two-thirds of the 8,000 children under the care of the federal govern-ment were eventually placed outside Florida in various institutions including orphanages and religious boarding schools. Now adults, the Pedro Pans' memories of their placements are mixed. The shorthand way of describing these experiences were that you either received a *good or bad beca*. The boarding schools seem to have been among the *good becas*. Here children were treated like students in boarding schools. The letters received by Sara Yaballí, who some called *Mamá* and others *Nuestro Ángel* (Our Angel) describe the mixed experiences. A boy from Matecumbe who was sent to Notre Dame in Morton Grove, says that it was a "good *beca*," but that Christmas had been very sad. Another in a

Kentucky boarding school had a good one and resolved his loneliness by saying, "My responsibility now is to study for the future of Cuba."[41]

But institutional placements were another story. Some remember stark, uncaring institutions run with little regard for cultural or personal differences, while others recall the camaraderie that developed among the various unaccompanied children. These may have been real boarding schools. The ones who seem to have had the hardest and even cruelest experiences were those placed in what had been orphanages.

By the early 1960s, the United States had been moving away from the institutionalization of parentless children in favor of placing children in foster homes.[42] Most of the children in these institutions had been placed with foster families, but those left behind were often the hardest to place, and we can assume they were the most troubled. These state- and church-run institutions had been left largely vacant, so they could easily accommodate many of the newly arrived Cuban children. But these places were geared to hard work and severe, if not questionable, disciplinary methods.

Letters to Yaballí from a boy in St. Joseph's Center in Reno, Nevada, said that his was not a good *beca*. For example, the children placed in a Nevada orphanage say the priests routinely beat them. Children placed in a Nebraska orphanage run by nuns were submitted to a cruel routine that included being awakened at 4:00 A.M., in the middle of winter, and forced outside to fetch buckets of water for mopping the floors. Another letter, from an orphanage in Cincinnati, said that it was not good there, either.[43] I came to learn why it was a bad *beca* from two of the Arruza brothers.

After we landed in Miami, Xavier was taken to his uncle's home in Coral Gables. The three older brothers were already there. But within weeks, the uncle decided that he could not handle them and he turned them over to Catholic Welfare. The boys were sent to Kendall to wait for a *beca*. Their parents, who were fighting in the underground, had insisted that the boys be kept together. Within a few weeks, they were summoned to the director's office where they were shown a picture of a beautiful building and told that they would be going to St. Joseph's in Cincinnati.

When they arrived at St. Joseph's, it was a dilapidated old building. Within weeks, one of the walls collapsed and they were then moved to the new facilities, what they had seen in the picture. The boys were separated by age, the two oldest placed with the high school students, the middle one with the middle school and Xavier, my friend who was seven, with the little ones. They were not allowed to spend time together. They only saw each other during lunch, but no one was allowed to speak. Nuns would patrol the large cavernous dining room forcing the boys to eat whatever was on their plates. The only other Cuban children there at the time were two sisters and a brother. The youngest one hated spinach, but the nuns forced him to eat it anyway. One day he vomited, and she forced him to eat his vomit. The younger children were awakened by this same nun who inspected their beds; if they had wet them during the night, she would beat them. The older boys' quarters were rough. Sexual preying and assaults, and ultimately, submissions were not uncommon.

The boys' letters to their parents were reviewed and censored, yet despite this they managed to let their father know that things were bad. In his Cuban arrest record is the following annotation: "In mid-1962, he visits Mongo Grau [Alsina], because of complaints he has received about mistreatment of one of his sons in St. Joseph's Orphanage in Cincinnati, Ohio. Grau Alsina advised him to write a letter with the information and send it via diplomatic pouch to Catholic Welfare. Expressing the strictness with which children in certain Catholic orphanages are being treated."[44]

Sometime after this, the boys were sent to a foster home. At last they were together, but the woman was elderly and found that she could not handle them. After a year, they were separated, the two youngest were sent to one home and the older boys to two other homes. At the end of the summer, the two youngest were also separated. José, the oldest, felt responsible for his brothers, but there was nothing he could do. Repeated conversations with the social worker assigned to them did not change the situation. In addition, the foster families were not receiving all the money they had been promised. Instead, the social worker would throw lavish parties, and the older boys were forced to dress in fancy uniforms, including white gloves, and wait on her guests. They speculated that she was pocketing the money.[45]

Other children were bounced around as well. When María Conchita Cadiz went from Florida City to a foster home in Columbus, Ohio, the foster family rejected her, saying that they had asked for a younger boy. She was then placed in a Catholic orphanage. "The rules were very strict," she recalled:

> They would wake us up at five in the morning and we had to clean the entire building. I had kitchen duty, which meant I had to clean the counter and even the window in the kitchen and the dishes afterward. The nuns would make us redo our tasks if they were not done to their liking. I never talked back to them. But the other girls did and they would get hit if they did. I was thirteen at the time. When I graduated from eighth grade, I had to leave the school. I was placed in a foster home. The family never thought that my parents would actually come. They grew very attached to me. When my parents arrived in 1966, they did not want to let me go.[46]

The Louisiana placements were particularly troublesome, as children were housed in institutions for delinquent youth and separated according to skin color.[47] Darker-skinned Cuban boys went to what was called Lafayette Home for Bad Boys, the lighter-skinned Cubans to a delinquent boys' home for whites only.

Raquelín Mendieta, daughter of a prominent Cuban political family, was sent out of Cuba when her father learned that she and her sister Ana had started to aid an opposition group. Raquelín was fifteen at the time and Ana twelve. (Ana, who died in 1985, would later become a world-renowned artist.)[48] Raquelín remembers traveling with a legal document that gave Catholic Charities guardianship of the sisters. On September 11, 1961, upon their arrival in Miami, they were transported to Kendall. There, the sisters, who in Cuba had been accustomed to sharing a bedroom and nighttime conversations, were placed in different units.

Raquelin Mendieta, Iowa, 1961. Courtesy of Raquelin Mendieta.

Raquelín's father had heard that there were people in the Miami camps spying on the children and reporting back to Cuban intelligence. He was afraid for them and wanted them out of Miami. The request was not hard to meet since most of the children were shipped to other states. He stipulated that they should not be separated.[49] After several months, the sisters, along with a group of other girls that included Lisette Álvarez, daughter of successful Cuban entertainers, were shipped to Dubuque, Iowa, to what was purportedly an orphanage but was in reality a reform school run by Franciscan nuns.[50] Upon arrival, the girls were stripped of their belongings and assigned to different dorms. Raquelín remembers:

> We were not allowed to eat meals together. Our mail was censored, any letter we sent our parents had to be handed over to the counselors, who would read it and decide which parts had to be rewritten. And there were cruel punishments. We had heard of the "hole," but it wasn't until Lisette Álvarez, another of the Cuban girls, got a letter from Cuba that really upset her, and she started crying and couldn't stop, that both of us were put in the furnace closet for hours. Another Cuban girl was beat up by a nun because she took a shower on a day she was not supposed to bathe. The same nun punched my sister repeatedly in the face as her head hit a door knob because we did not want to go roller-skating. We had wanted to spend an evening together watching television. She had escaped from Communist China and kept telling us we would never see our parents again.

The girls they found there were very troubled. One had been raped by a stepfather; another one had tried to kill her mother; others were emotionally disturbed. Finally, the Mendieta sisters were taken to a foster home:

> I never understood why they took us in, they had six children of their own. There Ana and I had our own rooms, but we were not al-

lowed to have anyone call us. We were told we were dirty Cuban refugees and we did not have the right to be friends with good American people. By that time, we had the stigma that we had been at the St. Mary's Home.

Like other siblings, the Mendietas tried to stay together:

Then they tried to send me to another boarding school and I refused to go without Ana. A very nice family put in a request to be our foster family and we thought we were going to live with them in Dubuque. The social worker came to take us to Dubuque. And we were so excited, we had friends there. Instead she took us to another institution in Cedar Rapids for the summer. There we met Thomas Shea, the first human being we had met who really tried to help us. He found Ana a wonderful foster home and helped me get a scholarship to Mount Mercy College. And that's where we were when our mother came in two years.[51]

Most of the eight thousand children were sent to institutions where life was severe, and we, those of us trying to reconstruct our exodus, are left wondering how many did not send letters or did not have a Sara Yaballí to write to.

The Helena Scandal

The Helena, Montana, placements have come to symbolize all that was wrong with the Pedro Pan program. The abuse of young men by the local priest throughout the years has become common knowledge among Pedro Pan children. Many have commented about what happened to some of the boys who were placed there. In addition, the nurse at Matecumbe had received letters from the boys begging her to help them return to the camps. Before hearing the actual stories of what had occurred in Montana firsthand, I found a paper trail that hinted at some of the problems.

From the outset, the state of Montana did not want to contract out its services to the Florida Department of Public Welfare, as was stipulated by the Children's Bureau, but wanted to deal directly with the federal government. In addition, the Montana Department of Public Service did not want to accept non-Catholic children, fearing it was more likely the communists had indoctrinated them. In a letter to Montana officials, Mildred Arnold, the liaison between the Children's Bureau and the states insisted that "in relation to the Department's concern with regard to the indoctrination of children, the parents are sending them to this country to escape this indoctrination."[52] Montana finally dropped its demand for only Catholic children.

Once the Montana operation was actually up and running, other problems surfaced. In one incident, two boys were expelled from the unaccompanied children's program two days after they graduated from high school and were shipped back to Miami. Several educators protested. Edith Miller, their math teacher, wrote to the Children's Bureau complaining about their treatment:

> No one met him at the plane, but finally he found someone to take him to the camp. The other boy, Frank, has been reduced to a brokenhearted, crying child. On the night of the seventh, after a terror-filled previous evening in which he was beaten about the face and his shirt torn off, Father Harrington took him away; we do not know where. All the boy wanted was to go to the post office to mail a letter to his mother. Is this America? It sounds like a chapter from communism. And these children were sent to the United States for freedom. How very strange this treatment must seem to them, and how sad.[53]

The principal of Whitefish High School also wrote to Senate majority leader Mike Mansfield on behalf of the boys: "Last fall some families in Helena, Montana, received Cuban children. The homes were not properly investigated to my knowledge. They had been placed in a family that had operated a day-care center and the welfare [agency] had revoked their license." The letter described how the mother of the family beat the boys. The principal wrote that he had appealed to Monsignor Harrington who was in charge of the Catholic Welfare Bureau in the area, but "he turned a deaf ear."[54]

That Monsignor Harrington was unsympathetic to the boys' plight came as no surprise to other boys in the program. Many had written letters to Sara Yaballí, the kind nurse who had nurtured them in Matecumbe. Some referred to the fact that the priest would not give them money for school registration and would make them work during the summers to repay him for this money. One of the mothers wrote to her asking for advice—her son wanted to leave Helena immediately; she had counseled her son to stay and study, and his father had told him to "be kinder to the Monsignor and accept his fate like a man."[55] Only he did not know what was really happening. To keep parents from worrying, children often would not provide details of their hardships. But other more desperate letters arrived, pleading for help in getting them out of Montana. According to the boys, the monsignor would have them come over to his residence late at night, he would get drunk and ask them to do unmentionable things.[56]

Senator Mansfield responded and asked HEW secretary Abraham Ribicoff to look into the allegations. The conclusion to the investigation reads: "Father Walsh has been in close contact with Monsignor Harrington, Director of Catholic Charities in Helena."[56] The boys "[were] not returned to Miami without previous warning and the appeal to return the boys to another family in Montana was denied." The report did recognize that there had been a staffing problem: Harrington only had one social worker for the one hundred children placed with his agency. As a result of the investigation, Harrington made plans to increase the staff.[58] But the charges of sexual and physical abuse went uninvestigated. The truth about these experiences was lost in a religious bureaucracy shrouded in mystery, vows of celibacy, and a desire to appear saintly.[59]

Once back in Matecumbe, Oscar Torres, one of the boys sent back to Miami, wrote to a friend, "This is awful. [When we] were here there was only 140 kids, now there are 431. I am sleeping in a tent on the floor without a pillow and the mosquitoes are awful. They say that they threw me out because I behave so badly. I know I'm not getting a scholarship in a hundred years. I need help now."[60]

Foster Home Placements

By the early 1960s, social workers had reached the conclusion that children were better off in foster families than in institutions. Child care agencies were in the process of retooling when unaccompanied minors from Cuba began to arrive.[61]

Table 7.2: Comparative Data on Unaccompanied Children in Foster Care by
Location and Type of Care for 31 December 1961, 1962, 1963, and 1964.

	12/31/61	12/31/62	12/31/63	12/31/64
Total Children in Foster and Group Care	2309 / 100%	3781 /100%	2796 /100%	2117 / 100%
In Foster Family Homes	486 / 21%	1444 / 38%	1163 / 42%	969 / 46%
In Group Care	1823 / 79%	2337 / 62%	1663 / 58%	114 / 54%
Children in Foster and Group Care in Miami Area	907 / 39%	1200 /32%	891 /32%	624 / 29%
In Foster Family Homes	87	162	178	162
In Group Care	820	1038	713	461
Children in Foster and Group Care outside Miami Area	1402 / 1%	2581 /68%	1905 /68%	1493 / 71%
In Foster Family Homes	399	1282	985	806
In Group Care	1003	1299	920	687
Number of communities in which children were placed	62	95	109	105
Number of states in which children were placed	30	38	41	40

The foster home experiences were mixed. Many host families offered loving and supportive homes and tried to soothe the pain of separation, but others exacerbated the children's sense of cultural and linguistic alienation. María Concha Bechily, whose parents had opted for staying in Cuba and fighting in the underground, ended up in a home in the Chicago area. Her parents had thought it would be only a matter of months before she and her two brothers would be sent to live at a relative's home. Maria recalls:

> I was supposed to come and go to the camps like everyone else. I was ten years old, not quite eleven. And, I knew people were leaving Cuba and all of us were told it would be very short term. So, I always thought it was a big adventure. I was totally in love with the concept of leaving and being on my own. Anyway, before we leave, my parents get word that the camps are not the best place to go. This is fall of 1961. At the time I had an uncle that lived in Miami. And he, I'm not sure how he got in touch with my parents, said, look, I don't want them to go to the camp, we're hearing stories that the camps are overcrowded. They don't have the best supervision. I want them to come to my house. I've got an apartment and they can stay with me. So when we left Cuba we went right to my uncle's house. This was December of 1961.

But life for newly arrived immigrants was extremely difficult. They, too, were being pushed out of Miami:

> And lo and behold by March 1962, my uncle is gone from Miami because his wife—he had a wife and two children—decided that this was not a good place to be. They leave, but don't ask me why, they decide they would join the Protestant resettlement program. They brought them to Evanston, Illinois. We were left in different homes in Miami. I am left at a family from Matanzas. My two brothers are left with a sister of my aunt from marriage. And they are waiting for them to send for us. Meanwhile my parents in Cuba

are hysterical. 'Cause they got us out of Cuba because they wanted us to be brought up in a certain kind of environment. Particularly being God-fearing Catholics. And we may start going to a Methodist church now and we may lose our Catholic faith. And so my father had enough clout from Cuba that he got us back on track into the system with the Catholic Church. If you could imagine that someone from Cuba could make this happen. So, we did come to Evanston, Illinois, because that's where my uncle was. And my parents felt that at least they can be near relatives, right? I arrived at my uncle's house on a Wednesday. On Thursday morning the social worker from Catholic Charities was there. And my older brother and I were back on track into the Catholic Resettlement children's program. My younger brother, because he was so little, stayed with my uncle.

María would face yet another displacement:

I was placed in a foster home in Lincolnwood and my brother was placed in a foster home in Wilmette. I sternly lobbied to stay together. I sternly said that I would prefer that. But there was no one really that could accommodate a brother and a sister. They kept siblings of the same sex, interestingly enough. My first six months in that foster home were the most miserable six months of my life. I cannot imagine worse. I can only say that if something terrible happened to my son right now, that would equal it. I cried every day. I was depressed. No one understood what I said. Nobody tried to understand what I said. The social worker from Catholic Charities didn't speak Spanish. And the little she spoke, she was so stupid. She would say things like, I visited Mexico and I didn't like the food, and her analogies, even for a twelve-year-old, I would only cry harder because I couldn't understand how an adult woman would compare a vacation in Mexico to my total despair. I felt abandoned by my parents. I wanted to go back to Cuba. I made attempts to go back to Cuba. Well, I told my social worker that I wanted to go back to

Cuba. That I didn't want to stay in the United States. That I really had nothing there and that I didn't want to stay. And she said I don't think that's possible. So I did attempt to go back through a couple of other adults. And everybody said, well that's not possible. You can't go back. There are no flights. Nobody will take you back. You know, your parents will be so absolutely mad at you if you do that. Because you know you are going to be reunited.

Some of the children were willful and resourceful. María was one of these:

So I decided that part of my despair and depression was the fact that I had been placed in a totally wrong home. The people that I was with were absolutely the worst. There was no physical or sexual abuse, but there was certainly emotional abuse. They did not in any way try to even be loving to me. Serious cultural clashes. They brought in a record and they played the record. They asked me to teach them some steps. So I started teaching them some steps as Cubans would do the cha-cha. Later on that evening that woman went ballistic with me. That I was being obscene. I remember the word "indecent." I remember her saying to me, do you know where babies come from? What do you think you were doing? Americans would do 1, 2, cha cha cha. And, Cubans do totally different, and I was teaching them what I had actually done in my own living room in Cuba when we had parties. They were just awful, repressed, terrible people. And I realized that Catholic Charities had done a very poor job of identifying this family and providing them with the tools that they needed for a twelve-year-old that didn't want to be there.

María took matters into her own hands:

So I decided okay, I got to get out of here. I was allowed to visit my uncle on a regular basis in Evanston. So I was dropped off at this home. And I would make their life miserable enough so that they would want to get rid of me on the weekend. And, so through my uncle's connections in Evanston, I met a woman who was Puerto Rican, who was the only Puerto Rican who lived in Evanston, Illinois. Married to an Anglo. Lillian Thompson, who had three children. And I met her because someone in the Methodist church had made contact with her to help interpret and be helpful with my uncle and aunt. But I pretty much said to her, if I don't move in here I will run away and no one will have me. I totally guilt-tripped her. But I was serious about it. So they took me in.

I always thought, and I thought about it while it was going on, and would say to my social worker, find me a Spanish-speaking family. That's all I wanted. Someone who could speak Spanish to me. That was so foreign to her. Because there was a large Mexican community in Chicago as you know. And there was a fairly large Puerto Rican community that had come in the fifties. I would say find me a family that speaks Spanish. That's all I cared. I didn't care if they were middle class, if they had two bathrooms in the house, if they had carpeting, if they took me to church on Sunday. I didn't care. I wanted somebody I could speak Spanish to. Be able to communicate, because I was not able to communicate.[63]

Dulce María Sosa was nine years old when the revolution triumphed. Like many other Cuban families, hers was jubilant. She recalls:

I was living in Central Covadonga, Las Villas. And I remember that there were *milicianos* [rebels] who would march in little parades. And I had a *miliciana* costume that my aunt had made and I would put it on and march behind them with a plastic rifle. That is what was happening. So we had to be part of it.

But soon her parents began to worry about what she was being taught in school.

I remember coming from school one day and telling my mother, Mami, they told us a story about a little boy who was very hungry and they locked him in a closet and they told him to ask God to bring him food. And he asked, and asked for it. But they wouldn't bring it to him. Then they told him to ask Fidel. And they brought it to him. And my mother, who had lived through the civil war in Spain, said this was communism.

As a temporary solution they decided to send her to live in Havana with her grandmother. Her father had had a brush with the police.

My father was arrested on one occasion because his last name was the same as one of Batista's henchmen. The truth is that my father was not involved in anything, my uncle was, but the decision was made to leave. So my uncle, who was already in Miami, arranged to send us visa waivers. And my younger sister, my brother, and I were to leave. I remember the day we left, and I left the first of July of 1962. My parents were to join us in three months. The youngest, who was five, stayed with my parents; she was very upset because she had wanted us to wake her up to say good-bye, but my mother felt it best to let her sleep. The next thing I remember is la *pecera* [the glass-enclosed departure area at the Havana airport] and my father holding his hands up to the glass to touch ours. Then we're on the plane, everyone was crying and someone started to say, "*Viva Cuba libre.*" We were all children except a few adults. When we got to Miami, it was raining and there was a lot of lightning.

Dulce María and her sister were separated from their brother.

They took my little brother to one camp and my sister and I to one I later found out was called Florida City. There we were put in two separate lines for vaccinations. It wasn't until I was sitting alone in my cabin that it started to sink in. We were supposed to go live with my uncle, who at the time was in California, but because he was single, we were not allowed to stay with him. Well, through the church they found a Mexican family who could have all three of us together and who spoke Spanish. It was perfect. We were going to be safe.

But what seemed to be a more culturally sensitive environment ended up being a place of sexual and repeated emotional abuse:

> I don't remember many of the incidents, but I do remember that it started with him kissing me as I was washing the dishes one night. I started to withdraw inside of me. I finally told my sister how he would stand outside the window of the bathroom looking in as I was bathing. And the social worker told me I was lying. That if I kept it up they would take me out of the house and put me with an American family. Well, I did not want to leave my sister alone, so I stayed. He continued. He was the one who drove me to piano lessons, and he would give me a dollar not to say anything. With this money I would buy little toys. Still today I do not remember full details of the abuse, but I collected hundreds of model cars. I have not ever been able to play the piano.[64]

The social worker refused to investigate the charges; instead, they threatened that if she complained, she would be removed from the home, and her younger sister and brother would remain there. For their sake, Dulce María did not raise the issue again.

The Official Myth about the Fate of the Children

Despite all of the problems children were facing, administrators of the programs continued to project it as a success. In October 1961, almost a year into the program, a staff member from the Children's Bureau visited Miami to review its operations. She reported problems regarding the relocation of parents, since many of them wanted to stay in Miami. Generally, however, her field notes suggest that the program was a success. She commented, "Father Walsh says that this has been the best-handled refugee crisis to date, since it had not required a tent city."[65] The needs of the unaccompanied children were being served not as though it were a refugee crisis but rather within a child welfare context.

In reality, while children were facing a host of problems, organizers and administrators seemed more concerned with ideological issues than with the children's welfare. In congressional hearings held in July 1963, Congressman Feighan of Ohio asked about the long-term plans for the care and protection of the minors. Ellen Winston, at the time commissioner of welfare for HEW, responded that the fact the children were in the United States showed what was happening to people and to normal family life in Cuba under a Russian regime. "Parents," she concluded, "had demonstrated a deep faith in the democratic way of life."[66] Lucille Batson, consultant for the children's program, reported the following in a meeting: "Father Walsh and Mrs. McCrary, his staff person, have been concerned about a 15–16-year old boy who can no longer live with his father and stepmother because of his ideology. The plan was to place him in St. Raphael's, where his attitude may be diluted and modified by the other boys. Father Walsh also reported on a seminary for boys in Puerto Rico where in a surprise test the majority of the boys unconsciously gave the classical communistic definition of capitalism."[67]

The zeal to save children from communism mobilized agencies throughout the United States to participate in the program. For instance, in a letter written to Senate majority leader Mike Mansfield, a high school principal stated: "I understand this movement [bringing unaccompanied Cuban children to the States] is a way of combating communism in Cuba."[68] The children's experiences thus were defined primarily by the need of the social service bureaucracies to retell the story of the children they saved from communism. To the extent that social workers contributed to this myth, and ideological concerns prevailed over the needs of the children, it was difficult to focus on what was actually happening to the Pedro Pans, even when public officials were asking questions about their plight.

In a report on refugees, John Thomas wrote: "These unaccompanied children were sent out of Cuba by their parents to avoid communist indoctrination. . . . It is a mark of faith of these parents in the warm heart of the United States that they sent their children alone without resources or relatives to this country. The remarkable thing about these youngsters is how well they have adjusted. As one social worker commented: 'We expected all kinds of problems and they just did not happen.' "[69] This would be the official spin on the Pedro Pan children: they were saved from communism, well-adjusted, and grateful to be in the United States.

The Lost Apple: *La Manzana Perdida*

Children grateful to be saved from communism would be the image that propaganda makers in Washington latched on to. After the *Miami Herald* published an article on the exodus in March 1962, they began to take a greater interest in the Cuban children. A few weeks later, the issue arose at a meeting of the interagency Caribbean Survey Group, which included representatives from the CIA, Richard Helms and William Harvey, as well as those from the Pentagon, United States Information Agency (USIA), and State Department. Robert Kennedy was chair. Discussions ranged from using the exiles as a means of gathering intelligence to potential kidnappings of Cuban government officials (Robert Kennedy wanted to know if this was a possibility), to using the unaccompanied children in the camps for propaganda purposes. Together the group made up the oversight committee for Operation Mongoose, the anti-Castro campaign put in place by President Kennedy after the failure of the Bay of Pigs, and part of its task was propaganda. The psychological warfare committee had representatives from the CIA, State Department, and U.S. Information Agency.[70] Their activities encompassed production and the distribution of materials that would include leaflets, comic books, editorials, books, radio broadcasts, and films.[71]

At the meeting, USIA's Hewson Ryan mentioned that there were eight thousand children (at this point) being sent out of Cuba in order to avoid communist indoctrination and the hard times experienced in

Cuba. General Lansdale chimed in that "we should exploit the emotional possibilities of the 8,000 children that were under the protection of the United States." They concluded that the refugee children would serve a good propaganda purpose—"one we should exploit."[72]

Plans were put in place. These included publishing comic books that depicted how the Cuban government was brainwashing children and how scared parents were about their future and producing a film on the children. But at a July 17 meeting, the USIA reported that the voluntary agencies and HEW were opposing any publicity on children in the Miami area for fear that Castro would not let others leave.[72] The following week Lansdale assistant, Col. James Patchell, announced: "USIA reported money appropriated, superb director appointed and highly professional staff organized to do the job, but were not given permission by volunteer agencies to take close-ups and therefore the project was dropped."[74] The CIA representative was concerned that filming the children would expose their parents in Cuba and place them in danger. However, Lansdale insisted, "They could shoot the backs of heads."[75] Lansdale prevailed, and the exploitation of the image of the children became a key objective of Operation Mongoose psychological operations. This would take various forms, including suggested visits by Mrs. Kennedy to the camps which "would show our concern for the plight of the children" and the production of documentaries.[76]

The USIA commissioned well-known documentary filmmaker David Susskind to produce a film about the children's camps. There were back-and-forth conversations with Father Walsh in Miami, who was concerned about the safety of the children's parents in Cuba. Finally he agreed to the filming.[76] Like other reports about the children, the film was to be produced in English and Spanish so as to be able to show it in Latin America.[78] The film, entitled *The Lost Apple* (*La Manzana Perdida*) after a popular Cuban nursery rhyme, begins with a little boy's arrival at the camp. The camera follows him through his initial interview with a counselor and his vaccination shots at the nurse's station. The narrator, identified as Carlos Montalban, describes to the audience the loneliness that the little boy must be feeling. He then turns his attention to the boy and asks him, "Now, why would Mama and Papa send you here, all alone?" The answer provided by the same narrator is: "Fidel Castro."

From here, the film strikes a happier note, as children are shown playing ball and attending English classes. In another scene, a young blond girl, chewing gum, approaches a counselor and asks, "Are there any *becas* [scholarships]?" The counselor says, "Not yet." She urges her to check back in a few days. The film shows announcements of *"becas"* posted on a large blackboard.

The climax of the film is a nighttime variety show. There is opening footage of a priest giving a speech about the evils of communism. Two girls follow: one reads *"Los zapaticos de rosa,"* a well-known children's poem by José Martí, and the other sings a patriotic song. It is Dulce Maria, the girl who would end up in the California home. It is her extraordinary performance, filled with an eerie, almost adult passion, that captures the heart of the audience in the film.

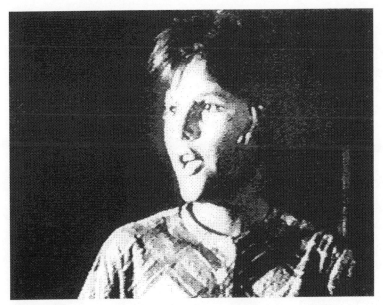

Dulce María Sosa. Image from the film *The Lost Apple,* 1963.

I remember the first time I saw the film. It was at a conference of Pedro Pans organized by Elly Chovel. We had swapped stories; it had been an emotional day. We had listened to speakers and I had given a presentation on the origins of Pedro Pan. But we were all left with the haunting memory of this young girl in the film who was only referred to as Dulce María. What had become of her?

Then a few years ago a California-based band headed by a Cuban woman performed at Miami's Calle Ocho Festival. It was rumored that Candy Sosa, the bandleader, was a Pedro Pan. Elly approached her and asked if she had been at the camps. "Was she in the camps? Did she remember singing at the camps? Did she remember the song she had sung? Later, a group of us met with Candy. She had been the child star of the film and she did not know, even remember, that she had been filmed. She sang the same song for us—'*Cuba mi patria querida . . .*' [Cuba my beloved homeland . . .]." Dulce María had become the professional singer Candy Sosa.

A few weeks after the shooting of the documentary, Dulce María and her sister and brother were sent to the Spanish-speaking California home where Dulce María was sexually abused.

We cannot gauge how many children were abused. From anecdotal evidence, sexual abuse does not seem to have been common, although there are cases of it. Physical and emotional abuses were more prevalent. Still, Dulce María's case illustrates how misplaced governmental priorities were at the time. The U.S. government and the social service agencies caring for the children appear to have been more interested in the ideological battle against communism than in the children's welfare. The children's complaints to supervisors about mistreatments and abuse in institutions and foster homes often went uninvestigated if not unheard. Those complaints did not suit the mythology spun in the ideological battle of the Cold War about children who had been rescued from the evils of communism—their real experiences, to be lived and suffered silently.

8

Doors Are Shut

Along with the increase of unaccompanied Cuban minors in the United States came the concern about reuniting them with their parents. Initially, Father Walsh wanted to establish an office in Havana to facilitate the orderly return of the children to their parents in Cuba. Alternatively, he urged that government funds be expended to care for the children while the parents arrived.[1]

Clearly, the process of reunification was not well thought through. A report from the Children's Bureau noted that "the first thing nearly every unaccompanied child has done on his arrival in Miami is to inquire about getting his parents a visa waiver."[2] Visa waivers for adults could be mailed to Cuba after a first-degree relative in this country or a volunteer agency signed for them on the parents' behalf. But the volunteer agencies had not established nationwide procedures for children to reclaim their parents; some families simply fell though the cracks. And the backlog of children waiting for placements was increasing, as was the push to get them out of Miami.

On April 29, 1962, an Associated Press wire story reported that one hundred children from Cuba would be "adopted" by Catholic nuns. Boston's Cardinal Cushing, speaking at a Society of St. Vincent DePaul community breakfast, said that the children would be arriving in Framingham, Massachusetts, by the Fourth of July. The church would receive six dollars a day from the federal government per child. The home for the children would be operated as an institution and not as a parochial school to avert criticism about the lack of separation between church and state.[3]

The news was greeted with anger from constituents across the country, many of whom made their opinions clear in letters to President Kennedy and their congressional representatives. Robert Griffith, a citizen from Massachusetts, wrote the following to the president: "This appears to be a raw, bold scheme by which the Roman Catholic Church undertakes to assure its future political power at the same time that it enriches itself at the expense of the U.S. taxpayer, all in violation of our church–state separation." Others were upset about the amount of money provided for the children's care. "What are you doing, letting those Cubans come here and paying them six dollars a day?" wrote Wayne Ladner. "This amounts to 2,000 dollars per year per child," Billy Kelley calculated in his letter. Lois Koetler, from Quincy, Illinois, wrote her senator, Everett Dirksen: "I am only allowed $600 a year for my child, I would like very much an explanation of this. I feel a great deal of bitterness." A Denver lawyer demanded to know under what law or presidential directive these children were allowed into the country and why these agencies were authorized to care for them. Others worried that the children were little spies sent by Castro to undermine the United States.[4]

Forty-four letters from eleven states were referred to the Children's Bureau by the White House. Fifteen of the letters raised questions about the payment of federal monies to the Catholic Church. Twelve questioned the authority of the program, ten stated that more was being done for Cuban children than for the children of U.S. citizens. There were also fifteen inquiries from members of Congress indicating that they, too, had received letters from angry constituents.[5]

October Missile Crisis: U.S. Responds with an Air Isolation Campaign

Paradoxically, at the same time that Americans were questioning their government's open-door policy, the economic embargo of Cuba imposed in early 1961 was beginning to have serious effects on the availability of consumer goods on the island, adding to the pressure to leave the country. Cuban exiles were worried that Kennedy's commitment was waning. In an attempt to reach out to Cuban exiles, White House officials held a series of meetings with the leadership of the Cuban Revolutionary Council. Although there was no concrete commitment to launch another invasion, the White House assured exiles that covert operations under the guise of Operation Mongoose were well under way.

In Cuba, meanwhile, the leadership had sought the support of the Soviet Union, and it came in the form of nuclear missiles. Numerous exile reports of the buildup of missiles, including one from Serafina de Giquel, one of the leaders of the network of former headmaster of Ruston Academy Jim Baker, reached the United States, but the White House did not act on them until October 1962.[6] Despite these reports, the Russians were able to build up their nuclear arsenal in the Western Hemisphere.

On October 22, in a national address, President Kennedy announced that in the face of the Soviet deployment of nuclear weapons in Cuba, he was ordering a quarantine of the island. The crackdown included cancellation of all flights in and out of Cuba. Countries friendly to the United States were encouraged to do the same. Cuba mobilized for an invasion.

For several tense days, the world waited anxiously as the two competing superpowers tried to negotiate a face-saving agreement. Finally, on October 28, Kennedy announced that he had accepted Khrushchev's demands, which included a promise by the United States that they would not invade the island of Cuba in exchange for the removal of the nuclear missiles.[7]

Relations between the superpowers remained at an impasse. The United States maintained its economic embargo of the island, prohibited travel to Cuba, and instituted an air isolation campaign to discourage flights in and out of the island. The air isolation campaign had as its purpose "to control the movement of subversive persons, propaganda materials, funds, and arms."[8] Cuba's air traffic was severely reduced. In effect, this meant that the United States would shut its doors to any new refugees from the island.

There had been debates about whether or not to cut off the immigration valve earlier in the year. In one meeting, President Kennedy asked if it was not better to shut the doors to the people trying to get out, so that they would be forced to stay and take action against the regime. General Lansdale, who had been in charge of Operation Mongoose, disagreed. For him the two thousand Cubans fleeing every week was a symbol of U.S. sympathy. They also provided important intelligence information.[9]

The State Department admitted that flights to and from Cuba served humanitarian purposes, but it was more important to isolate Castro's regime.[10] At the time, there were still 4,300 children in foster care and another several thousand living with friends or relatives, awaiting their parents' arrival.[11]

Requests for visa waivers were still pouring in. Father Walsh reported over 4,000 requests per week.[12] Walsh criticized the isolation policy, stating that the children would be the ones hurt. Parents were also fearful that their children would become too Americanized.[13] William vanden Heuvel, president of the International Rescue Committee, had testified to Congress that "the reunion of separated families is a basic attribute of any normalization of family life. Too many children are waiting for their parents; too many wives for their husbands." In addition, the visa waivers, particularly for children and youths, demonstrated the growing disaffection with a regime that claimed to favor them.[14] Ironically, the State Department had just started to issue visa waivers to entire families in an attempt to curtail the number of unaccompanied children under the care of the federal government.[15]

The Children and the Crisis

The week of the October Missile Crisis had been particularly hard for the Pedro Pan children whose parents were still Cuba. Children were afraid that Cuba would be bombed and that their parents would be killed. The situation in the camps was chaotic. The Marist Brothers asked leaders of the Juventud Estudiantil Católica to come speak to the boys at Matecumbe. Many members of the Juventud Católica were also members of Movimiento Revolucionario del Pueblo. They had not backed the U.S. invasion of the island. In Miami they were called Fidelistas sin Fidel and in Cuba they were repressed. Nonetheless, they continued to have a good relationship with many of the clergy that, while anti-Communist, maintained an anti-invasion posture.

By this time, Pancho León was living in Miami. Everyday after lunch, he would speak to the boys bringing them news. "We wanted to let them know that not all Cubans in exile were advocating bombing the island or for killing all those who had stayed. Our hope was to develop a nonviolent approach to Cuba amongst the Pedro Pans. With the help of Father Walsh and the Dominican Francisco [Titillo] Villaverde, we began publishing a journal called *Mensaje* (*The Message*) which was used to train the instructors at the camps, instilling in them a nonviolent approach toward the government in Cuba."[16] (Monsignor Walsh would continue advocating peaceful means of change for Cuba.)[17]

But the crisis created other problems as well. The abrupt ending of flights left many divided families in limbo. Children did not know if and when their parents would come to the United States. At the time, two of my cousins were waiting for the arrival of their father. My uncle, a onetime supporter of the revolution, was now working in the underground; being caught could mean his life. For those turning nineteen, the future was particularly nebulous, since they were no longer eligible for the children's program and not eligible for U.S. citizenship either.[18]

The distance between the children and the parents grew wider. Letters became less frequent or took longer to arrive, as they would have to travel to a third country before being shipped to the United States. Telephone lines between the two countries continued to deteriorate, making phone calling a frustrating experience. Reaching an operator was difficult, and even when you did it was almost impossible to get a line. If you were lucky enough to get through, you were limited to a few minutes of talk.

Attempt to Rescue the Parents

Around this time the United States initiated behind-the-scene maneuverings to get the Bay of Pigs prisoners released and transported to the United States in exchange for shiploads of goods. The results of the negotiations would provide an opportunity for some Pedro Pan parents to get out of Cuba, since the cargo ships used in the exchange would be returning from Cuba empty and capable of carrying people. The negotiations took months. Fearing a public backlash against negotiations with the Castro government, particularly discussions that would give the appearance that the United States was paying a ransom for the prisoners, the Kennedy White House established a committee of private individuals to give the public the impression that these were private and not government efforts. James Donovan, a Washington lawyer, was asked to chair the committee. The White House orchestrated the meetings and their publicity.[19] When Castro proposed a $62 million ransom, the State Department provided the Cuban Families Committee their public relations strategy: "The theme should be in terms of the fight to recapture human freedom and national independence rather than in terms of disabled Cubans to whom the United States owes a debt."[20]

Negotiations stalled and U.S. government officials disagreed on how to proceed. Attorney General Robert Kennedy had plans for the Bay of Pigs veterans: "The group would be a very valuable asset at some future time when the Castro regime collapsed." However, in July 1962, the CIA surmised that Castro's offer to release the prisoners was motivated by his need for foreign currency.[21] John McCone of the CIA's Directorate of Intelligence, cautioned "that payment of money or food would probably prolong the existence of the Castro regime, possibly for such an extended time that it would become permanent."[22]

The Cuban government was anxious to receive hard currency. One way to get it was by resuming flights in and out of the island. They agreed to release the prisoners and allow their family members to leave if the United States lifted restrictions on the Pan American flights. The president, in turn, was willing to resume the flights if Castro allowed the relatives of the Brigade members to leave.[23] But while the talks moved on, what the public knew was that the island was quarantined.

When flights out of the island were canceled, Concha Bechily panicked. Her three children were in the United States while she and her husband had continued their involvement in the underground, not only distributing visa waivers for children but also helping underground fighters escape the island. Their Havana contacts, Judge Oscar Piña and his wife, Petite Esnard, had been jailed. She had already gotten her and her husband's' papers in order and had purchased airline tickets to come to the United States at the end of October. She recalls:

> We had lost all hope of leaving. Things were very bad. People were being jailed, and we had been involved in many activities. The only way out of Cuba was through a third country or in small boats, and this was very difficult and very dangerous.[24]

In the States, her daughter, María, thought that she would never see her parents again. Everything was uncertain. While she could still communicate with her parents, it was becoming more difficult to get a call through. Sometime it took days. She knew there was no returning to Cuba, and she was determined to try to get her parents out.

> I realized that most of the social workers that I was dealing with were very limited. They were doing their job, but they weren't going to go out on a limb for me. I had to go out on a limb for me. So I had the idea that we could write letters. My older brother has always been very precocious. And, he's an excellent writer. He knew more English than I did because he had already studied English in Cuba, and had an interest. So I said to him, you know what, we need to do this ourselves. So, let's get the names of the two U.S. senators from Illinois, and let's write to the attorney general, who I knew was the brother of the president, and let's write to the president. And, let's just tell them our story. That we're here, that we're stuck

and that we need to get our parents out of Cuba. So, we started this letter-writing campaign.[25]

On special occasions, all the Pedro Pan children would gather in Chicago at a church. This gave them an opportunity to compare notes.

Well, I'll tell you one thing that Catholic Charities did right. They would provide us with opportunities to get together. Christmas, parties, el Día de los Reyes. They had picnics. We did get together on a regular basis. And, that was wonderful. This is when we would get the other children to sign the letters. I remember keeping tally of how many letters were sent. I know, I was totally obsessed with this.

Finally, Senator Paul Douglas of Illinois wrote her a letter telling her that her parents would be arriving on one of the cargo ships that had taken food supplies to Cuba in exchange for the Bay of Pigs prisoners. After months of negotiations and haggling, the two governments had finally reached an agreement.[26] People who had unaccompanied children in the United States would be given preference. Concha Bechily remembered the day they got a phone call from a Cuban official telling them they could leave:

We got a notice that we had to be in Havana in the first few days of June. But there was a strike in the port of Philadelphia and the cargo ship did not get to Cuba until the beginning of July. Then we were told we had to be at the port of San Francisco at five in the morning. We spent all day waiting. We were only allowed to take three changes of clothing and nothing else. The Cuban authorities strip-searched us to make sure that we didn't. After hours of waiting, my feet were so swollen. I had to take my shoes off and could not put them back on. I gave them away and put on a pair of sandals I had with me. We did not get on the boat until six in the evening. We were the last to get on.

We finally arrived in Fort Lauderdale and were taken to Opalocka where they processed our entrance. We were in Miami seven or eight days and we were told we would be taken to Chicago, where our kids were, and that we would be in charge of them immediately upon our arrival. We had wanted to stay in Miami, but this was not possible.[27]

On the last Red Cross supply ship, 325 parents, involving 348 children, arrived. Fifty-four of those children were still in foster care in Miami, and 100 outside of Miami. Of these, 66 were in Chicago, a fact that surprised Father Walsh, who had not known about the children's letter-writing campaign. María had saved her parents from going to prison.

Other parents were not as fortunate as the Bechilys. Pepe Arruza tried to leave on one of the cargo ships, but was told to wait by Mongo Grau, one of the Pedro Pan organizers. Three years later, he and Mongo were arrested in what Cuban intelligence called the "Case of *El Cura Manco*." Arruza's Cuban arrest record contains the following annotation:

> After the October Missile Crisis, Arruza visited Grau since he wanted to leave the country with one of the cargo ships. Grau advised against it, telling him things between Cuba and the United States were about to change. Several months later he again visited Grau. He was concerned about his sons: the older children had written to him, telling him that the younger siblings were forgetting their Spanish.[28]

Arruza would serve seventeen years in jail. His family would never be reunited.

Canceling Visa Waivers

The program that had reunited the Bechilys was greeted with contempt from Congress. Representatives were outraged that established immi-

María Bechily with her brothers and parents celebrating her fifteenth birthday, Chicago, 1964, shortly after their arrival.

gration procedures had been circumvented. Congress immediately called hearings. They grilled immigration and naturalization officials on the procedures that had been used to screen the passengers on the cargo ships, and they demanded to know about the visa waiver program from the State Department. Like their constituents, they also questioned the constitutionality of a federal program that paid money to the Catholic Church to take care of refugee children.

But what concerned Congress most was security. The fear was that Castro would use the opportunity to infiltrate spies into the United States. They wanted to know how Cubans on the cargo ships had been chosen and what role the Cuban government had had in putting people on the boats. In August 1963, officials of the State Department's Bureau of Security and Consular Affairs prepared a statement about the visa waivers. This was the first public statement by the U.S. government regarding the visa waiver program:

> Since the United States after the break in diplomatic relations had no consulate in Havana, the Secretary of State and the Attorney General decided that the requirement for visa would be waived on the basis of unforeseen emergencies as provided for in Section 212(d)(4)(a) of the Immigration and Nationality Act. A visa waiver procedure was put in place. This required the submission by persons in the United States (relatives, friends, church or voluntary agencies, group organizations, members of Congress) a request on behalf of a Cuban in Cuba. With information provided, State Department carried out a security screening. Over 617,000 visa waiver applications were received, 478,969 were granted as of July 31, 1963. 138,000 Cuban were declared ineligible . . . approximately 94,786 Cuban who received waivers under this procedure have entered the US. The visa waiver only allowed Cubans to enter the US, the actual admission was granted by a parole given by the Attorney General.[29]

Congressional representatives demanded to know specifically who decided which people boarded the ships. They were given a detailed description of how U.S. officials had reviewed the lists provided by the International Red Cross. Indeed, these screening procedures had delayed the departure of the ships.[30] The State Department explained that their main concern had been the repatriation of Americans still on the island, but since there had been extra room they had agreed to let parents of children institutionalized in the United States come on the ships as well.

Public pressure was mounting to keep the doors shut. Florida assistant attorney general Ralph Odum wrote to Washington, claiming, "We have serious problems dealing with Cuban refugees. Miami has about reached the saturation point in its ability to assimilate any more of these people. The problems include jobs, housing, schools, law enforcement, but I believe the most serious is the fact that many of the refugees seem determined to stay as close to Cuba as possible and help start a war in the Richard Harding Davis–William Randolph Hearst tradition."[31]

The fear of a runaway Cuban exile effort to overthrow Castro also worried some in Washington. Cutting off the immigrant flow could have the special benefit of creating enough pressure within the island to provoke an insurrection, so that outside effort would not be needed. McGeorge Bundy, national security advisor, was informed that Abba Schwartz, head of the Bureau of Security and Consular Affairs of the State Department, was recommending a suspension of the visa waiver program. Congress had been very upset about the lack of security procedures and what they perceived were unnecessary expenditures since there was now no transportation from Cuba to the United States. The Justice and Defense Departments did not feel strongly about the visa waiver program and stated that they would agree to a suspension. But others in the State Department reminded colleagues that visa waivers were now being granted to split families with the purpose of uniting them, to children for educational purposes, to persons of special interest to agencies of the United States, and to persons who were believed to be in danger. The political division of the State Department recommended that it was in the interest of U.S foreign policy to continue the policy of waiving visas.[32] The CIA concurred—suspension of the visa waiver program would be perceived as yet another example of Washington abandoning its commitment to a free Cuba, and it could be interpreted as the United States collaborating with Castro to keep Cubans jailed on the island.[33]

Members of an intra-agency committee appointed by the president during the missile crisis, decided to review visa waiver policies. On August 30, the Interdepartmental Committee on Cuban Affairs circulated a memo to Alexander Haig, lieutenant colonel of the U.S. Army and member of the group;[34] Joseph Califano, general counsel of the U.S. Army; W. F. Wendt of the U.S. Navy; and John Carpenter of the U.S. Air

Force. It asked for an answer to a request from the State Department about their position vis-à-vis the cancellation of the visa waiver programs. All agreed to the cancellation, in that there was no longer a military need for them. The final decision would be a political one. The authority of the attorney general to parole refugees in individual cases should provide sufficient flexibility to deal with any special situations that might arise. Technically, this marked the end of all Cuban visa waiver programs.[35]

For Father Walsh, the program had been over since the cancellation of flights the previous year. He had reduced his staff by fifty people because the caseload had noticeably decreased.[36] Wendell Rollason, who needed the visa waiver program to take care of the underground fighters, protested when he was told that the United States now wanted to shut off the immigrant valve with the hope of causing an internal combustion on the island. He had people in Cuba whose lives were in danger, and if the United States was going to shut the doors, he would find another country that would help. He went looking for assistance in Mexico, although he was warned repeatedly by his State Department contact, Frank Watterson, that if he did not stop trying to get people out of Cuba, he would regret it.

On September 21, 1964, Rollason was arrested in Mexico and charged with the bribery of government officials and of using fraudulent documents to get refugees out of Cuba. Rollason had dedicated his life to refugees and his reputation was impeccable. Indeed, on occasion he had written to State Department officials warning them about people selling visa waivers.[37] He had also made passionate pleas on behalf of the visa waiver program for adults and for children: "The increase in demands for visa waivers is based on the noblest of human emotions —love for another man, woman, or child. The demand within Cuba is based on the most understandable of human emotions—fear, fear of hunger, fear of oppression, fear of death, fear of the unknown." Rollason argued that the United States should leave the doors open. If Castro shut them, then he would have to pay the consequences.[38]

However, a spate of memos through the various agencies involved concluded that officially all visa waiver programs were canceled. The United States government had declined an offer by a British national to set up a ferry boat service to transport the 300,000 Cubans holding visa waivers to the United States. Most waiver holders had relatives and children here. Father Walsh had personally signed thousands of the waivers. Essentially, the U.S. government believed, the "crowded and potentially explosive situation in Miami and the pursuit of our isolation policy have counseled against further substantial inflow."[39] To continue allowing people in the United States without a possible early return to Cuba would create a refugee crisis. Social service agencies taking care of the children in the United States were reassessing the situation. Father Walsh wrote, "Two months ago, there was talk in the agencies about how to plan for the children when they go back. This is not being considered at this time."[40]

Rollason was admired by many people in Miami, including the Episcopalian bishop, who organized a campaign to get him out of jail which featured a high-profile visit by Miami's mayor Robert King High to Rollason's prison cell. The mayor was also warned by the U.S ambassador to Mexico not to cause any trouble.[41]

But even in jail, Rollason would not be silenced. He demanded meetings with the President of Mexico, Luis Echeverría.[42] He sent letters to the national security advisor protesting a report by journalist Jack Anderson that the administration was considering negotiations with Cuba: "The Revolution of Cuba was the revolt of the country's youth against the tyranny of Batista and the traditional corruption of its government. Most of its original men-in-arms are now in exile, in prison or dead. The United States must not compound the crime."[43]

LBJ: Isolate Cuba

On November 22, 1963, John F. Kennedy was assassinated. Vice President Lyndon Johnson, the pragmatic former senator from Texas, assumed the presidency. JFK's policy had relied on the Monroe Doctrine to justify its actions against Cuba, and Johnson, who had chaired meetings of the National Security Council that oversaw Cuba policy, shared this perspective. The Monroe Doctrine provided a historical justification to the U.S. position that it would not accept the presence of a Soviet-backed country in this hemisphere.[44] Still, Johnson wanted a more focused policy. The White House promptly issued a memo to various departments asking for evaluations of the program and broadly outlining its primary objective: a free Cuba. However, the administration wanted to keep Cuba in perspective and out of the public's eye. They wanted to demonstrate to the public that they were diligently working to get rid of the communist menace, without scaring the public.[45]

By the end of December, the president called a special meeting on Cuba. Representatives from the CIA, State Department, National Security Council, and the various branches of the armed forces were present. The president observed that there was no immediate possibility for an internal insurrection, and therefore pressure had to come from the outside. Various projects were discussed—including blowing up a power plant in Matanzas—to send a signal that Johnson would not abandon the Cuban cause. Representatives from the armed forces, including Cyrus Vance, were enthusiastic about a military action, but others, including the president, feared that these types of actions could backfire.

It was decided that covert programs should also be closely monitored. For the CIA, the goal remained replacing the Cuban government with one more compatible with the United States. Their mission was to create maximum pressure on the regime through all means short of direct intervention and use of military force. Covert programs would include intelligence gathering and propaganda aimed at stimulating low-risk sabotage by autonomous anti-Castro Cuban exiles so that the U.S. government could deny involvement.[46]

There had been a debate within the administration as to what to do with the exiles. The main umbrella group formed by the CIA was the Cuban Revolutionary Council, headed by Dr. José Miró Cardona. The council had received over $3 million from the United States covertly. At the time, the council was composed of about a dozen groups, although a CIA count had identified approximately four hundred exile organizations, most of which were described as consisting of a leader and his friends. The administration wanted exiles to concentrate on propaganda activities and not military actions, therefore Miró Cardona resigned.[47] There was also infighting among leaders of the council, with the military wing, headed by Manuel Artime, wanting independence from the political wing.[48]

Some members of the U.S government had advocated forming a freedom brigade with the Bay of Pigs prisoners as a way to demonstrate to the world the United States' commitment to a free Cuba.[49] The navy, army, and air force had drawn up plans and budgets and had found sites for the training of the brigade.[50] But fearing a runaway exile military group, a program of military and civilian opportunities was established for the members of the Bay of Pigs invasion brigade instead. The civilian portion offered them student loans, vocational training, special employment counseling, and English classes. As for the military initiative, Cuban exiles were recruited into the armed forces, including many Pedro Pans who had turned nineteen and were now out of the unaccompanied children's program. Strict security procedures were put in place for them, including a polygraph test to determine political loyalties and moral character.[51]

While exile leaders were demanding recognition of a government in exile, there was local pressure to get exiles out of Miami. Resettlement was still the federal policy, although only 50,000 refugees had been resettled and an estimated 125,000 remained in Miami.[52]

Johnson opted for a strategy to isolate Cuba economically, politically, and psychologically from the free world. But was it effective? At a White House meeting, Dennis Fitzgerald, speaking on behalf of the CIA, said he thought the blockade was effective in creating economic woes for the island, but that there were holes in the embargo that needed to be plugged. Equipment vital to the Cuban economy still reached the island via Canada and Great Britain. Johnson ordered a study on the effects of the embargo in order to develop a more cohesive policy.

Johnson was also worried about hemispheric relations and Cuba's continued role in aiding insurrectionist Latin America. McGeorge Bundy, his national security advisor, reported on developments in Latin America, especially Cuban intervention in Venezuela. The goal was to pressure Latin American countries to help the United States isolate Cuba and terminate any help that Cuba may have been giving to insurrectionists in Latin American countries. The Organization of American States would play an important role in this aspect of the Johnson policy, and the hemispheric strategy would become central to the Johnson plan. The intent, clearly, was to strengthen the Latin American nations so that they could, through individual and collective means, resist communist subversion. The Cuban government's effort to advance the communist cause in Latin American through propaganda, sabotage, and subversion had to be stopped with all available instruments, short of acts of war.[53]

In contrast to Kennedy's original Cuba policy, Johnson's was not exile-centered, rather it relied more on the government's foreign policy tools and responded to domestic pressures. Indeed, on the question of American students involved in an organization called Hands Off Cuba Committee who were traveling to Cuba, Johnson tentatively approved travel restrictions but suggested a policy of selective prosecution. And the door would not be entirely closed to conversations with the Castro government.[54]

However, Johnson was adamant that renewed immigration from Cuba was not to be encouraged. The administration was convinced that isolation would be a major factor in curbing Cuba's adventures abroad. And although it could be claimed that flights served humanitarian purposes, any action that lessened isolation of Cuba in effect bolstered Castro.[55] The doors would remain resolutely shut.

Other Avenues for Parents and for Children

Left without direct flights to the United States, Cuban parents with children in the United States tried to find other avenues out of Cuba.

The flights to Mexico and Spain provided an opportunity to leave the island, but getting from a third country to the United States was very difficult. This was expressed in a letter written by María Miranda to the Children's Bureau asking for help in getting her father a visa from Mexico to the United States. Lucille Batson, a representative, responded that she was sympathetic, but it was up to the State Department and the INS to grant those visas. At this stage, there was little coordination between the children's programs and other federal agencies.[56] The Episcopalian Diocese of Minnesota even hired a lawyer in Mexico to help organize transit visas for Cubans who had unaccompanied children in that state.[57] But since the visa waivers were canceled, Cubans did not have a way to receive transit visas from U.S. embassies. They would travel to these third countries and then apply for a visa to the United States. But once in Mexico, it was very difficult to enter the United States.

Some Cubans who made it to Mexico decided to try to cross the border illegally. In what was deemed as an undesirable development, the embassy in Mexico asked the State Department to stop paroling Cubans who entered the United States illegally. According to their records INS apprehended more than 1,000 Cubans along the Brownsville, Texas, border area from March 1963 to December 1964.[58]

Cubans making it to Spain also faced obstacles in their efforts to be reunited with their children in the United States. This was the case for my uncle and aunt and their youngest child. By the time they arrived in Spain, their children, my two cousins, had passed through Florida City, had lived for several months in a foster home in Albuquerque, and joined our family in Cleveland. But the reunion in the United States was delayed for about a year. The United States now insisted on counting Cubans against the Western European quota, and they had to wait their turn.

Cuba also made these third-country trips difficult. Candi Sosa's parents finally came through Spain three years after she and her sister had left for the United States. Her family, like others, had visas for Spain, but the Cuban government would issue exit permits only to some of the family members. Because of this, many families decided to send their children ahead, which created even more unaccompanied minor refugees.

The pressure to leave Cuba increased even further when the Cuban government called for compulsory military duty for all boys. The induction age was seventeen, but no one under fifteen was given exit permits. Even though, according to Father Walsh, the Pedro Pan Operation was over, the Catholic Church in Cuba continued trying to get kids out with the help of the Spanish Catholic Church. Carlos Manuel de Céspedes, who would later become auxiliary bishop for Havana, remembered that the church helped get travel documents so that children could travel to Spain.

Hugo Chaviano, a Chicago-based attorney, used this route to get to the United States through Spain, although, years later, he said that he had not been aware that his trip was part of a continuation of the Catholic Church's commitment to save youth from communist indoctrination.[59] This exit route was not easy. The flights to Spain were very expensive and seats were difficult to get. There were two flights a week. One, Iberia, flew direct from Havana to Madrid, the other, KLM, had a two-night layover in the Bahamas. The KLM flight was used for unaccompanied children when the airline was part of Jim Baker's network. But since the United States no longer wanted to encourage immigration, the tickets now had to be financed by the families. No one in Cuba had dollars, so they had to rely on relatives living abroad. Once in Mexico or Spain, there was no guarantee that refugees could work or even go to the United States quickly. Their relatives had to support them abroad. Unlike the U.S. program, third-country avenues did not become an outlet for massive migration of children.

Once in Spain or Mexico, there were even fewer infrastructures to take care of the unaccompanied minors. Hugo Chaviano was fortunate—he was taken in by a friend of his family who was able to secure a visa to the United States within a month. Hundreds of unaccompanied minors came through Spain's program.

U.N. Commission's Offer

The third-country processes were extremely slow and expensive, so other minors tried different approaches to get their parents out. Alfredo Lanier, who had been bounced around from home to home, wrote to Jackie Kennedy for help. "Everyone realized that after the missile crisis, the separation was going to be for a long time," he told me. "I was in New York with the crazy Cuban, the one who wanted me to iron his clothes for him at all hours, and going to a high school that was like out of *West Side Story*. So I started writing letters. I sent one to the International Rescue Committee and one to the United Nations High Commissioner of Refugee Affairs."

Records indicate that the White House was not oblivious to the plight of unaccompanied minors. On April 9, 1964, Gordon Chase prepared a memo for one of the president's aides that chronicled U.S. policy toward refugees since the revolution: "After the missile crisis, the U.S. did not change its policy of acceptance of refugees, however it did impose a rigid isolation policy on the island resulting in a reduction of flights and leaving only a few flights a week between Cuba and Mexico City and Spain. But if we had our druthers even these would not exist." The flow of refugees was about 800 per month, 300 via Mexico, 300 via Spain, and 200 via small boats from Cuba. Since Castro's ascension to power, roughly 13,000 unaccompanied children had entered the United States. At present, the number of unaccompanied children was about 2,600. "A person lost his or her status when his parents join him, or when he turns 19. We have no statistics readily available, but probably 40–50% have lost their status. There are approximately 8,000 children who had not been reunited with their parents."[60]

The official U.S. position was that there were no restrictions on the Cubans' entry into the United States, rather, the problem was leaving Cuba. The official White House response stated: "Our best hopes for speeding up the process of joining unaccompanied children with their parents is for an international organization (International Red Cross or the UN High Commissioner of Refugee Affairs) to talk to Castro and convince him that the parents who want to leave should be allowed to do so and should be given preference on the transportation that exists."[61] Essentially, there was no official change in policy.

Mr. Bundy was reminded by a staff person of the plight of approximately 8,000 minors, but was forewarned by another that "humanitarian types around government think this is a very unfortunate business and want to do something about it. At the same time proceeding to reunite them could lead to additional pressure for additional transportation which would dilute our isolation policy."[62] Still, the State Department had turned to the U.S. representative at the United Nations. He, in turn, had spoken with Manuel Urrutia, the regional representative for the U.N.'s High Commission on Refugee Affairs, who informed him that the commissioner had been trying to find a solution to the problem of divided families. In 1964, the High Commissioner of Refugee Affairs had offered to negotiate the exit permits for the parents and siblings in Cuba, and pay for the flights. It was an opening, one that had not existed since the cargo ships a year earlier. But the United States' response came in the form of a State Department statement, declassified upon my request, from the Lyndon B. Johnson Presidential Library National Security Files:

> As of the fall of 1963, it was estimated that between 9–10,000 persons still in Cuba with waivers who had unaccompanied children in the United States or had spouses. Volunteer agencies taking care of the children had asked the American Council of Volunteer Agencies for Foreign Service to draw up a list of priority cases. And they petitioned the State Department for permission to permit these persons to be moved directly from Cuba to the United States. The answer came from the State Department; while sympathetic, the proposal was not feasible because of higher security needs (blockade) and also because of the difficulty in setting priorities and securing the co-operation of Cuba.[63]

Sensing pressure from both the United Nations and the volunteer agencies, the State Department in July issued points on how to talk about the concerns of reuniting parents in Cuba with their unaccompanied children in the United States. The United States was willing to give 50 percent of the seats on available flights to parents and siblings and, in special cases, grandparents, of minor children now in the United States who wished to leave Cuba. The United States, through the United Nations, would furnish the parents' names to the Cuban government. In addition, the United States was willing to facilitate the movement of unaccompanied children from the United States to Cuba provided that all concerned, children and parents, were agreeable. This was particularly ironic since the United States had helped set up the program to help them escape from communism. However, the United States was not prepared to participate in any arrangement involving the provision of special means of transportation for the carriage of the persons described above other than those already in existence.[64] National security needs were more important than the needs of children. The doors would stay closed.

By 1964, food in Cuba was becoming scarce. UPI reporter John Virtue wrote that even sugar was being rationed. Severe shortages of the most essential consumer items, like soap, toilet paper, razors, and sanitary napkins contributed to the discontent. The old questions of *patria potestad* were still worrying parents and fueled their desire to leave the country. By now, Castro had taken over the Communist Party and all government institutions. While all private schools were closed, the government was spending millions to build new schools and bring 100,000 children from rural areas to Havana for schooling. But the curriculum was framed by communist philosophy and tremendous pressure was placed on the children to conform.[65]

Virtue concluded, "Among the most troubled people in Cuba are those parents who oppose the government and the things their children are taught in school. By trying to counteract the teaching during these formative years, the parent puts him in the confusing situation of being told one thing at school and something else at home. But if the child becomes a *gusano* or worm as Castro calls his opponents, life will not be as pleasant for him when he grows up nor on the other hand will it be for the parents if their child grows up to be a communist."[66] The pressure to leave Cuba continued to increase, but with few legal travel options, many became desperate, leaving illegally in small boats.

9

Reconstructing Home

Home is not where other people don't understand me
Home is not where I look and talk funny
Home is not where I wake up in the middle of the night with a pain in
    my stomach
Home is not where I wake up in morning with a pain in my head
Home is not where I want to be anymore
Home is not where my parents are anymore
Home is . . . where is home?

—*Teresita Echazabal*[1]

On September 28, 1965, Fidel Castro announced his willingness to allow Cubans in the United States to pick up relatives on the island. The
port of Camarioca, close to world-famous Varadero Beach, would be
opened on October 10. President Johnson's response came in the form
of a public proclamation at the foot of the Statue of Liberty: People of
Cuba who seek refuge in the United States would find it. However, there
were grave concerns behind closed doors at the White House. Still, at
the September 30 briefing at noon, the White House reiterated its support for reuniting divided families, indicating that about 1,000 refugees
a month were coming to the United States through third countries.[2]

    Castro was quick to denounce the United States for what he termed
"*un rejuego*" (a game) with refugees. In what would become a familiar
pattern in U.S.-Cuban relations, Castro blamed the United States for
building the refugee crisis: "This has taken place since they suspended
travel to Cuba, thereby prohibiting all those persons who had previ-

ously received permission to go live in the United States, many of whom had members of their family living there, and obliging them to attempt the trip under risky conditions—a fact they have exploited unscrupulously for propaganda purposes." He reiterated an offer made after the missile crisis to set up two flights a day or to allow relatives to pick up family through their own means. However, he left open the possibility for discussion with the United States.[3]

In the meantime, Camarioca was opened and approximately one thousand boats originating from Miami made the trip. Like other refugees, those leaving Cuba were forced to abandon their homes and property to the government. From Camarioca 2,979 Cubans left the island. The 2,104 people remaining when Camarioca was closed were transported to Florida on boats chartered by the United States.[4]

The administration assessed Castro's proposal. There were strong arguments for keeping the immigration valve closed. There was strong opposition from Miami locals against any more refugees.[5] In addition, the administration's campaign to keep transportation links between Cuba and the United States to a minimum wasn't as effective as they had hoped for. U.S. officials also wanted to reduce HEW expenditures on refugees, and they were worried that new travel could potentially inject large amounts of foreign exchange into the Cuban economy, which could bolster the Castro regime.

On the other hand, there was the issue of the president's public image. How could he deny refuge to those fleeing a communist regime? The president's advisors believed that in order to win the international propaganda battle, the United States had to preserve its commitment to create a refuge for exiles from communist countries. This could be accomplished by permitting the entry of a limited number of close relatives; for instance, parents of children who were alone in the United States. This way, the impact on Florida could be kept within acceptable bounds and the government could retain control of the movement. Surely the American public would support such a program.

The next few months would be filled with tension for the Pedro Pan children. "Emotional upsets and illnesses among the Cuban children have increased," reported the Children's Bureau. "Children who earlier in the program appeared to withstand the separation from parents, home, and country amazingly well have broken down. To some of these children, their being sent to the United States, especially when younger children remain at home, was parental rejection. They have interpreted their parents' failure to come to this country as further evidence of rejection."[6] Many felt like orphans. This sentiment was expressed by a child who sent a telegram to President Johnson: "We wish visas for our parents who are in Zulueta, Las Villas, Cuba. We have been in this country for more than three years like orphans and we would like to be reunited with our parents."[7]

In a surprising move, the Cuban government announced it was willing to allow Cubans to travel to the United States to see their relatives and to permit Cubans in the United States to visit the island. The proposal would have created a way for parents who, for whatever reason, had chosen to stay in Cuba, to at least have some contact with their children. The White House interpreted it as a propaganda ploy on the part of the Cuban government, since it also included a plea to the U.S. government to allow U.S. students—who like all U.S. citizens were also banned from travel to Cuba—to visit the island without fear of prosecution in the United States.[8]

An intense diplomatic war raged for months. There were disagreements regarding the scope of what would be discussed. Cuban negotiators, sending messages through the Swiss embassy, wanted to broaden the discussion to include travel in general.[9] The U.S. government's representatives argued about the method of transporting the refugees and whether or not the United States could have inspectors at Cuban ports.[10] There were also disagreements on how many could leave; Cuba wanted 12,000 a month, the United States 3,000.

The greatest discrepancy in the two countries' positions concerned who could leave Cuba. There was a tense struggle over the political prisoners languishing in Cuban jails. In previous discussions with the United States, Cuba had made an offer through Abba Schwartz, head of the Bureau of Security and Consular Affairs of the State Department, that they would exchange political prisoners for a pledge of noninterference by the United States.[11] But now they were only willing to consider exchanging them for prisoners held in Latin American countries. This was particularly unsettling for the many Cubans who had families and relatives in Cuban jails. Isabel Bequer, one of the women sponsored by the CIA in 1960 to travel throughout Latin America speaking about the Cuban government's threat of taking *patria potestad* over children, appealed to the president: "We beg you in the name of our families who died in the struggle against communism that you ask the Cuban government to give priority to leave Cuba to all political prisoners."[12] This included some parents of unaccompanied children, like those of my friends, the Arruzas, with whom I had traveled to the United States.

Finally, an agreement was reached. Priority would be given to Cubans with relatives in the United States, thus recognizing the importance of reuniting divided families. Cuba would accept the United States definition of immediate family members, which included parents of children under twenty-one, spouses, unmarried children under the age of twenty-one, and brothers and sisters under the age of twenty-one.[13] However, it would retain the right to refuse exit to certain technicians and professionals. Cuba insisted that young men of military age, fifteen to twenty-six, could not leave. In addition, the Cuban government considered itself obliged to protect and guarantee the complete education of minors of both sexes who were mature enough to decide for themselves that they wanted to stay. There had been cases of young teenagers refusing to leave with their parents.[14]

On November 5, both governments signed a Memorandum of Understanding. Bill Moyers, the president's press secretary, closely choreographed a press conference to present the agreement in the context of freedom and family reunification. The unaccompanied children's plight would become the justification for opening the doors for a new wave of Cuban exiles. Ironically, only five months prior to this, the appeals to the president on behalf of the children had been overruled by national security priorities.

As part of the agreement, Cuba would close the port of Camarioca and the United States would set up two flights a day, which came to be called the Freedom Flights. Every day for the next eight years, two planes filled with refugees left Varadero for the United States. For many Pedro Pans, this would be the end of their prolonged separations from their parents. But not all divided families were reunited. According to a Children's Bureau report, approximately three hundred unaccompanied children remained in the program in 1967. Left unaccounted were the Pedro Pans who had turned nineteen and were technically out of the program. We still do not know how many of them were not reunited with their parents.

For the Pedro Pans whose parents were still in Cuba, there was not even the possibility of visits. For a variety of reasons, some parents decided to stay in Cuba. Others were awaiting the release of a jailed spouse or were barred from leaving the country because of their professions. The proposal allowing Cubans access between both countries had been dropped along the way.

While the United States allowed refugees in, it prohibited travel back to Cuba. Cuba also refused to allow reentry for those who left, and repatriation and visits were out of the question. Therefore the only hope for unaccompanied children was their parents' arrival to the United States. In 1973, the doors were shut again. This time it was Cuba's decision. Furthermore, new family divisions would be caused by the Cuban government's policy of not allowing young men of military age to leave the country. Many families would have to decide between leaving the island or staying with their sons.

Children Anchors in the Relocation Program

The backlash was precisely what the White House had feared. In October 1965, *Miami Herald* headlines read, "Miami Already Has Too Many Refugees," "Miami Fears Effects of New Influx."[15] A survey conducted by the State Department of major daily newspapers concluded that most editors were suspicious of Castro's motives. Most speculated that he was trying to get rid of opposition. "One thing is certain: The proposal is not prompted by humanitarian concerns."[16]

President Johnson received hundreds of angry letters. One, written by Barbara Fallon, a Miami resident, said, "Flagler Street to Biscayne Boulevard is like a main street in Havana and an American feels unpleasantly like a foreigner." Another resident wrote, "We Americans learned to live with the Cubans—voicing their fervent dislike of the USA, living several families to a house, disregarding state laws, we even got used to their bold attitudes and their public rudeness." A tourism worker complained, "I used to make 75 dollars a week, now some Cuban has my job and is being paid 55 dollars a week." Theresa Muller, a seventh-grader, pleaded with the president. "I have had my fill of Cubans. We no longer consider this city Miami, but as 'Little Cuba'!" Another letter read: "I think you are making a horrible mistake in letting all this riffraff into this country. Castro is unloading these people."[17] After a visit to Miami, a Los Angeles councilman wrote, "Very much alarmed at uncontrolled admittance of Cuban citizens. Very dangerous decision, we may get trained agitators and saboteurs." There were exceptions: Dunkin Donuts, for example, sent a telegram offering jobs and training for 150 refugees. [18] And Fred Fox, director of Catholic Social Services of the Duluth, Minnesota diocese, in a telegram sent to the president, expressed, "Please convey the thanks of many Cuban children anxiously awaiting their parents—to the President for his Bold and courageous offer of yesterday, assure him of the cooperation of hundreds of resettlement agencies throughout the United States."[19]

The politicians, however, listened to their constituents. They did not want Cubans in Florida. Already, on October 5, 1965, Florida governor Haydon Burns had written to President Johnson urging an aggressive resettlement plan which included setting up a national monitoring system so that refugees would not be allowed back in Florida.[20] Robert King High, Miami's mayor, who had been an advocate of granting Cuban exiles citizenship, worried about the extraordinary burden borne by the Miami community and of the potential for racial unrest.[21]

He had received a letter from the Donald Wheeler Jones, president of the Miami Branch of the NAACP, offering his organization's support in resettling Cuban refugees to other parts of the country. Many African-Americans had lost jobs to Cuban refugees, he claimed. While sympathetic to the plight of Cuban refugees, he wanted to ensure that his community was guaranteed economic stability and jobs. He worried that giving Cubans freedom and opportunities could increase poverty in his community.

In response to local pressure, Mayor High appointed a committee that included representatives from media, business, and religious organizations to assess the refugee situation. The White House responded by setting up a meeting with representatives from the State Department and HEW to review and expand the resettlement program. Unaccompanied children would be key to the program's success.

Families were forced to leave Miami if they wanted to reunite with their children. Like the Bechilys, many of the Pedro Pan parents had wanted to have their children brought to them in Miami. It was logical that the parents wanted to stay in Miami; some had relatives there, most had friends. They were afraid of going to a place where they didn't know the language. Reunifications, in Miami or elsewhere, were plagued by bureaucratic snafus.

However, federal policy was firmly in place.[22] When Manuel Peres and Daisy Blench arrived in October of 1961, they tried to reunite with their daughters, Vivian and Daisy, who had been shipped to Queen of Heaven School in Denver. They wanted to find work and bring their daughters to Miami. "When we went to the office of the Catholic Relief Welfare to request that our daughters be brought over, the negative answer was definite," they wrote to Secretary Abraham Ribicoff of HEW.[23] Instead of bringing children to parents in Miami, parents were shipped out to where the children were living. Federal agencies involved in the resettlement were brought together with child-care agencies.

But even families willing to leave Miami frequently had to wait long periods before seeing their children. This was the case for the Álvaro López family. Mr. López first registered at Catholic Relief services and later switched to the International Relief Committee. He was assigned relocation to California, which he wanted, but had to wait three months. The Lopezes frequently asked that their twelve-year-old son, who was in group care in Sioux City, Iowa, be brought to Miami. Six weeks later, they had yet to see the boy, their paperwork held up in transit from one agency to another.[24]

The social workers sought a solution, asking the Children's Bureau to set a limit of two weeks for resettlement. If it had not occurred within that time, then the children should be brought to the parents. Catholic Welfare, in fact, skirted the procedures and returned some of the children to Miami despite the push by the federal government to make the parents resettle out of Miami.[25] Still, for the next three decades federal government programs would resettle Cubans all over the United States. Thus, Cuban communities emerged in places as diverse as Ann Arbor, Michigan; Dubuque, Iowa; Freeport, Illinois; and Helena, Montana; places where unaccompanied minors had been sent. Children were the anchors for the resettlement program.[26]

Reunifications

Olga, the Arruzas' mother, arrived in Cincinnati in 1966 with her youngest son who had been born at about the time the boys left. Her husband was in jail in Cuba. In the five-year period since she had sent her older sons to the United States, they had stayed with relatives, receiving camps, an orphanage filled with troubled youths and abusive nuns, and lived in three foster homes. Guillermo, the second-born, initially refused to live with her. José, the oldest, felt that he had let down his brothers. A year later he committed suicide.

María Bechily remembers the reunion with her parents with mixed emotions. The Bechilys arrived in Chicago, found an apartment and brought their three children together, who had been spread among different homes. But Concha, her mother, was worried about the friends she had left behind who had been with her in the underground. She knew many would end up in jail if they could not get out, and entering the United States was impossible. It would be months before she could turn her focus to her children. María recalled, "I remember my mother constantly sitting by the phone waiting to hear from her friends in Cuba."[27]

The Mendieta sisters were reunited with their mother and their brother in Iowa, where Raquelín was in college. Mr. Mendieta, who had been jailed, could not leave; they would not see their father for another fifteen years.

Many of the children of underground activists experienced their parents' involvement in politics as abandonment. Parents, in turn, felt that they were actually doing something for their children—creating a better society.

Some children felt that their parents wanted to go on with life as if time had not passed and they had not changed. For some, like Elly Chovel, this was disconcerting. When she left Cuba, her mother told her that she would be in charge of her younger sister, so Elly had shouldered the responsibility and developed a sense of independence. "My mother did not understand that I had been in charge for three years," Elly said, "and now she wanted me to go back to being her little girl. This was impossible."[28] The growth was irreversible and her mother could not accept her independence. Two years later, her mother had another baby.

In some cases, divorce separated families. In others, a parent had been jailed or had died, and the family structure was irrevocably altered. By the time Alfredo Lanier's parents made it to the United States, he was in his last year of high school. The Laniers were divorced. His mother moved to New York, ready to pick up where they had left off three years ago, but Alfredo was not the same boy who had left the island, and the family he had left behind no longer existed.

Carlos Erie's father died during the period they were separated. His mother finally managed to get out of Cuba, but their lives would never be the same. He had to drop out of school to work as he was now the breadwinner of the family. They moved to Chicago, where he took the night shift at the Conrad Hilton.

Candi Sosa dreamed of the day her parents would come and rescue

Elly Chovel (third from right) in Florida City, 1962. Courtesy of Elly Chovel.

her from her abusive foster father. She would finally be able to talk about her experiences without the threat of being separated from her sister. But her mother refused to believe what had happened—the truth perhaps too painful to accept.

I had been one of the lucky kids whose parents left before the doors shut. Even then, I remember the tension surrounding their arrival. We waited at home for them; I don't know why we didn't greet them at the airport. My mother and sisters arrived and I remember my mother was scared and nervous. Two militiamen had pulled my father from the plane, and she had had to make a last-minute heart-wrenching decision: whether to stay or leave without my father. There was no indication that he would be joining us soon. Alicia, one of my sisters, was crying. The baby, Lourdes, who was not walking when I left Cuba, was now running around all over the place. Everything was so chaotic. After months of waiting for my parents, that is the reunion I remember.

Several weeks later, my father arrived. Finally, we were together. Yet everything and everyone had changed, particularly my mother, who was preoccupied and often saddened by her worries for those left behind.

It was impossible for our families to return to where we had left off. Our parents longed for the world they had lost. We, the children, were immersed in a new culture, schools, and experiences. In some cases, we were speaking better English than Spanish. Many of us had become Americanized and rejected our parents' attempts to institute Cuban ways at home. Many of the older Pedro Pan children felt that they were now adults, not the children their parents wanted them to be. Some Pedro Pans dealt with the pain of separation by emotionally detaching from their parents and bonding with their foster families. Some rejected their parents when they did arrive, even asking to stay with their foster families.[29]

The parents, too, had suffered the separations. Some had clung to their babies refusing to let them grow up for fear of losing them as well. Others could not hear any of the horror stories, their guilt perhaps too great to accept. Most common, however, was the parents' need to assert their parental control. Except that their children had been forced to grow up without them. Indeed, they became interlocutors between their Cuban parents and American society. The balance of power in the family structure could not simply return to the way it had been.

This sense of personal and familial dislocation was to become the essence of exile for the entire community in the United States. But the language of politics would not allow us to speak of the pain of separation or, for that matter, question whether or not that separation had been necessary. The separations were justified by the need to have saved us from communism.

Returning "Home"

If the familial home was hard to reconstruct, some Pedro Pans went in search of the geographic home they had left. In the early 1970s, debate ensued as to whether Cuban exiles should engage in dialogue with the

Cuban government. Two groups led the discussions. One was the Instituto de Estudios Cubanos, of which Emilio Cueto, one of the Pedro Pan children and now a lawyer in Washington, D.C., was a founding member. The Instituto consisted mainly of young Catholics who had formed the backbone of the youth movement in support of the revolution in Cuba and, disaffected with the government's anti-Catholic stances, opted for exile.[30] The other group was composed of even younger exiles, like myself, who had become radicalized though the civil rights and antiwar movements and were in search of identity and alternative politics. Many of us were Pedro Pan children. Lourdes Casal, a sociologist and poet whose work put her in contact with many Cuban exile students, facilitated the union of the two groups and built the bridge to take us back home.

The idea of visiting Cuba was met with stiff opposition from the exile community, who felt it meant an endorsement of the system that had disrupted their lives and foreclosed the futures they envisioned. In their eyes, those of us who wanted to return were giving ourselves over to the very man who had betrayed them and their nation—the same one who had forced families to make the painful decision of sending their children alone to a foreign country.

The broader community battles were also waged within our individual families. These clashes cut sharply along generational lines and were especially violent because they unfolded amid a cultural revolution in the United States that pitted children against their parents. Our parents wanted us to follow Cuban ways, but they opposed our desire to return to Cuba. We had adopted an American posture of intellectual independence and defiance. Interestingly, the fact that we had become Americanized had not led us further from our homeland; instead, it was the political cultural vehicle by which we would return home.

In my first year in college, 1972, I started hearing of Americans who traveled to Cuba. I applied to the Venceremos Brigade, a group sympathetic to the revolution, but was rejected because Cuban exiles were not allowed to travel with the brigade. If the exile community did not want us to travel to the island, the Cuban government reacted negatively to our desire to return as well. Officials feared that we might be infiltrators, spies who could be used by the exile opposition to gather information about contemporary life on the island. They were also wary of our potential impact on the Cubans. After all, we lived in the country of the enemy. But many of us were insistent. Individually and in groups, we lobbied Cuban government officials at the United Nations and in other countries. I went to Mexico to talk to Mexican officials who were friendly with the Cubans at the embassy. Emilio Cueto traveled to France and, after getting himself invited to a reception at which the Cuban ambassador would be present, approached him and asked for assistance in returning to Cuba. While his immediate request was denied, eventually the Cuban government began authorizing the visit of a select number of exiles. Two or three individuals, usually from different organizations, were allowed to enter at any one time. They were informed by government officials not to tell anyone they were Cuban. Official policy, after all, defined all who had left as traitors.

Yet the news of these visits trickled throughout the island and through the exile community. In 1977, the Cuban government finally granted fifty-five reentry permits to a group of young Cuban exiles, mostly students, who had been working on a variety of political projects throughout the United States. Some had worked with *Areíto*, a magazine that had originated in Florida, and others with one from New York called *Joven Cuba*; still others had been activists in the civil rights and antiwar movements. I was invited to return on this trip but declined, rationalizing my decision by telling myself that my political work was now in the United States. In reality, I feared a confrontation with my parents.

The group called itself the Antonio Maceo Brigade. A few weeks later, I read the group's account of the trip in *Areíto*:

The name of Antonio Maceo, the mulatto general of the War of Independence, was chosen [as the name for the group] because of our desire to maintain a continuity with the history of our homeland . . . our rebellion against the foreign decisions and against the historical circumstances which uprooted us from our homeland . . . and our protests against the blockade which impedes our need to get to know the Cuban reality. Above all, the Antonio Maceo Brigade defended the right of all Cubans to travel to Cuba to become reacquainted with the new Cuba and define their relationship to the homeland.

I cried. I also remember reading *Contra Viento y Marea* (*Against All Odds*), a compilation of personal testimonies of this first group and feeling like someone had written my story as well.[31] It traced their departures from Cuba, their earlier experiences in the United States, and the political radicalization that led them back to the island. Pedro Pan features prominently in the book. An entire chapter was dedicated to the experiences of children who ended up in the camps. In the camps they had forged a camaraderie, but they were also fearful and lonely. Those sent up north often found that they were in places where no one spoke English. "Our parents had been afraid of losing their *patria potestad,* yet they had sent us alone, it was the same as if they had sent us to Russia or Patagonia. I felt used; the exodus of the children had been a propaganda coup for the Americans. And what was going to come out of the camps was an injured generation."[32] Pedro Pan would become part of our collective identity. The goals of the Antonio Maceo Brigade resonated deeply for me: to recapture for the nation all the children who had been taken away by their parents. To return home.

My First Return

At the time, my sister and I were living in Austin, Texas, meeting and organizing with other young exiles.[33] A thaw in relations between the United States and Cuba had resulted in a series of meetings between the Cuban government and Cuban exiles, which included discussions about releasing political prisoners and traveling to the island. In the autumn of 1978, we were invited as Antonio Maceo Brigade members to a meeting in Havana in which the Cuban government was to sign the accord of the meetings referred to as "the dialogue" with the exile community. This would be our first return. We were extremely nervous. We asked our parents for our old Cuban passports in order to get new ones. They refused, and so we were issued special reentry permits. What seemed to us a logical development in our lives—returning home— was an act of betrayal to our parents. Furthermore, the travel arrangements had to be kept secret for we feared terrorist reprisals. A Cuban airline was permitted to fly to the United States to pick us up in Atlanta. Since the air isolation campaign, no Cuban airline had been permitted to land in the United States. Everyone onboard was ecstatic yet anxious. When we landed, we spontaneously broke into a round of applause.

As soon as I deplaned, I knew I was home. The smell in the air, the humidity, the colors all seemed part of me. Everything appeared familiar—the outline of people's faces, the way they walked and talked, the small gestures with which they (we) punctuate our everyday conversation. Somewhere deep in my memory, I had kept these images intact.

We were rushed to the Hotel Riviera, an art deco structure right on Havana's Malecón, the city's seawall. My sister and I managed to find an old phone book and looked for the name of a great-aunt who lived in Havana. Fortunately her phone was listed. We dialed it and by no small miracle found it was still her number. When she answered, we told her who we were and immediately she invited us to her house. We spent the next few emotion-filled hours with four of her children and their children. This was our first family connection to the island in almost twenty years.

The purpose of our invitation, to attend the government-sponsored meetings, occupied most of our time. Brigade members caucused before the formal meetings to develop a list of requests we wanted to present to the Cuban government. It was our American political culture at work. Our main demands were a right to participate in island organizations, an institute to address the needs of those living abroad, and finally, repatriation. We also supported the release of all political prisoners. At the end, over 3,500 political prisoners were released, including Polita Grau and José Arruza.

In between family visits and official meetings, we were taken to see the movie 55 *Hermanos*, the documentary film that recorded the group's first return to the island. It chronicled a meeting between Armando Hart, Minister of Culture at the time, who was visibly moved as he spoke of his nephews, whose father had been captured and tortured to death by the Batista military. The boys had been sent to the United States. Andrés Gómez, a brigade member from Miami, asked him if he and others could return to the island not just for a visit but to live. Indeed, many wanted to make a permanent return.

Many of us felt a powerful need to return to Cuba. It seemed like the solution to the incoherence we all felt, to the tremendous sense of loss that haunted our memories. The Antonio Maceo Brigade grew rapidly. In less than a year, eight chapters were organized. I was invited to join the national committee in the spring of 1979, while the Brigade was in the midst of defining itself and organizing the second travel contingent. We were a tightly knit group; we felt a sense of unity we did not share with other exiles in the broader U.S. society, or even the American left, which still distrusts and despises Cuban exiles.

Our relationship with our island hosts, too, was tense. Our political styles were very different. We yearned to organize a broad-based political movement that could unite what we felt was a divided nation; we wanted to provide a bridge. They, in turn, were leery of the exile community and more interested in confrontation.

Our strongest disagreements concerned who to bring on future brigade trips and what to do once we arrived in Cuba. We felt that young Cuban exiles needed to experience the revolution for themselves before being forced to make a specific commitment. Our Cuban hosts insisted on allegiance to political positions in support of lifting the embargo.

We wanted more free time so that brigade members could reconnect with their families. This was precisely what Cuban security forces did not want. Family visits were a sign of ideological weakness in us, they said, and dangerous particularly if the families were not supporters of the government. The system discouraged contact between exiles and island relatives. For almost two decades, people in the island had been punished for maintaining contact with relatives who had left. The institutional and ideological practices of this policy ran deep.

The strongest advocate of a more open position was Carlos Muñiz, a twenty-six-year-old Cuban who had been a Pedro Pan and was living in Puerto Rico. (Carlos and his sister had traveled on a visa waiver. Their mother, who had been widowed, traveled on the same flight. She could not provide for them and believed that her children would be given a scholarship. Once in the United States, she realized that they would be sent to an orphanage, and she reclaimed them from Catholic Charities.)[34] On April 26, 1979, a few months before our second contingent was to arrive in Cuba, Carlos was shot to death in Puerto Rico. Omega 7, a U.S.-based anti-Castro organization, took credit for the shooting. Although there had been prior bombings of homes and businesses of exiles who had advocated for peaceful coexistence with the Cuban government, Muñiz's death marked a declaration of war. We simply became more defiant, and over two hundred young Cuban exiles traveled to Cuba with the second contingent of the Antonio Maceo Brigade that summer. The dream of going home and of becoming part of the nation exerted a powerful pull.

The political intrigue made the homecomings even more intense than they otherwise would have been. For some the trips were disconcerting, perpetuating a sense of permanent loss. Still others saw through the political manipulations. But others, like myself, had a sense of mission and community, which bonded our group in a special way. In Havana, we met Cuban exiles from Spain, Venezuela, Mexico, and from various sections of the United States. We were a political phenomenon, children of the exiles returning home. Our commitment was to reclaim for the nation the children who had been sent away, particularly those parents who were still in Cuba.

Finding Parents

Through the years I have been researching this project, I have received letters and messages from dozens of Pedro Pans and their relatives. One came from a family in Cuba. The uncle was trying to find his niece who had been sent here in 1961. They had lost contact. The mother had died, and he was tying to let his niece know. I also received a letter from a young woman who ended up in British Columbia. She, too, had come to the United States as a child. Could I help her check to see if her mother was alive? Others, like a mother in Santo Suárez, who had put her six-year-old girl on a plane and was then unable to leave, just needed to know more about the exodus, how and why it happened.

We simply don't know how many Pedro Pans were never reunited with their parents or waited decades before seeing them again. At a forty-year reunion in Miami in the fall of 2001 the question was asked of Father Walsh, who said he didn't know of many cases. But when we asked the group of fifty Pedro Pans, six had not seen one or both parents since the day they arrived in the United States.

Emilio Cueto was finally able to see his mother in 1978, seventeen years after he had come to the United States. Rafael Ravelo was a social worker at a community organization in Chicago. In 1961, he was separated from his family, and the separation would last for eighteen years. In 1977, thanks to the thaw in relations between the United States and Cuba, and the community's lobbying efforts, visits were finally permitted. He remembers the jumble of emotions he felt when he learned that there was a possibility of visiting his family in Cuba:

When Carter announced that Cuba and the United States were going to start having flights for reuniting families, it was all over the news, and there were places opened. There were a couple in Chicago, announcing that they would facilitate these trips. Oh, God! I immediately . . . I got scared, very scared, because so many years had gone by, all of the sudden I started thinking that I wasn't going to recognize my mother, that I wasn't going to recognize my sister, that I had changed a lot because I left at thirteen and I was thirty. It was a huge change in my life, and I didn't know whether they were going to feel comfortable with me, so it was a very scary type of feeling but also very exciting, too. It was like, I don't care what happens, and I just have to get this over with and see them.[35]

The Antonio Maceo Brigade gathered the applications for travel and made recommendations to our Cuban hosts. They were the ones who gave the reentry permits. Ravelo received one:

I think in a matter of two months I was in Cuba. The only problem was that it was so restrictive. They only gave us a week. And in a week, it was horrible, because in a week so many things open up and then you were gone. And what it did, it made us relive the separation again. We needed like a month. The first three days, I remember being in Cuba and feeling like a total stranger, which was a weird feeling, and then, little memories would come back, "Oh wow, that was there." It didn't come suddenly, it took three days, even my house, I just remember those little decorations that didn't change in eighteen years, and they were still there.

For Rafael, like for many of the young exiles, being in Cuba felt natural. Recovering our relatives, even the distant ones, would become a very important part of the brigade experience. We also had to confront major changes in the way we remembered our lives on the island. Rafael remembers:

Two things happened, one was, I was amazed that after eighteen years I felt comfortable with my family in three minutes. That was just amazing. Even though my family was no longer the same: my parents had divorced and they were not speaking to each other. This made it very difficult for me.

Still I felt tremendous, tremendous affection, from all people in my family and from people who didn't know me. I had nieces and nephews who were sixteen, seventeen, and they had no idea who I was, but it didn't matter because I got there and instantly they all knew me. There was a lot to catch up on, they told me stories that happened while I was away, when I was a kid, and that was very comfortable, but that was really hard, too, because we only had one week, the experience was one week of emotional display. Because we would be up until four o'clock every day, the whole idea was, we have a week, we are not going to waste it sleeping.

But for Pedro Pans like Rafael, whose parents were still in Cuba, the recognition of what had been lost—the years of family intimacy and shared experiences—made these trips particularly difficult.

I remember that in my room there were like twelve people sleeping on the floor. For me that was so important. And for them it was so

Rafael and his mother, Havana, Cuba, 1982.

important. They wanted to jump in the bed and be with me. It was the touching, they didn't want one minute to go by and waste it, because I was there, they wanted to make sure they were there the twenty-four hours. And they would be in bed with me; my mother would be in bed with me! I remember one night I woke up and my mother is looking at me. She was just looking at me and she would caress me face . . . that was real hard . . . so that was the first time it was real hard.

Our trips were short, and they sometimes only helped to underscore the distance that remained.

I also relived the pain of leaving them. When the day came for me to leave, the night before there was all of this crying, and my sister would come and there were all of these conversations in one side of my house and it was all about me and the people would come and you could see the sadness, and tomorrow at six o'clock we had to be at the airport.

Nonetheless, returning also let us experience life as it was going on in Cuba. We were no longer dealing with only memories or ghosts. This had the effect of shortening the psychological distance.

Rafael remembers returning to Chicago:

I remember getting back to Chicago and feeling whole. You know, it's hard to describe that experience. It's not that I didn't feel whole before, I didn't even know it, there was this vacuum that I felt. It was a sense of completeness, that the branch was connected to the trunk of the tree. And then, I remember saying, I can die now. That was the first thing I said, now I can die.[36]

Other Pedro Pans wanted to return to Cuba permanently. Ena Torres was living in San Francisco at the time. In the early 1960s, her mother had been admitted to the psychiatric hospital and Ena had been placed in a Catholic orphanage in Havana. When the clerics had been expelled from Cuba, they had closed the orphanage and had sent the kids to the

United States through Operation Pedro Pan. When Ena returned, her mother was still hospitalized in Cuba. Ena wanted desperately to stay in the island, to take care of her.

The answer to our pleas came directly from Fidel Castro. He was aware of Operation Pedro Pan and would describe it as follows:

> Over 14,000 Cuban children were virtually kidnapped by the United States when counterrevolutionary groups, organized from the very beginning by U.S. intelligence agencies, surreptitiously published and distributed false government bills to spread the criminal lie that children's custody would be taken away from the parents. Panic was sown among many middle-class families, who were frightened into sending their children away secretly, without visas of any kind, on the same legal and regular airlines that flew directly to the United States. These children separated from their parents were met there and sent to orphanages or even detention centers for minors.[37]

Still, when asked by some of these children, then young adults, if they could return to live in their homeland, Castro responded by telling them that the country would be better served if they returned to their U.S. communities and worked there on behalf of the revolution. In effect, the Cuban government would not permit repatriations, even of those whose families were still on the island.

If the children of Pedro Pan had shown the world the desperation of parents living under communism, we could testify to the horrors of capitalism, of the exile community, and of life in the United States. We should take up the banner of reclaiming for the nation the children who had been robbed.[38] Castro's position would never essentially change. In a strange twist of history, we, the children of the Pedro Pan exodus who became the symbol of the horrors of communism, would end up becoming a propaganda coup for the regime from which we had been saved. There would be no coming home.

10

Pedro Pans Search for Memory

I feel an immense anguish this morning. It is the confrontation with reality—my reality and that of my circumstances. I realize my great necessity of being in Cuba and wanting to insert myself in its culture and history. Culture is the memory of history, to have access to my roots and feel free to explore them.

—*Ana Mendieta*[1]

Acts of remembering the past are both personal and political.[2] In some countries torn apart by the Cold War, attempts at national reconciliation have included debates about the children's memories. In Argentina and in El Salvador, for instance, children of political prisoners were literally snatched from their mothers and given to military officials.[3] These children have lived their entire lives believing that their present families were their real families, when in reality they had been their parents' assassins. Could countries reconcile their past and move forward without telling these children the truth, indeed, fill in their interrupted family memories?

In countries where the conflict erupted into wars of ethnic cleansing, like in the Balkans, children's bodies became the site where the worst violence was committed. Headlines like "Little Ones Lost" stated that "a most unimaginable terror is reserved for the smallest of refugees."[4]

In reality, these debates are battles to define historical memories. Cuba is an island nation ravaged by a revolution. If the battle over the children's minds in the 1960s had been a way to contest the country's political future, interpreting the exodus became a way to control its history.

Forty years after the first Cuban refugee children arrived alone in the United States, a debate about the exodus waged across the Florida Straits. The abrupt exodus of over 14,000 children had left an open wound and engendered powerful political myths. For the exiles, Operation Pedro Pan became part of the collective narrative of origin of the community, one that was closely tied to a supreme sacrifice—Pedro Pan parents separating from their children for the sake of saving them.[5] For the island-nation, it was yet another example of the unscrupulous psychological warfare waged against its revolution by the powerful United States.[6] For some Pedro Pans, these explanations provided a way to justify, and perhaps explain, their suffering.

Finding information about the program in order to arrive at a clear interpretation is difficult. Although there are freedom of information laws in the United States that make government documents available, there are many exemptions to this law, especially when it comes to the CIA, the agency in charge of the Cuba project during the years of the operation. In Cuba, where there are no such laws, research projects are conducted through a governmental agency.

The need to understand what really happened has motivated many Pedro Pans to delve into the past. However, because the operation played out on the world stage of the Cold War, documents about this time period have been nearly impossible to obtain. Part of the U.S. government's record of the operation was destroyed in a fire at a government warehouse in St. Louis. Other documents have not been released to the public because the operation was classified. Nor has the Catholic Welfare Bureau, a critical participant in the program, made its records public. They did donate the individual caseworkers report to Barry University in Florida, but these can only be accessed by the individual, not the public. The financial records will be made public in the future.

Both the U.S. and the Cuban governments are still interested in spinning the facts. The battle has moved from saving children's minds to controlling the narrative of the exodus. The defensiveness of both the

Cuban and the U.S. government regarding Operation Pedro Pan only underscores the fact that it was a program with deep roots in the national security apparatuses of both governments. The intensely politicized Cold War battleground engendered a culture of secrecy in the name of national security. Still, it is imperative to try to understand what happened.

The Island's Ideological Guardians

For me, part of my journey to understand the event was organizing a research team that included voices both from the island—and from the exile community. By the time I started this research, I had moved from organizing trips of young Cuban exiles to the island to promoting academic exchanges with the University of Havana. The end of the Cold War allowed collaboration among scholars from different sides of the fault lines. One major project examined the October Missile Crisis by bringing Soviet, Cuban, and U.S. scholars and policymakers together at a conference which ultimately helped to provide a more comprehensive understanding of what actually occurred. For instance, U.S. policymakers learned that the Soviets had had more missiles than what they had estimated. Another project attempted piecing together the history of the Bay of Pigs invasion.[7] I strongly believed that in order to reconstruct history it was necessary to hear voices from all sides of the divide. The task was not easy; I had become well aware that no matter how hard we tried to reconcile our differences, something always disrupted the process, such as an irrational action by either government. I felt we needed to go way back, to understand the moment of rupture, and that was another reason why I began my research on Operation Pedro Pan.

But travel to Cuba was, and is, complicated. There are U.S. travel restrictions; Cuba sometimes denies the reentry permits needed for exiles to return. Despite the obstacles, I was able to travel to Cuba frequently during the initial phase of the research project. The Ministry of the Interior (Cuba's domestic and foreign intelligence, police, and immigration apparatus), the agency that grants or denies reentry permits, had final say over whether we would be allowed to visit. Reentry to the island was contingent on our collaboration with an island-based institute. Indeed, interviews in Cuba had to be approved and former state security officials were prohibited from meeting with "foreigners." This included Cubans living in the United States. Thus, I brought on board Mercedes Arce, then director of Cuba's Centro de Estudios de Alternativa Política, a university-based information center funded by the Ministry of the Interior. At that time it was the only institute authorized to work with Cuban exile scholars. It was the only center permitted to study the exile community at all. This, after all, was a classified subject in Cuba, synonymous with "*la contrarevolución*."

Despite the Centro's obvious links to the Ministry of the Interior, I believed that Mercedes and her colleagues were reform-minded and committed to normalizing relations between the exile community and the island. In addition, I was enthusiastic about working with Mercedes because our family experiences ran opposite : while my parents left at the time of the revolution, hers had returned to Cuba from Venezuela. But there were warning signs from the beginning. Our proposal, eventually funded by the John D. and Catherine T. MacArthur Foundation, required the approval of her superiors, who were already suspicious of what they believed to be CIA-controlled American foundation. Mercedes' participation was approved, but her superiors were offended by the phrase, "the inevitability of change of leadership in Cuba," which was included in the proposal. Further, the spirit of the project was one of reconciliation, and this, too, was suspect for ministry officials.

I had hoped to promote exchanges among our students and our children. But while U.S. students working on the project traveled to Cuba, students from the island were not allowed to leave Cuba or enter the United States. Since Mercedes and I both had daughters rather close in age, I thought it would be good to incorporate them into the project. But again, though I could bring my daughters to Cuba, Mercedes was not permitted to leave the island with her daughter. The Cuban government restriction, supposedly a reaction to the exodus of children in the early 1960s but in reality a fear of defections, prohibited parents from traveling abroad with their children.

A year into the project, my colleague in Cuba was fired from her job-part of a larger political purge. The Cuban community project, Comunidad Cubana en el Exterior (or COCUEX, the bureaucratic acronym), of which the Centro was a part, had become one of the most lucrative businesses on the island. Money from visiting exiles and re-mittances sent by Cubans to relatives on the island poured into the economy. Carlos Aldana, a high-ranking member of the politburo and the third most powerful man on the island (after Fidel Castro and his brother, Raúl), had managed to combine his bureaucratic power with an economic base. In the summer of 1992, while Castro attended the Olympics in Spain, Aldana attempted a bureaucratic coup (not a polit-ical nor a military one, as was reported in Miami). Mercedes referred to the coup as the "Queen Elizabeth" model: it aimed to create a change in real power while Castro remained as figurehead. The plan failed, and all those involved, including Mercedes, were fired and sent to work in agriculture.

Mercedes, however, was allowed to continue working with me on the project. The reason is that the Cuban government was trying very hard to woo American foundations at the time, and the complete "dis-appearance" of Mercedes would have seriously hampered these efforts. Nonetheless, Mercedes was politically vulnerable, which made it ex-ceedingly difficult for her to ask questions that could lead to a critical perspective of the role of either government in Operation Pedro Pan. In addition, after she was removed from her university position, she began collaborating with Cuba's Film Institute (ICAIC) to produce a documentary on Pedro Pan. Somehow my field notes ended up in the hands of Gail Reed, an American reporter living in Cuba. These field notes, which included some names that had been given to me in inter-views that had not yet been checked, were used, misspellings and all, in an article she wrote in 1994 announcing the film.[8] I tried to include a Cuban exile filmmaker in the project, Miguel González Panda, a professor at Florida International University and an oral historian who was willing to collaborate with filmmakers in Cuba.[9] They refused to work with him, however. As a young man, González Panda had participated in the Bay of Pigs invasion. Subsequently, a documentary made by ICAIC, in collaboration with Mercedes, cast the entire operation as a sinister CIA plot.[10]

A few years later, Estela Bravo, an American who had lived in Cuba since the early 1960s, produced a second documentary on Pedro Pan. For years, Bravo had been one of the few persons in Cuba authorized to deal with the topic of the Cuban community abroad, a topic of high security clearance for it was synonymous with *"la contrarevolución."*[11] Her version of the exodus was not much different than ICAIC's. It portrayed the Pedro Pan children as victims of a dirty war against Cuba. A year later, in the heat of the Elián González saga, the Cuban government published a book written by two researchers of the Ministry of the Interior.[12] The book, like ICAIC's documentary, was critical only of the United States and failed to raise questions about the actions of the Cuban government that contributed to the exodus.

The Legal Battle to Reconstruct the Past: Uncovering Official Secrets

What began as a straightforward research project ended up as a battle to reconstruct the context in which our exodus unfolded. Along the way, there have been many that have supported the quest, others who have either been silent or not fully forthcoming. In the United States, many Cuban exiles who were in the underground have been extremely helpful in our efforts to reconstruct the details of Operation Pedro Pan. The American organizers who had been in a position to know and make decisions about the program have been more guarded. While they answered our questions and gave extensive interviews, their stories changed, sometimes contradicted themselves, and ultimately left many unanswered questions. Monsignor Walsh was willing to give several interviews and even participated on a panel with me and others on various occasions. But he did not provide any new information, only confirming what was raised to him. It is true that his story did become more layered each time we spoke; he could simply have refused to talk to us like so many government officials. Still, many holes remain.

Wayne Smith, a friend and colleague, first led me to Penny Powers, the British intelligence officer who was instrumental in the operation. Smith was the liaison to the Catholic Church and U.S. vice consul in Havana during the Pedro Pan era, yet for years he would not talk about the children. Much later, he claimed that the CIA was involved and that he believed that it had been a ploy to disaffect the middle class. He claimed, "We subsequently found out that the CIA had begun this sub-rosa program of simply allowing a Catholic priest to sign what amounted to visas for people's children, children of the Peter Pan Operation."[13] The real story appears to be much more complex.

The former U.S. government bureaucrats, who remembered the most insignificant details of U.S. policies toward Cuba in the early 1960s, could not recall or would not discuss the Cuban refugee children's program. The program, after all, had been referred to as a classified project and government employees signed oaths of silence regarding this type of information. Faced with this silence, I needed to pursue other means of uncovering the facts of the operation. With the help of excellent archivists, I searched the libraries of the three presidents who were in office during the operation, as well as the libraries of the State Department and other federal agencies housed in the National Archives in Washington. I filed countless Freedom of Information Act requests. Some requests are still outstanding; others resulted in declassifying critical documents.[14]

In the United States, the least cooperative agency in providing information has been the CIA, the agency in charge of U.S. participation in efforts to overthrow Fidel Castro during the years of Operation Pedro Pan. Some of the declassified documents demonstrated that the CIA was kept abreast of virtually everything relating to Cuba and its refugees, including the children. Father Walsh has stated that prior to the Bay of Pigs, the CIA had operational interest in bringing children of the Cuban underground to the United States. If that were true, there has to be a paper trail. I requested information on Operation Pedro Pan and any documents they had that referred to the exodus of children. However, the CIA has steadfastly refused to admit or deny the existence of any documents on the ground of national security.

On January 12, 1998, I filed a lawsuit contending that the CIA, the agency in charge of the Cuba project from March 1960 to May 1961, must have records of the movement of unaccompanied children from the island to the United States, and that these records should be made public.[15] Unfortunately, the issue in court was a very narrow one: whether the CIA had conducted an adequate search for my request. It was our task to demonstrate that the CIA's search was not reasonable.

In preparing our lawsuit, we gained disturbing insight into the way the CIA handles information requests, which raises serious questions about the agency's compliance with the Freedom of Information Act. We discovered that most of the indexes and filing systems used by the CIA are classified information. Not even the chief archivist of the State Department has the necessary clearance to review the indexes. Furthermore, the cryptogram names for CIA operations are classified, making it virtually impossible for a citizen to guess keywords on which to request a search.[16] Their initial search was to plug in Operation Peter Pan and Operation Pedro Pan. Only after I sued did they admit this "code" name was not one used by their agency.[17]

Ultimately, the CIA produced a few documents that have been extremely valuable. The first, located less than twenty-four hours after I filed the lawsuit, is a report of a social worker in Miami telling the CIA of the drastic reduction of children in a particular week of June 1962.[18] We knew that the CIA had established a station in Opalocka, where incoming refugees were debriefed. People from the Miami community also systematically reported to officers stationed there.[19] The social worker's recorded conversation is the first document we have which shows that the flow of children from Cuba to the United States was used as an intelligence gathering tool to assess what was happening on the island. The document provides a window into events on the island preceding the October 1962 Missile Crisis, a period about which we have little information. It is during this time that the U.S. government instituted a series of policies that, in effect, shut the immigration valve. As a result, 8,000 children were stranded in the United States without their parents.

I received a second version of the same document that identified the source as a person involved in social work who was knowledgeable about the children. I wondered if Monsignor Walsh had been the source of the information. I asked him and he said no. Coincidentally, I found a Children's Bureau document dated June 29, 1962, that reports a conversation with Walsh: "Father Walsh was in the city [Washington, D.C.] en route to Chicago. Said he had no special problems, just wanted to see people in the Division and in the Commissioner's office to report his observations of a sharp change in trend. For the first time since October 1961, there has been a marked decrease in the number of unaccompanied Cuban children coming to Miami."[20] This was the same information contained in the CIA document.

Another CIA document corroborated statements made by Polita Grau, the head of Rescate de la Niñez, the main organization coordinating the children's exodus after the Bay of Pigs invasion. Grau claimed the CIA knew of and collaborated with the group.[21] A third document turned out to be the least redacted copy to date of Operation Mongoose, the program instituted by President Kennedy after the Bay of Pigs fiasco, propaganda plans that stipulated that refugees, particularly children, were to be used as key propaganda objectives.[22] This document is significant because it references a film about child refugee camps and makes the footage available for public use. Until then, the filmmaker's family had sought royalties for its use. The film is the first government document to confirm the centrality of the young refugees in the propaganda battles; the film was subsequently titled *The Lost Apple*.

The CIA acknowledged finding other documents regarding the children, but the judge upheld the CIA's right to keep them secret. Documents that would indicate operations leading to the evacuation of agents and their family would be protected from public access. Another search triggered by a Freedom of Information Act request to the Federal Bureau of Investigation yielded documents originating in the CIA. Again, I asked that they be declassified, but the agency refused, citing national security reasons for their decision.

Two important legal questions that have a direct impact on how we reconstruct events of the past have emerged from my efforts to gain access to government documents. The first involves what constitutes a relevant and significant document. For researchers of events shrouded in secrecy, every document is a valuable piece in the larger puzzle. While not addressing whether or not the documents given to me responded to my request, the judge did find that because I did not discover "a gold mine" of information, what was turned over was considered insignificant and, as such, not responsive to my request. In my opinion, every document pertaining to Cuban refugees is extremely valuable because so much material was destroyed in the fire at the St. Louis National Archives warehouse.[23]

The second question involves what constitutes a reasonable search. Under the best of circumstances, the search for forty-year-old records is extremely difficult and may require a special set of guidelines. The "reasonable" standard for a government agency such as the State Department, which maintains a public library of released documents, cannot be the same applied to an agency such as the CIA, which does not even allow its own Freedom of Information officer to browse through its files.

Few people who have sought help from the courts in prodding the CIA's vast files of information have been successful.[24] They are slow in responding to requests. (The CIA offered my lawsuit as an excuse for its failure to process other Freedom of Information Act requests.)[25] Although the Freedom of Information Act is intended to open up government records, the exemptions for the CIA make it virtually impossible to obtain documents from this agency.[26] Despite executive orders and congressional mandates to open up Cold War records, the agency continues to plead the "mosaic rationale": to reveal any document may unravel their tightly held secrets.[27]

What is clear is that the agency chose to spin my request as a political battle. Internal memos made available to me as a result of the lawsuit indicate that the CIA was waging a public relations battle and acting defensively about its role in Operation Pedro Pan. The CIA had just released thousands of pages of documents about events regarding Cuba in the early 1960s, including those about the Bay of Pigs and the October Missile Crisis. Why would it be so secretive about the unaccompanied children's program, even though important officials like Jacob Esterline, one of the commanders of the Bay of Pigs, wrote a letter stating: "The best thing to clear away the dark shadow that hangs over the Bay of Pigs would be to declassify the whole damn record. And let the public see what actually happened—for the sake of history, and, frankly, closure to this tragic event."[28]

It is inconceivable that other visa waiver programs were run and financed by the CIA and their surrogate organizations, and the one for children left to its own. Why not release the information that was found but not released? Generally, the CIA may fear that any information on Pedro Pan could lead to unraveling the entire anti-Castro tapestry. Some have suggested that the CIA was trying to protect identities of agents still working for them. One archivist commented to me that foreign operations conducted in collaboration with friendly governments like Great Britain are the hardest to pry open.[29] And clearly Penny Powers, Great Britain's intelligence officer, was a key organizer of the operation. Maybe there are documents, like Arruza's communiqués, that would indicate that the children weren't being taken care the way the United States promised they would. This would add to what many Cuban exiles have perceived as the great betrayal of the United States—the lack of support during the Bay of Pigs invasion. It could be damaging for current promises that they may be making to other agents around the world.

Undercover activities involving children may be the most sensitive of all categories. What is clear is that many of the parents who were fighting in the underground trusted the CIA with their children's well-being. We have documentation that, in at least several cases, information was sent to the U.S. government about the plight of these children. But for unknown reasons, the situation was not taken care of. As underground fighters either risked their lives or languished in jail, some of their sons and daughters were being physically and emotionally abused while under the care of the Catholic Church and the U.S. government. Maybe they are afraid of the public outrage or the consequences of grown children remembering and suing the government and its allies.[30]

Lingering Doubt

Many unanswered questions about Operation Pedro Pan remain. The order of how events unfolded is not clear; for example, there are several versions of the chronology of this story: In one, a boy named Pedro Menéndez approached Father Walsh during the month of October 1960 raising concerns about more unaccompanied refugee children. In another, members of the American Chamber of Commerce approach Father Walsh to help take care of unaccompanied children. Jim Baker, too, was inconsistent and tentative about the origins of his involvement. The chronology of events is significant because it would help clarify some of the lingering questions as to how the program originated.

There is also doubt about when the program actually started. In the oft-cited chronology of the first thirty days of the program, Father Walsh reports that the first group of children arrived on December 26, 1960, although there were already children from Baker's list in Miami who had arrived on tourist visas.[31] John Thomas, a Cuban refugee coordinator, refers to the December group as the first "official" children (his quotes), implying that there were others who had already arrived.[32] Ruby Hart Phillips, the *New York Times* correspondent in Havana, wrote that around December 15 1960, her sister had assumed guardianship of a six-year-old girl and was leaving Cuba for Miami. "Hundreds of children were being sent out of Cuba and the authorities were not pleased to see an American taking one."[33] There was a group of over fifty Cuban girls who had arrived in an Ursuline school in New Orleans in

October of 1960. And a November 27, 1960, article in the Cuban magazine *Bohemia* notes that students from Villanueva were being taken to
the United States in a program sponsored by the State Department. Was
there a connection between this program and the official Operation Pedro Pan? Had the Catholic Church already started making arrangements to bring students to the United States? There were special visas
established for nuns and priests. What was the connection between
these and the other visa waiver programs?

One baffling enigma is why there was a visa waiver program aimed
at children while there were visa waiver programs simultaneously
aimed at the general population. Although family reunification was not
a cornerstone of immigration policy at the time, it was an accepted fact
that the family unit was important for children. This program, even in
the short run, created family separation.

The children's program was run through Father Walsh who was
authorized to grant visa waivers to anyone under eighteen. The other
programs ran through opposition groups and granted visa waivers to
friends and family members of the opposition. Could it be that bureaucratic politics played a role in shaping distinct programs? Or was
there a separate program for children because it was a well-concerted
ploy to train a group of Cuban children as future democratic leaders of
Cuba? Was it a program to keep the underground focused and not worried about their children? Was it a means to control the underground?

There could be bureaucratic reasons why two separate programs
existed. The general program may have needed an initiating petition
from a relative in the United States; Pedro Pan did not, and therefore it
was open to anyone on the island under the age of eighteen. In addition,
the blanket visa waiver given to Father Walsh was possible because
children were not perceived to be a security threat, while adults were.
Therefore, security concerns could have facilitated the creation and the
perpetuation of two separate programs.

There is some evidence to suggest that there was interest on the part
of the church and the government to have a group of elite leaders safeguarded for democracy. Both Penny Powers and Jim Baker allude to this

in their letters to the U.S. government. They could have perceived the program to be one of training the future leaders of Cuba.

Parents fighting in the underground were concerned about their children, and if they were caught, what would happen to them? Certainly, in this regard, it makes sense that a program was established to take care of the children of those in the underground. Having the children in the United States could have provided CIA handlers who did not trust Cubans a means through which to control them.

Another lingering question about Operation Pedro Pan is why it mushroomed after the Bay of Pigs. Clearly, the program was first set up for a group no larger than 500. However, from April 1961 to October 1962, over 14,000 children came to the United States. Obviously if it was a mechanism to evacuate young men of the underground, the increased repression in Cuba increased the number of youths trying to flee.

Monsignor Walsh had suggested that the CIA lost operational interests after the Bay of Pigs, and therefore the activists and organizers kept doing it without any accountability.[34] Surely, the secrecy of the Operation facilitated this. But the CIA continued to be involved in anti-Castro operations. Government documents subsequent to the Bay of Pigs clearly demonstrate that the U.S. government had multiple interests in the children—from being involved in procuring visa waivers for young members of the underground to using them as intelligence-gathering vehicles and even as propaganda as in the film *The Lost Apple*. In the summer of 1961, Congress held a hearing and the unaccompanied minors program was thoroughly discussed, although Father Walsh asked that the question regarding numbers of, be left off the record. The unaccompanied children were discussed in almost every congressional hearing on Cuban refugee problems until 1965. The government was not unaware of the program.

If it was not neglect, then were the numbers deliberately increased so that the Cuban government would not be able to automatically detect who the underground was through the departing unaccompanied minors? The concern that Cuban intelligence could use the program as a way of detecting the underground had been raised in its early stages.

Members of Baker's group were questioned about sending children to the United States. And while many in the United States thought they had duped Cuban intelligence with the response that Cuban students had always gone to the United States, surely the sheer number of children traveling would have been an indication that something else was occurring. The increased numbers did provide a cover, but there is a question as to whether this was intentional.

Others have suggested that Operation Pedro Pan was a CIA propaganda ploy. I believe that the evidence points to the fact that the origins of the program were not propagandistic, but rather military. This does not mean that the CIA was not involved, or for that matter, in charge of the program. And the increase in numbers, in part, was due to U.S. propaganda efforts to destabilize the regime, particularly the campaign to convince parents that they would soon lose *patria potestad* over their children, including decisions on how to educate them. Parents were clearly fearful of losing their authority over their children, and this fear was fueled by real events as well as U.S.-directed propaganda. The propaganda was successful because certain Cuban government actions lent credibility to it. The shutting of the schools and the increased repression certainly provoked many families to make the decision to send their children to the United States. Parents believed that their children's minds were important to safeguard. Most important, they believed that their children would be safe. They trusted the United States and the Catholic Church. Once in the States, the children did provide cannon fodder for propaganda wars.

Why, one might wonder, didn't Cuban officials stop the exodus? In effect, if Cuban officials refused to let parents send their children abroad, they would have usurped their authority. But perhaps more important, the Cuban government benefited from the exodus. It helped to denationalize the disaffected. Children provided them with information about the opposition.

Perhaps these various explanations regarding the origins and expansion of the program are not contradictory. Clearly, ideological concerns were at the forefront for many activists as well as government officials. In addition, Operation Pedro Pan provided CIA handlers with leverage over Cubans in the underground. Parents could continue their political activities more freely not having to worry about their children. And the exodus provided Cuban officials with information and a way to externalize disaffection. The secrecy of the program made it easier for a relatively small group of individuals to exert their ideological will on history. The interests of the activists, parents, U.S. bureaucrats, CIA agents and Cuban officials coincided. Indeed, the coincidence of a broad range of governmental and private interests may help explain the massive nature of the exodus.

Pedro Pans: Revisiting the Exodus

The debate about Operation Pedro Pan being a humanitarian rescue effort versus a sinister plot does not foster a deeper understanding of the program or its consequences. In these renditions, children are victims of either communism or capitalism, and victims, as we know, are usually seen as powerless and voiceless. Without doubt, many of the children suffered, but to reduce them to victims is to continue to effectively deny their voices once more. Some Pedro Pans chose not to speak about their experiences; while not necessarily denying the past, they prefer to look forward. Others, like Xavier, the boy I traveled with and finally found again almost forty years later, simply cannot remember the journey or what life was like with his parents in Cuba.

But these were powerful experiences that narrow political positions cannot contain or silence.[35] More complex explanations are starting to emerge that will help many Pedro Pans to remember. Yvonne Conde wrote a book using surveys of 442 Pedro Pans.[36] Teresita Echazabal created a website for Pedro Pans "dedicated to all those wounded children, and it gives voice to the issue of healing their fragmented souls."[37] Flora González wanted to return to the island to create a present in her past. She writes in her short story "A House on Shifting Sands": "I retain an inexplicable emptiness of all farewells. I feel like a young girl, alone in an airport, in search of adventure. I carry with me the fragile but portable house of a mother tongue. Instructions to build and rebuild are easy: take sand, add water, and build a castle."[38] Román de la Campa included his experiences in a book about his relationship to the island. He writes, "I have often marveled at the irony that we ended up in camps after all—not in Eastern Europe, but in distant sites that our parents had never heard of, and without their direct knowledge."[39] For him this moment is not one of remembering, but rather of forgetting: "My Jacksonville experience turned out to be forgettable in many respects. I could feel my life changing through subtraction—an accumulation of losses that left me in an existential void, not unlike the process of learning English, which ultimately required unlearning some Spanish."[40] Carlos Erie has recently written a memoir about what was lost—the Cuba of his childhood.[41]

Others like Francisco Méndez-Diez have explored their experience through art. In "Los Cacharros" a small boy leads a grown dog, and in the background (memory?) lies a mother dog and her pups. Like other Pedro Pans, Francisco, who was thirteen when sent to the United States, felt that he had to grow up too quickly.[42] Ana Mendieta, who created earth silhouettes in nature, some in Cuba, describes her art as a search for origin: "There is no original past to redeem: there is a void, the orphanhood, the unbaptized earth of the beginning, the time that from within the earth looks upon us. There is above all the search for origin." [43] Her sister, Raquelín, who is also an artist, says that through her art, Ana "was free again to experience her identity: her heart and her soul."[44]

Still others have dedicated their time to bringing the now grown children together. Elly Chovel, for instance, felt that Pedro Pans needed to come together to recollect their own memories.[45] She felt a strong connection to other Pedro Pans. Time and again she heard similar stories: most of the Pedro Pans she met were grateful to be in the United States and not in Cuba, but there was still a sense of loss, of dislocation. And there were many unanswered questions.

Elly knew of Monsignor Walsh. She had been in contact with Catholic Welfare to get her parents out of Cuba. When they arrived,

"Los Cacharros" Francisco Méndez-Diez.

Monsignor had written to her that he was delighted that she had been able reunite with her family. He told her that he would like to hear from her from time to time to know how she was doing.[46]

In late 1990 she met Monsignor Walsh at a dinner in his honor. She asked him if it would be all right to organize a gathering of Pedro Pans. It had been attempted before, but the efforts had been unsuccessful. Elly insisted. There were children in South Florida who were in circumstances similar to the Pedro Pans of decades ago. Hundreds of unaccompanied refugee children from the Caribbean and other parts of the world were under the care of Catholic Welfare in the Miami area. She had a recurring dream, about a place where children lived together, played, and did not feel so alone. Perhaps a group of Pedro Pans could help actualize that dream by relieving the experience of the new unaccompanied children; and perhaps by helping to ease their sense of loneliness, Pedro Pans could come to terms with their past as well.

Chovel's Operation Pedro Pan group is a cross section of Cuban
exiles: bankers, doctors, secretaries, realtors, professors, musicians, and
artists. They represent different political positions, often disagreeing on
the most sensitive topic for exiles: politics and the island. But for the last
ten years, the group has come together to sponsor events for the new
refugee minors, some of whom are Cuban children, like themselves.
They have also raised money for the construction of a Children's Village
in Miami, similar to the one in Elly's dream.

Elly also felt that we Pedro Pans needed to do something for ourselves. We had to know our histories, even if it meant resurrecting
painful moments. She began organizing annual encounters of Pedro
Pans that drew people from around the world. For several years, a
smaller group met the last Saturday of every month at Versailles, the
Cuban restaurant in the heart of Miami's Little Havana, in order to explore how and why their exodus had occurred.

As part of the annual conference, Elly launched a history project.
She invited those who had been involved in the underground to share

Monsignor Walsh, Elly Chovel, and James Baker, Miami, 1992. Courtesy of
Operation Pedro Pan, Inc.

their recollections. Many were dying and she feared that their stories would go untold. She invited those of us who had a more critical perspective of the project to debate the organizers. While Elly understood the political risks of challenging the myths, she felt strongly that we needed to know what had happened in order for collective healing to occur; indeed, both Elly and the group's efforts made my research journey possible.

Because our experiences have been filtered through a political mythology, recollecting and retelling them remains difficult. One of many myths surrounding the Pedro Pans is that we are overachievers —that we grew up before our time. The list of those who contributed to this book—professors, social workers, realtors, journalists, and lawyers—certainly would add credibility to that perception. But there are many others we don't know about. Scholars who study the long-term impact of abrupt separations from family suggest that once we have a fuller story, the picture will be more complex.[47]

In the fall of 2001, over sixty Pedro Pans gathered at Barry University in Miami to celebrate forty years of their journey to the United States. We did not know that this would be the last time that Father Walsh would be there, sometimes hesitant about the discussion, but present nonetheless. And how had the experience affected these Pedro Pans? Many believed that it had made them stronger, more independent. Some felt they had grown up too fast, and still needed to live out their adolescence. Often they had a sense of duty to succeed. Many admitted that it was difficult for them to reconstruct a place called home, and that it was hard to sustain emotionally intimate relationships. The experience of separating from their parents had affected their relationship with their own children. Some said they were overprotected, while others felt that they had raised them to be independent, almost as if readying them for an unexpected separation. Pedro Pans are torn on the question of whether or not they would have made the same decision as their parents, but they know that they are different people because of the experience.

At the conference we also spoke about our similarities to other immigrants and exiles. Olga Drucker, the author of a book about the Kindertransport, shared her experiences with us. And though no one compared our exodus to hers, there were similarities in how children experienced separations from their parents. Ultimately there was virtual consensus that we still lived through a very unique set of circumstances that was framed by a political reality we could not easily influence. Ironically, those tense relationships continue to affect many Pedro Pans, especially those with relatives on the island.

As Rafael Ravelo later remarked:

> What makes our situation unique is that we can't go back when we want to. My mother had three strokes in the last three years, if she were seriously ill, I couldn't go. When my father died, I tried to get back. I called Washington, did whatever I could, didn't get the visa. That is the problem, knowing that they can't come here either. Several years ago, I got real sick. The doctor said I might not make it through the next two weeks. My sister applied to come but the U.S. didn't give her entry. So I was still alone.[48]

Still, as Ravelo meditates on his experience, he arrives at complex notions of culture and identity that many Pedro Pans share.

> All of these years, two things have happened to me. I have reconnected with Cuba but I now feel I'm a citizen of the world. I don't think that I would have ever gotten there had I stayed in Cuba.[49]

Perhaps more complex notions of identity can engender complex notions of politics, if not a more open approach to politics. There are many political opinions reflected among the Pedro Pans, particularly regarding Cuba, but there is also a culture of tolerance that is less publicly acknowledged among other exile generations. Maybe the shared past allows us to respect one another's political opinions. Maybe the need to understand our own personal histories in a more complex way has fostered the openness. Perhaps it is the understanding of how fragile our own histories are woven that makes us more empathetic to each other. After all, we all began our journeys in the same way; those of us who ended up with good *becas* could have as easily ended up with a bad ones. Take for instance the contrast in fate between Xavier's experiences and mine. He was on his way to a relative's home but was unexpectedly not welcomed. Instead he was placed in an orphanage with severely disturbed youths and a cruel administration. When my foster family could not care for me, a relative took me in until my parents came. For sure, camaraderie exists among many Pedro Pans, as well as a shared commitment to understand our histories. The result is that we have begun to develop a fuller grasp of the origins of the exile community itself. We hope that a reexamination of the myth of origin of our exile can lead to a more comprehensive understanding of ourselves and our communities.

Conclusions: Rethinking Our Notions of Childhood

More than forty years after our extraordinary exodus, relations between our home and our adopted country remain tense. Pedro Pans, the children who were saved from communism, remain a symbol and still affect the continuing tense relations between the United States, the exile community, and Cuba. The 1960s conflict over who would control the minds of Cuban children is today played out by attempts to control the narrative of our journeys. Cuba excludes from their rendition the reasons why our parents feared the regime, including religious persecution, summary trials, and executions of young men. In the United States, government officials and religious refugee organizations hide behind the mantle of national security, even as they publicly embrace their official version of our exodus—a flight to freedom. Our understanding of the largest exodus of unaccompanied minors in the Western Hemisphere cannot be reduced to either a sinister program designed to steal children away from a budding revolution or, conversely, a humanitarian mission devoid of politics.

In this book, I chose to narrate a more nuanced story. I included the military and political interests that influenced the children's exodus and contextualized parents' fears—not only as a response to their circumstances, but also as a product of how children were conceived during this period.

Operation Pedro Pan was phenomenal in so many ways. The U.S. origins of the children's exodus were part of a massive covert program aimed at overthrowing the Cuban revolution. This program included provisions for immigration and evacuation of agents. The U.S. government, mainly through the CIA, ran visa waiver programs. These programs relied on historically unprecedented relationships with private and religious refugee relief organizations; one Catholic priest was given the power to issue blanket visa waivers to any Cuban children under sixteen. All this was to be temporary until Castro's government was overthrown and the children returned to their parents, many of whom were underground fighters. The invasion failed, but the secret immigration mechanisms were left intact until 1962, when the United States ordered a quarantine of the island and halted all flights. By that time, over 14,000 unaccompanied refugee minors had entered the United States.

There is no one overarching narrative that can capture the complexities of our parents' emotions or our individual experiences. Even though our collective story has been bound by a very well guarded mythology born of revolution, persecution, disillusionment, and fear, there are, in reality, as many stories as there are Pedro Pan children. Each one should be shared and reflected upon. To do this honorably, we need to continue to break the silence that has shrouded our journeys.

The secrecy imposed by political and institutional interests has made it particularly challenging for children who experienced the most difficult times to tell their stories. The government denies involvement; the Catholic Church denies that abuse ever happened. When children complained to their social workers, they were asked not to tell, a practice not just reserved for Cuban refugee children but for many other children as well. Abusers were protected and children, even when they were proven right, were asked to remain silent. As such, children were stripped of the only defense they could have had-to talk honestly about the abuse. This "don't talk" request is demonstrative of the ways in which society has constructed children, as vehicles for the future and not as individual human beings with emotional needs.

Our exodus, as it was individually lived and experienced, was a contest of ideas over the future of nations battled over the control of children's minds. Therefore, we need to reexamine the philosophical underpinnings, which convinced parents and activists about the righteousness of saving children's minds, frequently at the expense of their emotional well-being.

Operation Pedro Pan: Contesting Nations through Children

Q What compelled parents to send their children to an unknown country, expecting a quick reunion but not knowing for certain if that would happen? The answer, in part, is that the opportunity existed to send children ahead, but the fears parents had about what would happen to their children under communism are critical to understand their motives.

The decision parents made to send their children abroad was closely tied to what they wanted for themselves. They, too, were frightened about what would happen in their lives. The arbitrary nature of change in Cuba following the revolution wreaked havoc and uncertainty in people's lives. For some parents the fear of physical safety for their adolescent boys was real. Many were involved in the underground and, if caught, they could face firing squads. Others feared radical changes in the family itself, particularly the authority parents had to make decisions about their children. The propaganda campaign that claimed the state would usurp *patria potestad* from parents was effective. (The 1978 Cuban constitution includes a family code that recognizes parents' right to *patria potestad* over their children. However, they can lose it for a variety of reasons, including "abandoning national territory and, therefore, their children.")[1] The militarization and overpoliticization of education, and of society in general, scared parents into thinking that it would be possible to lose their children to the state. The children needed to be saved.

But why the fear of brainwashing? The search for an adequate explanation to this exact question has led me to consider how children were socially constructed during this time period, which would make it urgent for parents and underground organizers to guard children's minds. Therefore, it was the promise of a better future and the role that children would play in that future that contributed to the urgency expressed by the organizers of the exodus.

*children were seen
as the future of
the nation.*

Parents were fearful of what would happen to their children's minds. These fears were grounded in a set of beliefs about children and their place in society. The idea that most influenced Operation Pedro Pan was the European modernist project's proposition that human beings could indeed impact their own future. Children were building blocks to this new future. In this way, their education was the determining factor for the destiny of a nation.

The women of the underground believed that they were involved in the noble cause of saving children from indoctrination. Their participation in Operation Pedro Pan, a peak experience in their lives, combined their desire to overthrow the Castro government with what was ultimately a gendered role: taking care of children. *Rescate de la niñez!* (Rescue the children!) became their battle cry. They, too, believed that children's minds mattered greatly to the future of a country. Jim Baker, an American educator deeply enamored with Cuba, had spent his career building an independent school that could contribute to bringing democratic thought and practices to the island. For him, saving children from communist brainwashing was an extension of his commitment to protecting the future for democracy.

For Jim Baker and Penny Powers, Operation Pedro Pan was about educating the future leaders of a democratic Cuba. For the Cuban government, children were the vehicles for undoing the past. In both cases, plans called for removing children from their families and placing them in Catholic Church–run institutions in the case of Pedro Pan and state-run boarding schools in the island. Not surprisingly, Penny Powers believed that the way the children were being mistreated jeopardized the entire plan. The military aspect of the plan would be compromised because worried parents would not continue fighting in the underground, the ideological because children would not learn the lessons of democracy. However, Baker told me that he was more concerned about what would happen to the children in Cuba: "The destructive effects of communism was the predominant factor in my thinking in those days."[2]

For Father Walsh, religious and political beliefs combined to give him a sense that the children were better off in institutions and away from their parents than in Cuba, where they lived with their families but in an authoritarian state. Although the prevailing wisdom in child psychology was that children were better off with their parents, Operation Pedro Pan was organized in such a way as to break the family apart, a concept that philosophers since Plato had contemplated as a means to create a just society.

Longer argument

Cuban parents and the organizers of Operation Pedro Pan believed that the children would be better served in a democratic country rather than in an authoritarian state. Clearly, they may have had idealized notions of life in the United States, and they trusted their priests. Moreover, they believed what they were told: that their children would receive scholarships to boarding schools. Perhaps most important, they believed that the future of their families and their nation depended on how their children were educated. They had all become heirs to the political project of modernism that claimed that children's minds were the building blocks of future.

Operation Pedro Pan, however, would be conceived in a uniquely American context that had its own political history. During the 1950s, the United States entered into an intense war with the Soviet Union that contested not only territory and military might but also conceptions about the place of government and individuals in society. Given

Sub-argument

the importance that modernism placed on children's roles in creating the future of nations, control over their minds became a central point of combat in the Cold War. Through Operation Pedro Pan, children would be saved from communism, and democracy would spread to an authoritarian island. Saving Cuban children from the clutches of communism would combine the ideals of a democratic republic and the romantic self-image that Americans had of themselves.[3]

Like the immigrant children of the "Orphan Trains" and the Native American students of the U.S. government-run boarding schools, Cuban refugee children would be schooled in the ways of democracy, their minds detoxified from the evils of communism. They would be future leaders of a country made in the image of the United States. In contrast to the American children, refugee children were not building the nation, but rather the empire.[4]

The irony of the struggle for the minds of Cuba's children was that both sides shared in the method of creating a better future: the education of children. In 1962, children in the refugee camps were told that they were the future of Cuba, the "New Man" of the next century. Ché Guevara would champion the notion three years later. In what would become one of his most read essays he said, "We will create the man of the twenty-first century. The basic clay of our work is the youth."[5] But the idea actually had its roots in radical Catholicism.

Not surprisingly, the state's authority in educating children was a feature of both versions of the rational/modernist project. In liberal democracies, education became compulsory. Private and public institutions coexisted even as the state influenced the curriculum taught in private schools. However, parents were given a choice of whether to educate their children in public or private institutions. Through elected representatives, individuals could have a voice in conceptualizing public education. In socialist countries, private schools were abolished and the state assumed total control of the curriculum. Their greatest difference concerned who would control the decision making and be in charge of creating the new man. And this is what framed the political battle to save the children.

In part this campaign was so massive because children have been powerful vehicles through which nations have been contested. Their innocence makes them desirable political objects. Indeed, safeguarding children's innocence would become the reason for struggling to control their minds. This has been possible because of the mythological pull they have on our psyches. Children are windows to the future and simultaneously evoke a past for which we are nostalgic. It is perhaps our own anxieties about losing the past that compels us to project our fears onto our children. Protecting them gives us a way to feel meaningful. In times of national anxieties, the thought of protecting children is comforting, of course; simultaneously, it is a way to try to control a changing world.

Lingering Misconceptions about Children

Since 1965, Cubans have continued to come to the United States because it holds the promise of better economic opportunities and political freedoms. In addition, the over one million Cubans already in the United States offer an anchor for others. There are still divided families: those that never found each other again; those that did but who cannot travel easily back and forth, sometimes due to U.S. policies, at other times because of Cuban policies. Then there are the boys who stayed behind, the ones the Cuban government would not let out because of military duty. Families with relatives on both sides are affected by these tensions.

Every immigration wave since has also had its share of unaccompanied refugee minors. Over several thousand unaccompanied minors made their way to the United States during the 1980 Mariel boatlift.[6] In the 1990s it was the children of the rafters, some of whom lost their parents in treacherous journeys.[7]

For the exile community, this continues to be a testament to the horrors of communism and, specifically the Castro regime. Children continue to be used as political pawns. For instance, in 1994, the Clinton administration changed it policy toward Cuban refugees. Instead of automatically admitting them into the United States, Clinton ordered their detention. Over three thousand children were detained, many of whom ended up with their parents in Guantánamo. Conditions at the base were difficult—it was hot and sandy, and families were living in tents. Others were detained with their families in Krome, the Immigration and Naturalization Service's Detention Center in Florida. Some exile leaders wanted to take the children to Puerto Rico and place them in temporary foster homes, just as the Pedro Pan children had been. Ileana Ros-Lehtinen, a congressional representative from Miami, issued a press release asking members of Operation Pedro Pan to take the children into their homes. "The children who are detained are also victims of Castro and escaped from their homeland searching for freedom. These children are the future of Cuba."[8]

But the Pedro Pan children, now grown, knew what it felt like to be separated from their parents. Elly Chovel wrote to the *Miami Herald*, "As a former child of Operation Pedro Pan, I beg of all people of conscience: Do not let the children be used as pawns in the political games played by adults in Miami, Washington, Tallahassee, and Havana."[9] The grown Pedros Pans lobbied against the idea. The children's lives were not in danger. What would happen if the temporary stay turned out to be years? Monsignor Walsh weighed in as well. He wrote Congresswoman Ros-Lehtenin:

> It is regrettable that this premature announcement was made without its implications being studied. Your proposal is that children, who are in Krome with their parents, be released and taken into the homes of strangers. As a child welfare agency, we would have very grave questions regarding any plan to separate these children from their parents, even for a short period of time. Advocacy efforts would be better directed at getting the whole family paroled into this country on humanitarian grounds.[10]

Monsignor Walsh had also learned from our experiences. Eventually, these children and their parents were paroled to the United States.

But the issue resurfaced again when one child, Elián González, the boy rafter whose mother lost her life on her journey toward a better future, came to symbolize the tragedy of immigration crisis, becoming an example of the lingering misconceptions about children. Almost immediately, the exile community and the Cuban government again compared a child refugee to Pedro Pans. The child would lead an exile back home; conversely saving the nation through his innocence. For Pedro Pans, he recalled our own family separations. He reminded us of how we, too, had been used as cannon fodder in ideological battles; we the yellow ribbons of the Cold War, he the symbol of hope for an end to forty years of dictatorship. We saw ourselves in him, alone in the United States in the middle of a political maelstrom. We were, however, divided on the fate of the child.

There was a critical difference in the situations: the choice made by

Elly Chovel with the children of Guantanamo Base, 1994. Courtesy of Operation Pedro Pan, Inc.

not coherente

the parents. In the case of Elián, his mother, surely in an act of desperation that reflects real life in Cuba, chose to leave with him, on a raft. She did not send her child alone. Her vision was life in the United States together with her son. He was not an intended unaccompanied refugee minor. In contrast, our parents made the decision to send us here unaccompanied. They were afraid that the Cuban government would take away parental authority over their children.

Once Elián's mother died, his father publicly expressed his desire to have his son returned home. And in an ironic twist of history, his expressed wishes were threatened by some of the very people who had once sent their children ahead, fearing that they would lose the right to decide their children's future. Instead, they proposed placing Elián with distant relatives he had briefly met on two occasions, a family riddled with emotional and legal problems, and to be educated in a school, Lincoln/Marti, that proudly professed a strong ideological curriculum.[11] Clearly, parental rights, freedom of thought, and the child's emotional needs were not factors in keeping Elián in the United States. Unfortunately, the church decided to remain silent on this case, although Monsignor Walsh repeatedly reminded us that the situations were very different.

If there was a similarity between Operation Pedro Pan and Elián González, it was in the compulsion to place children in the middle of political controversies and use them as political examples. This is still possible because, even forty years after our exodus, our conceptions about children and what their needs are remained unquestioned. Advocates of keeping Elián in the United States continually raised his right to live and be educated in a free country. Yet few spoke of his right to live with his father, by all accounts a nurturing parent, a right that would safeguard Elián's emotional well-being, not his mind. Indeed, one advocate of the position that Elián should stay claimed that because he was younger then the majority of Pedro Pans, Elián would have an easier time adjusting.[12] The work of child development psychologists has demonstrated time and again that the younger a child is at the time of separation, the more of an emotional impact it will have. Adults' political priorities, and perhaps ignorance, not a child's emotional needs, once again framed the debate about the fate of a child.

Throughout the twentieth century, child psychologists established the importance of children's early emotional development and the importance of the family during those years. The high cost of separating children from their parents had been clearly demonstrated during World War II. But somehow the political exigencies of modernism and its promise of reshaping a future eclipsed this understanding. A new conception of childhood has not yet taken root.

Reconceptualizing Children

The concept of the modern child was predicated on the assumption that children possessed a unique innocence and a mind that could be molded.[13] It is the idea of innocence that makes people yearn to save children, the dramatic force behind Operation Pedro Pan, and it is the malleable mind hypothesis that makes them political objects. In modernism, children acquired a political meaning as well—they were the keys to nation building. The modernist conception of childhood is what contributed to placing children at the center of the public's imagination and thus in the middle of political struggles. If by placing children in a prominent place in the public's imagination we made them vulnerable to manipulation, do we simply remove them? Or can we rethink a social space that both gives children rights and also understands and protects their vulnerabilities? Where is the boundary between the private and the public, and how can this be defined to protect and ensure children of their rights?

To fully explore these questions, we must first take note of the profound changes in the structures and ideas that gave birth to the modern child. Some claim that childhood is a category that no longer exists, since postmodernity has changed some of the basic elements that socially confined it. Postmodernity is characterized by the declining ability of nation-states to organize our economies, cultures, and, to a certain degree, our politics—a change that challenges the political role that children played in modernism, that is, as keys to nation building. Global cities are now important anchors of the world economy. In addition, innovative means of transportation have made it easier to travel from one part of the world to another, increasing contact among people of different backgrounds. Changes in technology have radically changed the ways that information is presented and distributed.

Other social, cultural, and legal structures that contributed to the formation of modern childhood have undergone dramatic changes in this new era. The family has been reconfigured as women have entered the workforce, thus changing the place of children in the nuclear family. In addition, there has been an erosion of legal distinctions between adolescents and adults when it comes to the criminal justice system. Legal changes in how we define crime and a criminal is an indication of this erosion. The juvenile court system, an institutional recognition of the differences between youths and adults, is losing ground as more and more youths are being tried as adults. In 1996, over 46 states had passed laws authorizing the prosecution of fourteen-year-olds as adults. In the last ten years, the number of adolescents doing time in adult prisons has doubled. Teenagers charged with the same crime as adults are punished more harshly.[14]

The boundaries demarcating adulthood and childhood have always been hazy, a fact that has oftentimes been controversial. For instance, there was a public furor over Freud's groundbreaking work demonstrating children's sexuality and, most recently, over Sally Mann's photographic images of her children and Robert Maplethorpe's photographs of children in poses and situations in that ambiguous intimate zone they share.[15]

Yet these boundaries may be more eroded today since one of the important elements that contained childhood in modernism is disappearing: access to information. Television and the Internet have made it easier to access information. Images have supplanted the text, thereby making it possible to present information in simpler forms. Children's sense of time has also been expanded. They have easy access to contemporary culture as well as culture from other eras. The result is that there are now more shared territories between children, youth, and adults. If childhood was a category of the Renaissance that was made possible, in part, by society's ability to compartmentalize and regulate information through text, childhood is no longer confined in the same ways.[16]

Because of these changes, some scholars argue that childhood as we have known it during modernity is disappearing and a new construct is emerging, indeed maybe multiple constructs of childhood and youth are evolving.[17]

All children are affected by these changes, because all children live in postmodern times, but there are class and racial differences in the rate of acceleration with which these changes are occurring. In Cook County, Illinois, 99 percent of the youths automatically transferred to adult court in the year 2000 were African-American or Latino.[18] Alex Kotlowitz in *There Are No Children Here* narrates the lives of two

African-American brothers growing up in one of Chicago's gang-plagued public housing projects. Their childhood has little resemblance to any ideal of modern childhood. The same can be said of children who have survived wars, or those who work long hours in sweatshops through out the world.[19]

And there are also still streams of refugee children being sent alone to European countries, the United States, or more prosperous neighboring countries by parents hoping to start an immigration survival chain for their families. All these children may be losing their childhoods quickly.

These changes are reflected in how children are portrayed. Last century's most circulated image of children was Betsy Cameron's photograph of two children sitting at the water's edge. A little boy of no more than three years old has his arm around a little girl's shoulders. The children are seen from behind, unaware that they are being watched. The sky and the horizon at a distance give a feeling of serenity.[20] In contrast we now have the hyper-sexualized child replacing these modern photographic images of innocence. In some cases, it is the criminalized youth that predominates. In most of these images, parents are absent from the scene.[21] These commercially constructed images of children seek both to sell to children, as well as to use children to sell.[22] Markets, not political agendas, have created an image-driven construction of childhood in which children are simultaneously consumed and consume, still without political rights that can safeguard their particular needs.

Few would argue that there are no differences between children and adults, but what are the differences, particularly in times when the distinctions that used to define childhood are eroding, and how should these differences be respected? If the innocent child made children vulnerable to political manipulations, what is the alternative?

Recognizing that children have this information may help us understand that the postmodern child is an informed child, but still a child. Children, like adults, have emotional feelings. In contrast to adults, emotional traumas take a harder toll on children since they have limited emotional tools with which to process trauma. Indeed, it is now clear that children have special needs and sensibilities, experiencing the world differently from adults. Emotional support and intellectual stimulation can make a difference to the rest of their lives, including the formation of moral intelligence that some claim is critical in just societies.[23]

The goal is to imagine children as informed beings who have special needs. In her series of paintings entitled *Childhood*, Elena Climent suggests this and a bit more—an informed, vulnerable, and playful child, protected in an intimate and familiar world. Her children reside in a protected and private space, usually the home. Individual rights are inferred in this private world.[24] Privacy was something not afforded to the modern child whose mind becomes the domain of the public, as was so evident in the struggle over Cuba's children. Yet while residing in the private realm, her children are allowed to be children. Giving children rights does not necessarily mean taking childhood away from them. They play. However, they are not isolated. They have windows to the world; there are boats, dreams, and, most important, books and pencils. They are children who are reading and who are playing. They have special sensibilities, which allow them to hold in awe even the smallest, most quotidian, object or gesture. It is this unprejudiced gaze of the world that makes them vulnerable but gives them the capacity to learn.

Children and Politics

What implication would a reconceptualization of children who are informed, yet emotionally and cognitively vulnerable, have on where we place children in society? Are there different ways that we can rethink their place while understanding their uniqueness and without sentimentalizing them? What would be the boundaries between the private and the public child? How would we educate postmodern children? And have we lost all hope of creating a better future because of the failures of modernism in protecting children's emotions?

Some would argue that we should seriously consider the place of

children in politics itself. Children are missing from the liberal democratic project.[25] Therefore there is budding interest in finding ways that
children can be included and counted in the electoral arena.[26] After all,
our notion of participatory democracy is predicated on informed citizens, and if children are informed, shouldn't we create a forum so they
can participate in politics? Children do have a political life that, in part,
begins with a sense of place, usually the nation, and includes feelings
about authority figures and information about politics.[27] There appears
to be particular stages of development in political attitudes, even as
these vary for children of different communities and countries.[28] And
children's political development is closely tied to their overall development. Children are generally more astute than usually credited.

But there are those who have vehemently opposed the politiciza-
tion of childhood. The argument in American racial politics between
Hannah Arendt and Ralph Ellison is worth reviewing. Arguing against
placing children on the front lines of desegregation in Little Rock,
Arkansas, Arendt claimed that children could only be protected in the
private realm. It was here, away from public manipulation, that intimacy and love could flourish, she believed. She concluded that inte-
gration should not begin in public schools, which placed children in
the front lines of the battle and allowed adults to abdicate their political responsibilities. She felt that these battles should be fought in the
adult world, not in the school yards. Ralph Ellison reminded her that
getting hurt was part of the "Negro experience" and that, as such, children had already been brought into the public realm in negative ways.
Mobilizing them politically could empower them, he observed.[29] Indeed, the fact may be that when the world is in turmoil, children will
invariably become involved.[30]

Children reside both in the public and in the private realms. In the
public realm, children can have a protected voice, but the public should
simultaneously respect the private emotional needs that until now have
been best realized through the family.[31]

But vital questions need to be explored. How do we decide how
families best raise children? Who teaches the children, and what are

children taught? These questions have become even more urgent in to-day's world. Can we reach some form of consensus about what we want in our future citizens? Modernism's political goal of creating a better future by developing informed, engaged, and independent-minded individuals need not be implemented in ways that compromise a child's well-being. The respect for the individual child is present in the thinking of modernist theorists such as John Dewey and José Martí, if not in those like Benjamin Rush, an early American thinker on the subject who called for youths to be Republican machines and Fidel Castro who declared, "Our youth will be builders of communism and forgers of a New World."[32] Education conceived as a means to empower individuals takes on a very different form than education structured to create a political future. It could even be argued that the latter is not about empowering individuals but about harnessing the uncontrolled present, children and youth.

Nations and empires can be contested through children, because, in reality, children, have no real voices, or at least voices that are heard, which makes them particularly vulnerable to manipulation. This is especially true for the more than two million children who have been displaced by wars and civil strife. It is also true for refugee minors, who are doubly marginalized by their immigration status and their age.[33] Given the symbolic power of children their actual powerlessness is tremendously ironic. It is crucial to find ways in which children can be real children, with effective rights and emotional support.

International law provides a legal framework for the fundamental human rights for children. It recognizes, for example, a child's right to participate in decisions about his or her life regardless of immigration status. Perhaps this more global human rights perspective can provide an alternative to the modernist conception, which did include protection of children, but without their right to participate.[34] To this legal framework can be added an understanding of the developmental stages through which children traverse. This understanding could help us discern what protections children need at each stage; and what responsibilities can be expected of them and what rights should be granted to them.

The Promise of a Better Future

In the modernist project, the focus was on controlling the future, and the promise was that it would be better. This was to be done by manipulating the present, particularly those aspects not compromised by the past. Children, as constructed in modernism, became the perfect vehicles for change. But ideological and political needs eclipsed children's emotional needs. Adults projected their priorities onto children without taking into consideration the uniqueness of children. Ironically, again, in trying to protect their innocence, children were treated as adults. It was assumed that they would process the experience of separation like adults who had more emotional tools to help them cope. Children were forced to take on adult responsibilities, as older siblings became surrogate parents, and younger ones were expected to act older than their age.

While each family has its own individual style, all children became pawns of a political struggle, icons for ideological warfare. In Cuba, they were vehicles for nation building for the emerging revolution and a means to guarantee ideological hegemony for the U.S. empire in its geopolitical war with the Soviet Union, a fight that found a strong ally in the Catholic Church, which also had a long tradition of educating children. The revolution aimed to place children and their education in the public realm. In contrast, parents fought to maintain the right to have children within the private realm. Ultimately, the choice that the Catholic Church and U.S. government gave them to protect their claim effectively removed the children from the family and placed them right in the center of politics.

Many parents assumed that the separation from their children would be temporary: either the situation in Cuba would change or they would soon be able to follow their children. But heightened national security concerns about Communist spies infiltrating the United States spared the children who were not considered dangerous. The very tightly controlled immigration procedures at the height of the Cold War were relaxed for them, if not their parents. This was the window through which the program proliferated. A coincidence of ideological and institutional interests, both in Cuba and in the United States, contributed to its massiveness.

Most parents who wanted to leave the island, given an opportunity to travel with their children would have chosen to leave together; however, this was not an option.

Instead, the Catholic Church and the U.S. government were trusted to take care of their children. A close partnership with the United States, particularly on refugee programs, had brought the church resources and also allowed it to continue its educational mission. The church was given unquestioned moral authority over the care of children in part because for centuries it had been in the business of caring for orphans. A shift in social service philosophy under way in the 1960s, from institutions to foster care, meant that large-scale orphanages run by the church were available for Cuban refugee children. In 1998, Pope John Paul II visited Cuba. One of his most pointed criticisms was aimed at the state education system, which, he stated, "takes preteens away from their families and ships them to 'boarding schools' on the island, making family contact nearly impossible." He admonished the Cuban government for substituting itself for these children's parents.[35] The same could have been said of Operation Pedro Pan.

The presumption underlying both the revolution's attempts to *sub-* build a new society through children and the opposition's attempt to *argument* save them from communism was that children's minds were more important to protect than their hearts. Both societies believed that human beings had the power to reshape their societies and themselves, and both promised a better future. The process, however, compromised the emotional well-being of an entire generation. It also put in peril social projects aimed at bettering the world through education, because it did not protect the critical elements of this project, the children.

Tragically, many good people who were committed to worthy ideals ended up creating a program that, in effect, turned parents' worst fears—that their children would be taken from them—into grim realities. Children's unique emotional needs, which included being with their families, particularly in times of war, were ignored. Many suffered abuse, whether physical, sexual, or emotional, at the hands of those who had been entrusted with their care. And when they were reunited with their parents, time had taken its toll, and parents did not find the children they had shipped off. Rather, many had become Americanized, alienated from their culture and resentful of their perceived abandonment. Indeed, they had been stripped of their childhoods. Unlike the children of *The Lost Apple* who are saved from the clutches of communism to have a happier life and the promise of a better future, children experienced journeys, not of salvation but of loss of personal innocence. We can only hope that a better understanding of our losses can lead to more comprehensive views of children and their needs, and to more humane social and political projects that could create a better future.

Postscript

One of the saddest moments I can remember was when we buried my grandmother, Rita. We had been anticipating her death—she was ninety-one years old. She was born in 1895 and lived through the independence of Cuba, the Republic, the revolution, and an exile. She had always longed to return to Cuba. But like many exiles, it was, for her, simply impossible while Fidel Castro was in power. Instead, we buried her in Dallas, Texas, far away from her birthplace. I felt that her history—our history in exile—was somehow geographically misplaced, and perhaps lost forever. In fact, the feeling that time was reclaiming our history compelled me to document our past.

There has been a passing of an era in this last decade. Many of the individuals who participated in our exodus and whom I interviewed have died, but unlike my grandmother, whose story was never told, we are fortunate that they shared their stories with us. Monsignor Walsh was always willing to talk about the exodus. I regret that he will not see the publication of this book, to which he contributed his memories and insights. James and Sybil Baker, Penny Powers, Ester de la Portillo, Sara del Toro de Odio, Ramón and Polita Grau, Wendell Rollason, Tony Comellas, and Enrique Baloyra all contributed their recollections of the events that led to our exodus; without them, we would have a less complete picture.

Some of the parents I spoke with have also died; Eliseo Diego, Felicia Alegría, Valentín Díaz, Secundino González, and Raquel Otis; and Antonio and Concha Bechily, who helped me understand the dilemmas faced by parents who deeply loved their country and their children. We also lost Miguel González Pando as he was beginning to work on a documentary aimed at telling a more complex story of our exodus.

I began this research journey by interviewing my mother, María Isabel Vigil, who tried to help me understand what is still difficult for me to imagine, sending your child to an unknown country. Pablo Armando and Maruja Fernández, Bella García, Tata Mendieta, and Raquel Costa, explained to me why they had opted to stay. Some of their children also shared their stories, Maruga and José Alegría, Josefina Diego, and Teresa Fernández. Rolando Estévez spoke to me about how it felt to watch your parents leave.

I am thankful to the women of the underground, whom we know so little about. Their stories transformed my perspectives on the aftermath of the revolution; Teté Cuervo, Margarita Castro, Evora Arca, Nenita Carrame, Albertina O'Farrill, Alicia Thomas, and Adelaida Everhart. Other underground activists helped me understand the moment of rupture; they include my uncle Aurelio Vigil, my cousin Pancho León, José Arruza, Natalia de Lasa, Arturo Villar, and Antonio Veciana.

We may need to comprehend history in broad strokes, but this is not the way that we live it; rather, history is experienced in many intimate moments. Many Pedro Pans trusted me with their moments. I hope I have written about them in ways that create a deeper understanding of our exodus. Some of the Pedro Pans I spoke to include my cousins Cuca and Carmen Vigil, Yuyi Abrantes, Loli Soler, Sergio and Leonor Esnard; childhood friends Ignacio and Xavier Arruza; close friends María Concha Bechily, Raquelín Mendieta, Rafael Raveló, Alfredo Lanier, Hugo Chaviano, Emilio Cueto, Ramón Bueno, Hilda Díaz, Flora González; new acquaintances Carlos Erie, María Conchita Cadiz, Teresita Echázabal, Elena Wagner, Francisco Méndez-Diez. Before her death, I spoke at length to Ana Mendieta about her journey. Before her death, Raquel Mendieta Costa, who watched her cousins leave in Operation Pedro Pan, shared with me what it was like to stay—and grow up and raise her son—in Cuba.

It is the network created by Operation Pedro Pan Group, Inc., the Miami-based organization for now adult Pedro Pans, that has facilitated a more collective process of rethinking our past. The caring and the delicacy with which this group of Pedro Pans engage with one another has set new standards of tolerance and comprehension in the exile community.

Finally, this would be a very different book had it not been for Elly Chovel, who has insisted that we have the right to know our past, and that this process should be one of healing, not of recriminations.

Appendix A

CATHOLIC WELFARE BUREAU
DIOCESE OF MIAMI

FATHER BRYAN O. WALSH, S.T.L
EXECUTIVE DIRECTOR

REV. JOHN J. NEVINS
ASSISTANT DIRECTOR

REGIONAL OFFICES
MIAMI   FORT LAUDERDALE

595 N. W. FIRST STREET — SUITE 207
MIAMI 36, FLORIDA
FRANKLIN 9-2593

Fecha _____

A QUIEN PUEDA INTERESAR:

Se hace constar que:

a _____
_____

nacio _____

le ha sido concedida la "Visa Waiver" por el Departamento de
Estado a peticion del Catholic Welfare Bureau, Inc.

Pan American y K. L. M. Royal Dutch Airlines han sido noti-
ficadas. El solicitante debera dirigirse a dichas oficinas para
hacer la reservacion y comprar su pasaje.

_____
(Rev. Fr.) Bryan O. Walsh
Director

Fig. 6

Miami, **Noviembre 29, 1962**

Nos complacemos en informarle que el Departamento de
Estado y el Servicio de Inmigración y Naturalización
de los Estados Unidos de América, han aprobado la Visa Waiver solicitada por Usted en favor de:

NOMBRE: **FRANCISCO MANUEL FERNANDEZ VAZQUEZ**

FECHA DE NACIMIENTO: **Julio 24, 1943**

Usted deberá enviar al interesado constancia de ésta
comunicación por duplicado.
La aprobación antes mencionada será comunicada a las
empresas de aviación (PAA y KLM) en el compendio de
una semana.
Ha sido un placer el haberle podido servir de ésta
forma.

Muy atentamente,

Albert K. Trout, Jr.
Departamento de Visa Waiver

**WAIVER
GRANTED**
BY
DEPARTMENT OF STATE
AND
IMMIGRATION AND
NATURALIZATION SERVICE
Date NOV 2 9 1962 By

25

Adelaida B. Everhart
13140 S.W. 82nd Ave.
Miami, 56, Fla

Appendix B

The Pedro Pan Archives are the property of Catholic Charities, Inc., of the Archdiocese of Miami, Florida These papers, occupying 900 cubic feet, are housed at the Barry University Archives and Historical Collections, in Miami Shores. Processing and cataloging of the papers has begun. The Pedro Pan Archives include four types of materials:

1. Individual and/or family case records These are the social workers' case files maintained at the Miami office; they also include social workers' reports on foster care or group home placement elsewhere. These records are confidential and open only to the individual to whom they refer. They can be examined only with the written permission of the individual client. Of the 7200 case files, 1400 remain to be cataloged.

2. Financial records. These have not been processed yet and are not accessible for the time being. They are expected to yield valuable information on placements and may enable individuals to recall names of other Cuban children who were in care with them at a foster home or group care facility.

3. General information and correspondence. Not yet processed.

4. Staff personnel records. Not yet processed.

As funding is available, the statistical and demographic material from the case records will be collected and placed on a CD, so that it can be more readily available to academic researchers. It is hoped that this will be accomplished by 2004. Again, Catholic Charities, Inc., of Miami is bound to respect the confidentiality of the individual case files.

At present the Pedro Pan Archives are staffed by two Dominican sisters who volunteer on a part-time basis. Beginning July 1, 2002, a full time data entry person will be working to complete the case files, perfect the database, and burn the CD. Every effort is made to respond to individual requests, but resources are very limited. As funds become available and a fulltime professional archivist and specialized personnel are hired to staff the Pedro Pan Archives, accessibility will be greatly improved.

Inquiries regarding the Pedro Pan Archives should be addressed to
Sister Dorothy Jehle, OP
Barry University Archives and Special Collections
11300 NE Second Avenue
Miami Shores, Florida 33161-6695
djehle@mail.barry.edu
Telephone 305/899-3027

5/28/02

Notes

Prologue

1. "Señora Santana," an old Spanish nursery rhyme popular throughout Latin America.
2. A promotional card publicizing a Cuban government account of Operation Peter Pan says, "*Este libro es la historia de 14,000 Eliáncitos.*"
3. "Veinte Preguntas Sobre la Verdad de Cuba," written for el Frente Revolucionario Democrático, a CIA-financed umbrella group, 1960, National Archives, JFK Collection, CIA Segregated Files, RG 233, 95th Congress, Box 37, is a pamphlet that talks about how communism will take children's innocence from them.
4. Mark Silva, "Presidential Candidates Leap into Debate over Boy," *Miami Herald,* 11 December 1999.
5. Everett M. Ressler, Neil Boothby, and Daniels Steinbeck, *Unaccompanied Children: Care and Protection in Wars, Natural Disasters, and Refugee Movements* (New York: Oxford University Press, 1988).
6. Dorothy Legarreta, *The Guernica Generation: Basque Children of the Spanish Civil War* (Reno, Nev.: University of Nevada Press, 1984).
7. Olga Levy Drucker, *Kindertransport* (New York: Henry Holt and Company, 1992).
8. Michael Fethney, *The Absurd and the Brave: CORB—The True Account of the British Government's World War II Evacuation of the Children Overseas* (Sussex, Eng.: The Book Guild, 1990). Also Ruth Inglis, *The Children's War Evacuation* (London: Collins, 1989).
9. Ressler et al., *Unaccompanied Children*, pp. 40–55.

Introduction

1. Fidel Castro's movement is named for the date in which he began an armed struggle to topple Fulgencio Batista by assaulting Moncada military quarters in Santiago de Cuba on July 26, 1953.
2. Edwin Potter, "8,000 Kids Saved from Brainwashing," *Miami Herald,* 8 March 1962.
3. Interview with Noemi Booth, Havana, Cuba, 1993.
4. R. Hart Phillips, *The Cuban Dilemma* (New York: Ivan Oblensky, 1962), p.305.
5. Gene Miller, "Peter Pan Means Real Life to Some of the Kids," *Miami Herald,* 9 March 1962.
6. "Cuban Children Helped in Florida," *New York Times,* 27 May 1962.
7. Ann Yeoman, *Now or Neverland: Peter Pan and the Myth of Eternal Youth* (Toronto: Inner City Books, 1998).

8. J. M. Barrie, *Peter Pan: The Complete and Unabridged Text* (New York: Viking, 1991), p. 26.
9. Ibid., p. 171.
10. Speech, President George W. Bush, Tuesday, 17 September 2002, http://www.whitehouse.gov/news/releases/2002/09/20020917-7.a.ram.
11. This is clearly changing. In the fall of 2002, the popular *CSI Miami* television series had an episode featuring a Pedro Pan and Monsignor Walsh.
12. The parallels in the situation are haunting, although these children were being brought to the United States to be put up for adoption. Agency for International Development, "Operation Babylift," Washington, D.C.: United States Government Printing Office, April–June 1975.
13. *The Lost Apple*, director, David Susskind, Paramount, funded by USIA, 1963.

1. Children and the Destinies of Nations

1. Philippe Aries, *Centuries of Childhood: A Social History of Family Life* (New York: Alfred Knopf, 1962). Also see Lloyd deMause, ed., *The History of Childhood* (New York: The Psychohistory Press, 1974). Debates around Aries' work concerning the similarities or differences between families then and now do not necessarily change his observation that as a social category childhood is more distinguishable in the Renaissance. For a critique of the family relations aspect of Aries' work see Steven Ozment, *Ancestors: The Loving Family in Europe* (Cambridge: Harvard University Press, 2001).
2. Plato, *The Republic of Plato*, trans. Francis MacDonald Cornford (London: Oxford University Press, 1941).
3. Rose-Marie Frenzel, *Jugando: Un libro de arte para niños* (La Habana: Editorial Nueva Gente, 1977).
4. Aries, *Centuries of Childhood*, p. 345.
5. For an extensive study of this time period see Lawrence Stone, *The Family Sex and Marriage in England 1500–1800* (New York: Harper and Row, 1977).
6. Anne Higonnet, *Pictures of Innocence: The History and Crisis of Ideal Childhood* (New York: Thames and Hudson, 1998), p. 23.
7. Giovanni Levi and Jean-Claude Schmitt, *A History of Young People: Ancient and Medieval Rites of Passage*, vol. 1 (Cambridge: The Belknap Press of Harvard University Press, 1997).
8. Priscilla Robertson, "The Home as a Nest," in deMause, *The History of Childhood* 2 (Winter 1974).
9. Benedict Anderson, *Imagined Communities: Reflections on the Origin and Spread of Nationalism* (London: Verso Press, 1983).
10. Neil Postman, *The Disappearance of Childhood* (New York: Vintage Books, 1994).
11. Peter Gay, ed., *John Locke On Education* (New York: Columbia University, 1964), p. 4.

12. Jean Jacques Rousseau, *Emile*, trans. and ed. William Boyd (New York: Columbia University Press, 1956).
13. Immanuel Kant, *Education* (Ann Arbor: University of Michigan Press, 1960), p. 11.
14. Sigmund Freud, *Civilization and Its Discontents*, trans. and ed. James Strachey (New York: W. W. Norton, 1961).
15. Sigmund Freud and Albert Einstein, *Why War? Letters Commissioned by the League of Nations*, trans. and published by the Chicago Institute for Psychoanalysis, 1978.
16. Leon Berstein, *Jefferson's Children: Education and the Promise of American Culture* (New York: Doubleday, 1997), p. 77.
17. Jodi Campbell, "Benjamin Rush and Women's Education: A Revolutionary's Disappointment, A Nation's Achievement," *John and Mary's Journal* 13 (2000).
18. "Thoughts Upon the Mode of Education Proper in a Republic, by Dr. Benjamin Rush, From A Plan for the Establishment of Public Schools and the Diffusion of Knowledge in Pennsylvania; to Which Are Added, Thoughts upon the Mode of Education Proper in a Republic. Addressed to the Legislature and Citizens of the State." Philadelphia: Thomas Dobson, 1786. In *Essays on Education in the Early Republic*, ed. Frederick Rudolph (Cambridge: The Belknap Press of Harvard University Press, 1965), pp. 9–23.
19. James Block, *A Nation of Agents: The American Path to a Modern Self and Society* (Cambridge: The Belknap Press of Harvard University Press, 2002); Richmond Mayo-Smith, "Assimilation of Nationalities in the United States," *Political Science Quarterly* 9 (December 1894), 649–70.
20. Horace Mann, *On the Crisis in Education*, ed. Louis Filler (Yellow Springs, Ohio: Antioch Press, 1965), p. 87.
21. Ibid.
22. John Dewey, *Democracy and Education: An Introduction to the Philosophy of Education* (New York: Macmillan Company, 1916).
23. Alan Ryan, "Pragmatism, Social Identity, Patriotism, and Self-Criticism," *Social Research* 63 (Winter 1996): 1041–53.
24. Jean Piaget, *The Moral Judgement of the Child* (London: Routledge Kegan Paul Ltd., 1932).
25. Paula Fass, *Outside In: Minorities and the Transformation of American Education* (New York: Oxford University Press, 1989).
26. The characterization appeared not only in reports and news stories but popular literature as well. See Lori Askeland, "The Means of Draining the City of These Children: Domesticity and the Romantic Individualism in Charles Loring Brace's Emigration Plan, 1853–1861," in *American Transcendental Quarterly* (June 1998): 145–62.
27. See Stephen O'Connor, *Orphan Trains: The Story of Charles Loring Brace and the Children He Saved and Failed* (New York: Houghton Mifflin, 2001); Marilyn Irvin Holt, *The Orphan Trains: Placing Out in America* (Lincoln, Neb.: University of

Nebraska Press, 1992); Donald Dale Jackson, "For City Waifs, A Bittersweet Trip," *Smithsonian* 17 (August 1986): 94–103.

28. For a more positive account of the program see Kristine E. Nelson, "Child Placing in the Nineteenth Century: New York and Iowa," *Social Service Review* 59 (March 1985): 107–20.

29. Bruce Billingham, "The Unspeakable Blessing: Street Children, Reform, Rhetoric, and Misery in Early Industrial Capitalism," *Politics and Society* 12 (1983): 303.

30. Clay Gish, "Rescuing the Waifs and Strays of the City: The Western Emigration Program of the Children's Aid Society," *Journal of Social History* 33 (Fall 1999): 137.

31. Billingham, "The Unspeakable Blessing," p. 305.

32. David Wallace Adams, *Education for Extinction: American Indians and the Boarding School Experience, 1875–1928* (Kansas City: University of Kansas Press, 1995), p. 18.

33. Ibid.

34. Philip Shenon, "Aborigines are Suing for Stolen Childhoods," *New York Times*, 20 July 1995; Clyde Fransworth, "Australians Resist Facing up to Legacy of Parting Aborigines from Families," *New York Times*, 8 June 1997.

35. Clyde Ellis, *To Change Them Forever: Indian Education at the Rainy Mountain Boarding School, 1893–1920* (Norman, Okla.: University of Oklahoma Press, 1996).

36. Brookings Institute report of 1928 quoted in *Wub-E-Ke-Niew, We Have the Right to Exist* (New York: Black Thistle Press, 1995), p. 113.

37. See John Higham, *Strangers in the Land: Patterns of American Nativism* (New Brunswick, N.J.: Rutgers University Press, 1955).

38. Frank V. Thompson, *Schooling of the Immigrant,* vol. 1 in *Americanization Studies: The Acculturation of Immigrant Groups into American Society,* ed. William Bernard (Montclair, N.J.: Patterson Smith, 1971).

39. Michael Kirshner, "Progressivism and Americanization: The Education of Adult Immigrants, 1911–1920," master's thesis, Northern Illinois University, 1987.

40. Thompson, *Schooling of the Immigrant,* p. 383.

41. Paula Fass traces the federal government's interest in educating African-American children in chap. 4, *Outside In,* pp. 115–55.

42. Azza Layton, *International Politics and Civil Rights Policies in the United States, 1941–1960* (New York: Cambridge University Press, 2000).

43. Dorothy Legarreta, *The Guernica Generation: Basque Refugee Children of the Spanish Civil War* (Reno, Nev.: University of Nevada Press, 1984).

44. Mark Jonathan Harris and Deborah Oppenheimer, *Into the Arms of Strangers: Stories of the Kindertransport* (New York: Bloomsbury Publishing, 2000); and Olga Levy Drucker, *Kindertransport* (New York: Henry Holt, 1992).

45. See Patricia Y. Lin, "National Identity and Social Mobility: Class, Empire, and the British Government Overseas Evacuation of Children During the Second War," in *Twentieth Century British History* 7 (1996): 310–44.

46. See Nicolas Gage, *Eleni* (New York: Ballantine Books, 1983).

47. Anna Freud and Dorothy Burlingham, *War and Children* (New York: Medical War Books, 1943).

48. William M. Tuttle Jr., *Daddy's Gone to War: The Second World War in the Lives of America's Children* (New York: Oxford University Press, 1993).

49. Ibid., pp. 12–13.

50. The September 1943 issue of *Annals of the American Academy of Political and Social Sciences* 229 is dedicated to studying "The American Family in World War II."

51. Laura Malvano, "The Myth of Youth in Images: Italian Fascism," in *A History of Young People: Stormy Evolution to Modern Times*, ed. Giovanni Levi and Jean-Claude Schmitt (Cambridge: The Belknap Press of Harvard University Press, 1997), pp. 232–80.

52. Eric Michaud, "Soldiers of an Idea: Young People Under the Third Reich," in Levi and Schmitt, *A History of Young People*, p. 257.

53. Robert Coles, *Children in Crisis* (Boston: Little, Brown, 1967), p. 325.

54. Fred Greenstein, *Children and Politics* (New Haven: Yale University Press, 1969), p. 4.

55. Tuttle, *Daddy's Gone to War*, pp. 122–27.

56. Quoted in ibid., p. 111.

57. Erik Erikson, *Childhood and Society* (New York: W. W. Norton, 1950), p. 16.

58. See the work of Fred Greenstein, *Children and Politics* (New Haven: Yale University Press, 1965); Robert Hess and Judith Torney, *The Development of Political Attitudes in Children* (New York: Anchor Books, 1968). And from a more psychoanalytical perspective, Eric Erikson, *Identity, Youth and Crisis* (New York: W. W. Norton, 1968).

59. Karl Marx, *The Early Economic and Philosophical Manuscripts, 1844* (Moscow: Progress Publishers, 1974).

60. See the work of Andrew Baruch Wachtel, *The Battle for Childhood: The Creation of a Russian Myth* (Palo Alto, Calif.: Stanford University Press, 1990).

61. Margaret Mead and Elena Calas, "Child-Training Ideals in a Post-Revolutionary Context: Soviet Russia," in *Childhood in Contemporary Cultures*, ed. Margaret Mead and Martha Wolfenstein (Chicago: University of Chicago Press, 1955), pp. 179–204.

62. V. I. Lenin, *On Youth* (Moscow: Novosti Press Agency Publishing House, 1969), p. 21.

63. Ibid., p. 41.

64. Ibid., p. 8.

65. Stuart R. Schram, ed., *The Political Thought of Mao Tse Tung* (New York: Prager Publishers, 1963), p. 337.

66. Sergio Luzzatto, "Young Rebels and Revolutionaries, 1789–1917," in Levi and Schmitt, pp. 174–231.

67. The idea that children could be detached from previous generations went contrary to the notion of the succession of generations. L. Moskvichov, *La sociedad y la sucesión de las generaciones* (Moscow: Editorial Progreso, 1979).

68. Robert Graham, S.J., *The Vatican and Communism During World War II: What Really Happened?* (San Francisco: Ignatius Press, 1996).

69. For a contextualization of the doctrine during World War II, see Pedro Ramet, ed., *Catholicism and Politics in Communist Societies* (Durham, N.C.: Duke University Press, 1990), p. 11.

70. Encyclical Letter of Pope Pius XI, "Atheistic Communism: Divini Redemptoris" (New York: The Paulist Press, 1937), p. 7.

71. Quoted in Anthony Rhodes, *The Vatican in the Age of the Cold War* (London: Michael Russell Publishing, 1992), p. 28.

72. Ibid., p. 30.

73. Alan W. Scheflin and Edward M. Opton Jr., *The Mind Manipulators* (Essex, England: Paddington Press, 1978), p. 219. This text discusses the origins of mind-control experiments.

74. Although many of the documents about the program were destroyed, some were eventually turned over to a Senate committee chaired by Senator Church.

75. Peter Grose, *A Gentleman Spy: The Life of Allen Dulles* (New York: Houghton Mifflin, 1994), p. 392.

76. Scheflin and Opton, *The Mind Manipulators*, p. 226.

77. Office of the Superintendent of Public Instruction, "Education for a Free World: Combating Communism Thorough Study of American Ideals in Our Public Schools" (Washington, D.C., 1962).

78. Report of the President's Committee on National Goals, *Goals for Americans* (New York: Columbia University Press, 1960).

79. For an understanding of the role of the Vatican, see Francis X. Murphy, "Vatican Politics: Structure and Function," *World Politics* 26 (July 1974): 542–59.

80. See Kathleen Gefell Centola, "The American Catholic Church and Anti-Communism, 1940–1960: An Interpretive Framework and Case Studies," dissertation presented to the State University of New York at Albany, 1984.

81. See Charles Loring Brace, *The Dangerous Classes of New York and Twenty Years' Work Among Them* (New York, 1872, reprinted, Washington, D.C.: National Association of Social Workers, 1973); and Marilyn Holt, *The Orphan Trains: Placing Out in America* (Lincoln, Neb.: University of Nebraska Press, 1992).

82. The Partido Socialista Popular (Cuban Communist Party) enjoyed a relatively privileged position during most of Batista's tenure. Several Batista cabinet members were open members of the Party, as was Luis Wangüemert, a political analyst whose commentaries were broadcast nightly. The Communists controlled major unions. And since the Party did not support the revolutionary process, calling it a "putschist" effort on the part of middle-class rebels, it did not suffer severe repression at the hands of the military.

83. José Martí, *La Edad de Oro* (Miami: Ediciones Universales, Sexta Edicion, 1988), p. 12.

84. José Martí, *On Education: Articles on Educational Theory and Pedagogy, and Writings from the Golden Age*, ed. Philip Foner (New York: Monthly Review Press, 1979), p. 34.

85. Ibid., p. 35.

86. Ibid., p. 93.

87. 26 of July Movement pamphlet entitled *"Qué es la Revolución?"* included in a Foreign Service Despatch, 27 October 1960. National Archives, Department of State, 737.00/10–2760.

88. Fidel Castro's 1953 *History Will Absolve Me*, published in English in New York by Center for Cuban Studies, p. 31.

89. Constitución de la República de Cuba, 1940, in Leonel-Antonio de la Cuesta, ed., *Constituciones Cubanas desde 1812 hasta nuestros días* (New York: Ediciones Exilio, 1974).

90. Jaime Suchlicki, *University Students and Revolution in Cuba 1920–1968* (Coral Gables, Fla.: University of Miami Press, 1969), pp. 70–75.

91. Gerald Poyo, "Catholics and the Revolution," paper presented at Notre Dame University Conference on Cuban Catholicism, the Island and the Diaspora, Spring 2002.

92. La Voz de la Iglesia en Cuba, *100 Documentos Episcopales* (México: Obra Nacional de la Buena Prensa, 1995), pp. 26–31.

93. Ibid., p. 28.

94. Manuel Maza, "The Cuban Catholic Church: True Struggles and False Dilemmas," master's thesis, Georgetown University, Washington, D.C., 1982, p. 79.

95. John Kirk, *Between God and the Party: Religion and Politics and Revolutionary Cuba* (Tampa, Fla.: University of South Florida Press, 1989), p. 65.

96. Richard Fagen, *The Transformation of Political Culture in Cuba* (Stanford, Calif.: Stanford University Press, 1969), p. 12.

97. See for instance Karen Wald, *Children of Ché: Childcare and Education in Cuba* (Palo Alto, Calif.: Ramparts Press, 1978) and Marvin Leiner, *Children are the Revolution* (New York: Viking Press, 1974).

98. Juan Marinello, ed., "La educación en la revolución," in *Fidel Castro on Education* (La Habana, Cuba: Instituto Cubano del Libro, 1974), p. 110.

99. Julie Marie Bunck, "Castro and the Children: The Struggle for Cuba's 'Virgin Minds,'" paper delivered at the 1987 Annual Meeting of the American Political Science Association, September 3–6, 1987.

100. Ibid., p. 30.

101. For an extensive discussion on labor unions, see Marifeli Pérez-Stable, *The Cuban Revolution: Origins, Course and Legacy* (New York: Oxford University Press, 1993), pp. 127–30.

102. Martin Carnoy and Joel Samoff, *Education and Social Transition in the Third World* (Princeton, N.J.: Princeton University Press, 1990), pp. 58–61.

103. Secretary of State Christian Herter, telegram sent to U.S. embassy in Havana, 9 October 1959. National Archives, State Department Files, Embassy Cables, 1959.

104. For an extensive biography of the director see Peter Grose, *Gentleman Spy: The Life of Allen Dulles* (Boston: Houghton Mifflin, 1994).

105. National Archives, Foreign Service Despatch #10, Amembassy Habana, 21 July 1959, Department of State Records.

106. *U.S. News and World Report*, 21 March 1960.
107. *New York Times*, 8 June 1960.
108. *Acción Cubana*, ed.-dir. Rocaner, 31 December 1959.
109. See Leslie Dewart, *Christianity and Revolution: The Lesson of Cuba* (New York: Herder and Herder, 1963), pp. 143–46.
110. In a memo to the pope dated December 19, 1963, Artime describes himself as a Marian member of the Catholic University Group of Havana and former president of the student section from 1952 to 1958. Obtained from the National Archives, JFK Assassination Collection, Document ID, 1994.03.07.11:20:04:400007, Originator Agency, CIA. However, in an interview quoted in Judy Artime's thesis he Artime is identified as the president of ACU. Judy Artime, "'The Golden Boy': Dr. Manuel Francisco Artime Buesa," master's thesis, Columbia University, 1996, p. 8.
111. Haynes Johnson, *The Bay of Pigs: The Leaders Story of Brigade 2506* (New York: W. W. Norton, 1964), p. 24.
112. Justo Carillo, *A Cuba le Tocó lo Peor* (Miami, Fla.: Universal, 1993).
113. Artime, "'The Golden Boy,'" p. ii.
114. State Department, Joint Statement State/USIA Guidance on "United State Information Policy Toward the Castro Regime in Cuba," 15 September 1959, National Archives, State Department Embassy Files, 1959.
115. CIA document, "A Program of Covert Action Against the Castro Regime," 16 March 1960.
116. National Archives, JFK Assassination Files, CIA Files, Cuban Exile Organizations, Box 64, R2–B.
117. National Archives, JFK Assassination Files, document 1993.07.31.10.23:20:250028, Box 14, Vol. File 11, 14 April 1961.
118. Eugenio Rolland Martínez would later become one of the infamous Watergate burglars. Artime, "'The Golden Boy,'" p. 22.
119. Ibid., p. 20.
120. Ibid., p. 36.
121. CIA memo, date and topic deleted, but archived in JFK assassination records, Rush R 95th Congress, Record Group Number 233, Box 37, Segregated CIA Collection.
122. Foreign Service Despatch. From: American Consulate, Santiago de Cuba, Consulate Despatch 78, 8 March 1960. National Archives, Department of State, Country Files, Cuba, 737.00/3–860.
123. Johnson, *Bay of Pigs*, p. 29.
124. Foreign Service Despatch. From: AmEmbassy, San José. To: The Department of State, Washington. Desp. No. 64. June 9, 1960. Subject: Platform of Movimiento de Recuperación Revolucionaria. Reporter: AACohen:mmh. It was signed by Dr. Manuel Artime Buesa, Major Ricardo Lorie Valls, Major Antonio Michel Yabor, and Major Higinio Díaz. Martha Hayward, trans.
125. Peter Kornbluh, *Bay of Pigs Declassified* (New York: New Press, 1998), p. 108.
126. Included in a Foreign Service Despatch, 9 April 1960, from Santiago de Chile, #740.

127. Veinte Preguntas Sobre la Verdad de Cuba, Frente Revolucionario Democrático, CIA-financed umbrella group, 1960, National Archives, JFK Collection, CIA Segregated Files, RG 233, 95th Congress, Box 37, p. 14.

2. The Military Origins of Operation Pedro Pan

1. Letter sent to author by James Baker, 25 May 1998.
2. Morris H. Morley, "The U.S. Imperial State in Cuba, 1952–1958: Policymaking and Capitalist Interests," *Journal of Latin American Studies* 14 (May 1982):143–70. Morley argues that these were the determining factors in the U.S. posture of support toward the Batista regime. Others have argued that strategic Cold War politics dictated these policies. In reality, it was probably a combination of factors, for they are not necessarily contradictory.
3. Taped interview of James Baker, former head of Ruston Academy, May 1998.
4. Baker could not recall the name of the person (or he was not authorized to reveal his name), but he remembers the encounter. Baker told me different accounts of this meeting, in one he said it was one son and in another two sons.
5. Baker interview, 1998.
6. Interview of Natividad Revueltas, Havana, Cuba, January 1991.
7. Paul Bethel, *The Losers* (New Rochelle, N.Y.: Arlington House, 1969), p. 56.
8. Arensberg would become the executive director of a CIA-backed Washington anti-Castro organization called Cuban Freedom Committee
9. Jack Anderson, "Soldiers of Fortune," *Parade*, 12 June 1960.
10. Taped interview, Gerry Patrick Hemming, Florida, May 1998.
11. "Try to Message: Return from Hills," *Times of Havana*, 11 March 1957.
12. "Parents Surprised By Boys' Return," *Times of Havana*, 13 May 1957.
13. Cushing hid Rufo López Fresquet who became a minister in the first cabinet. Bethel, *The Losers*, pp. 58–59.
14. Official Report of the Department of State, CMA/C Division. John F. Kennedy Presidential Library, Arthur Schlesinger Jr. Papers, White House Papers, Box 5.
15. Earl Smith, *El Cuarto Piso: Relato sobre la revolución comunista de Castro* (Santo Domingo: Editora Corripio, 1983).
16. *Columns*, Ruston Academy Yearbook, 1959.
17. Letter from James Baker to Senator Wayne Morse, 27 March 1959 sent to Roy R. Rubottom, assistant secretary of state by U.S. ambassador to Cuba Philip Bonsal, National Archives, State Department, Embassy Files, 350–Cuba, 1959.
18. Official Report of the Department of State, August 1960, "Responsibility of Cuban Government for Increased International Tensions in the Hemisphere." John F. Kennedy Presidential Library, POPK, National Security Council Files, Presidential Office Papers, Box 35.
19. Ibid., p. 13.
20. Foreign Service Despatch from American Embassy, Department of State, Desp. #1230, 6 December 1960. Reported by William Bowdler.

21. Ibid., p. 2.

22. *Columns*, Ruston Academy Yearbook, 1959.

23. Bethel, *The Losers*, p. 56.

24. Letter from Clarence Moore to Hon. Abraham Ribicoff, Secretary of the Department of Health, Education and Welfare, 1 February 1961. National Archives, Department of State files, 837.05100.

25. Bowdler, Desp. #1230, 1960.

26. CIA memo F. M. Hand, 19 March 1956, National Archives, JFK Assassination Files, Record Group 233, Box 40, Leo Cherne Files, also see Robert Scheer, "Leo Cherne, Our Man with the CIA," *New Times*, 19 March 1976, p. 16.

27. Eric Thomas Chester, *Covert Network: Progressives, the International Rescue Committee and the CIA* (New York: M. E. Sharpe, 1995), p. 184.

28. Congressional Hearings on Migration and Refugee Assistance held by House of Representatives, Subcommittee of the Committee of the Judiciary, 3 August 1961.

29. Christopher Simpson, *Blowback: America's Recruitment of Nazis and Its Effects on the Cold War* (New York: Weidenfeld and Nicolson, 1988), pp. 202–3.

30. Department of State, Incoming Telegram, classified secret and declassified, No. 1726, 13 October 1960, State Department Public Affairs Library.

31. Letter from Thomas Mann, Assistant Secretary of State, acknowledging receipt of letter from Bonsal on the Miró Cardona matter, 18 October 1960.

32. Department of State Memorandum, No. 2540, 19 December 1960, p. 89.

33. Outgoing Telegram, Department of State, 21 October 1960, National Archives, State Department Records, 737.00/10–21–60.

34. Notes of June Cobb, 7 June 1960, National Archives, John F. Kennedy Assassination Files, CIA Record Group 233, Box 14, Folder F.

35. Department of State, Memorandum of Conversation, 29 November 1960, p. 2. Edwin Vallon, Robert Stevenson, Robert Hurwitch, and Frank Devine from the State Department were at the meeting. The names of the Cuban participants were classified, although they were identified as members of the Frente Democrático Revolucionario.

36. Ibid., p. 2.

36. State Department Freedom of Information Public Library, Memorandum of Conversation, 23 March 1960.

37. Ibid.

38. State Department Freedom of Information Public Office, Foreign Service Despatch #100, 21 April 1960.

39. Department of State, Memorandum of Conversation, 1 November 1960, reported by John Hanes Jr., National Archives, State Department, Country Cuba, 737.00/11–60.

40. Ruby Hart Philips, *The Cuban Dilemma* (New York: Oblensky, Inc., 1960), p. 269.

41. Philip W. Bonsal, *Cuba, Castro and the United States* (Pittsburgh: University of Pittsburgh Press, 1971), p. 116.

42. Ibid., p. 142.

43. The *Miami Herald* ran a series about the plight of the refugees at the end of November 1960 to underscore the point.

44. Memorandum of Conversation, Department of State, 23 November 1960. Harvey Pike and Robert Stevenson, CMA, National Archives, Department of State. 737.00 11–2360xr 911.7237.

45. Letter from William Macomber, Department of State, to Senator Keating, 2 December 1960, National Archives, Department of State, 737.001/11–2160 CS/RA.

46. For an extensive account of this period, see Félix Masud-Piloto, *With Open Arms: Cuban Migration to the United States* (Lanham, Md.: Rowman and Littlefield, 1988).

47. Taped interview with Maria Teresa Cuervo, 1 March 1993.

48. Document from the Department of the Navy received from a Freedom of Information Act request, entitled "Security Implications of the Influx of Cuban Refugees," n.d..

49. Written communication from Gerry Patrick Hemming to Dana Sukenik, lawyer for *Torres vs. CIA,* February 1988.

50. Andrew Wixson, "Portrait of a Cuban Refugee," *Studies in Intelligence* (Summer 1964): 41.

51. Joint report of James Hennessey, INS, Al McDermitt, Department of Labor, John Hurley, "Cuban Refugee Situation in Dade County." Miami, Florida, 8 November 1960. Eisenhower Presidential Library, Confidential Files, Box 42, Subject Series, Mutual Security Assistance, 1960–1963.

52. Letter from Joe Hall to Tracy Voorhees, 26 November 1960. Eisenhower Presidential Library, Confidential Files, Cuba, National Security, 1960–1963, Box 42.

53. Report from John J. Fitzpatrick to Tracy Voorhees, 22 November 1960, Eisenhower Presidential Library, Confidential Files, Cuba, National Security, 1960–1963, Box 42.

54. Report of the Welfare Planning Council, 22 November 1960, written by T. E. Winterstee, Secretary for the Cuban Refugee Committee, to Tracy Voorhees, Eisenhower Presidential Library, Confidential Files, Cuba, National Security, 1960–1963, Box 42.

55. Eisenhower Presidential Library, Confidential Files, Subject Series Mutual Security Act, Box 42, 1960–1963, 22 November 1960.

56. Memorandum for the President, Douglas Dillon, Acting Secretary of State, 1 December 1960, Eisenhower Presidential Library, Confidential Files Box 42, Mutual Security and Assistance.

57. A memo to Arnold from Martin Gula, 19 December 1960, indexed in the Children's Bureau Files, National Archives, 0-2-0-7-1 (2), 0-1-5-1-8.

58. Memorandum from Secretary of State to the U.S. embassy in Havana recalling the ambassador. Lyndon B. Johnson Presidential Library, National Security Files, Gordon Chase Papers, Box 5, #11, dated 17 October 1960. In the fall of 1960, Ambassador Bonsal had been recalled to the United States and Daniel Braddock was the chargé d'affaires.

59. John Hanes Jr. Papers, 1950–1970, Box 6, File Republican National Convention, 1960, Eisenhower Presidential Library.

60. Reference to this trip is found in Aaron Levenstein, *Escape to Freedom: The Story of the International Rescue Committee* (Westport, Conn.: Greenwood Press, 1983), p. 101. Also Eric Thomas, *Covert Network: Progressives, the International Rescue Committee, and the CIA* (Armonk, N.Y.: M. E. Sharpe, 1995), p. 185.

61. Chester, *Covert Network*, pp. 186–87.

62. *Columns*, Ruston Academy Yearbook, 1959.

3. The Plan to Save the Children from Communism

1. Lynn Geldof, *Cubans: Voices of Change* (New York: St. Martin's, 1991), pp. 225–38.

2. Bryan O. Walsh, "Cuban Refugee Children," *Journal of Inter-American Studies and World Affairs* 13 (July–October 1971): 388.

3. Taped interview, Monsignor Bryan Walsh, 25 June 1992. Also see John Hubbell, "Operation Pedro Pan," *Readers Digest*, February 1988, pp. 99–102. And Marjorie Fillyaw, "Cuba's Child Refugees," *Ave Maria*, April 1962, pp. 20–25.

4. Walsh, "Cuban Refugee Children," p. 387.

5. Ibid., p. 388.

6. Ibid., p. 390.

7. The uniqueness of the administrative mechanisms are described in Michael McNally's *Catholicism in South Florida, 1868–1968* (Gainesville, Fla.: University of Florida Press, 1984), pp. 147–49.

8. Baker Memo to P. Bonsal, 1961. There had been a lively debate over whether the State Department should be involved in caring for the refugees.

9. "Villanueva," *Bohemia*, November 1960.

10. Telephone interview with Alicia Oyarzun Peláez, November 2002.

11. Central Intelligence Agency, Telegram, date excised but references Cuban events of the summer of 1960, National Archives, John F. Kennedy Assassination Files, Record Group, 233, Rush R, 95th Congress, Box 37, Segregated CIA Files.

12. Taped interview with James Baker, May 1998.

13. Received from the FBI in a Freedom of Information request, Outgoing Telegram dated July 22, 1961, to All Diplomatic Missions in the American Republics.

14. Walsh, "Cuban Refugee Children," p. 391.

15. U.S. Memorandum, from C. P. Torrey, of the CMA/C Division of the State Department to Ambassador Bonsal, Feb. 7, 1961, National Archives, Children's Bureau, the visa was issued on the basis of Form I-20 issued by the Dade County schools.

16. Walsh, "Cuban Refugee Children," p. 394.

17. Taped interview with Gerry Patrick Hemming, January 1998.

18. Father Walsh asked me repeatedly how much I learned about what Cubans knew of the operation.

19. Telegram from Secretary of State Christian Herter to Ambassador Philip Bonsal, 17

October 1960. Lyndon Johnson Presidential Library, National Security Files, Gordon Chase, Cuba Background Material, Box 35, No. 11.

20. Intelligence Report No. 8385, "The Situation in Cuba." Bureau of Intelligence and Research, Department of State, 27 December 1960, U.S. State Public Affairs Library.

21. After James Baker left Cuba, he went to work in Miami. For a period of time, he helped with the transportation of children from the airport to the camps. For one summer, he also became the recipient of messages from his committee. He was filling in for Julio Ulloa, a friend who worked for the CIA and was the regular "mailbox" but was off doing something else.

22. National Security Council Minutes, 7 July 1960. Washington, D.C.: Foreign Relations of the United States, 1958–1960, Volume VI, Cuba, p. 990.

23. Dispatch from U.S. embassy in Cuba to the Department of State, Havana, 16 December 1960, p. 1180. Washington, D.C.: Foreign Relations of the United States, 1958–1960, Vol. VI, Cuba, p. 1182.

24. Upon my return, I mentioned to Elly Chovel that Penny Powers was in a very old and cumbersome wheelchair, and she organized a donation drive among Pedro Pans to buy a new one and ship it to Cuba.

25. Abba P. Schwartz, The Open Society (New York: William Morrow and Co., 1968), p. 177.

26. Taped interview, Penny Powers, Havana, Cuba, June 1993.

27. Schwartz, The Open Society, p. 112.

28. Memorandum for Mr. McGeorge Bundy, 30 August 1963. Tab A, "Cuban Visa Program," John F. Kennedy Presidential Library, NSFPPD, Box. 39–40.

29. Instructions to William Finan, Assistant Director for Management and Organization, Bureau of the Budget, 23 January 1959, Eisenhower Presidential Library, Robert K. Gray Records, Box 2.

30. Taped personal interview, Alan Moreland, director, Department of State Visa Office 1962–1965. August 1993, Washington, D.C.

31. Walsh, "Cuban Refugee Children," p. 400. Walsh states that he and Baker called Washington. In a taped interview, however, Walsh said that they had received a call from the State Department.

32. Ibid., p. 401.

33. Phone interview, Robert Hale, former visa officer in the State Department, May 1992. He subsequently told me he could not recall anything about the children.

34. Taped personal interview, Monsignor Bryan Walsh, Miami, Florida, May 1998

35. Taped personal interview, Monsignor Bryan Walsh, Miami, Florida, June 1992.

36. Incoming Telegram from U.S. embassy in Kingston, Jamaica, 20 January 1961, received from the FBI under Freedom of Information Act, topic Cuban refugees.

37. Ambassador Philip Bonsal letter to Robert Stevenson, 20 February 1961. National Archives, State Department Records, Group 59, 737.00/2–2061.

38. For instance, Adelaida Everhart gave me a copy of a visa waiver that had been

issued to Francisco Manuel Fernández Vázquez, nineteen years old on November 29, 1962. It was written in Spanish and signed by Albert Trout Jr., Department of Visa Waiver.

39. James Baker memo to Philip Bonsal, received 7 February 1961, National Archives, Department of State, Cuba Country Files, 1961.

40. Ibid.

41. Ibid.

42. Ibid.

43. Ibid.

44. Memo from J. Edgar Hoover to Messrs. Tolson, Parsons, Belmont, and DeLoach, 27 January 1961, received through a Freedom of Information Act, FBI, March 2000.

45. Annex B, Revised Cuban Refugee Program, 29 April 1961, Department of Health Education and Welfare, in John F. Kennedy Presidential Library, Ted Sorensen Papers, Classified Subject Files: 1961–1964: Cuba General 5/0/61/5/24/61, Box 48.

46. National Archives, Children's Bureau Files, March 23, 1961, 0-2-0-7-1.

47. Geldof, Cubans: Voices of Change, p. 235.

48. Herbert Matthews, The Cuban Story (New York: George Braziller, 1961), p. 22.

49. Taped interview with Adelaide Everhart, May 1998.

50. Ibid.

51. Interview, Monsignor Carlos Manuel de Céspedes, Havana, Cuba, March 1992. In Cuba, church priests and nuns were key to the identification of children who could participate in the program. They turned children's names in to key contacts and occasionally distributed the visa waivers. After commercial flights to Cuba were stopped in 1962, the church continued to play a part in sending children out of the country, but instead of flying them to the United States they traveled to Spain. Monsignor Manuel de Céspedes helped to send children to Spain. In order to receive a Spanish visa, a letter from the parish priest was needed.

52. Memo from H. R. Wellman of the U.S. embassy in Cuba to Robert Stevenson, Visa Section, State Department, September 1960, 350 Cuba Files.

53. Taped interview with María Teresa Cuervo Miami, Florida, November 1992 and March 1993.

54. Report of the Department of State, CMA/C Division. John F. Kennedy Presidential Library, White House Arthur Schlesinger Jr. Papers, Box 5. The U.S. embassy described his death in the following manner:

> On the evening of the attack on the Revolutionary Palace (March 1957) the body of Dr. Pelayo Cuervo, the popular leader of the Ortodoxo Party, was found badly mutilated in a fashionable Habana suburb. There were definite indications that Batista police had murdered him, probably as a result of a petition he had sent to the United Nations condemning the Batista regime. Dr. Pelayo Cuervo's death came as a severe shock to the Cuban citizenry and the opposition demanded a full-scale investigation.

55. Taped interview with Margarita Castro (Oteiza), Miami, Florida, March 1993.

56. Sara's daughter, Silvia, would be a key witness in the Kennedy assassination investigation, see Noel Tyman, *Bloody Treason* (Menlo Park, Calif.: Laurel Publishing, 1997), pp. 322–27.

57. Taped interview with Jim Baker, May 1998.

58. Phone interview with Manolo Ray, March 1993.

59. To Oscar Guerra from G. W. Phillips, Department of State Reference slip, July 20, 1961. Declassified documents acquired by the Department of State Public Library. Department of State, Memorandum of Conversation, 21 June 1961.

60. Taped interview with Wendell Rollason, June 1993.

61. Letter to Dr. Manuel Antonio de Varona from Robert Hurwitch, Officer in Charge of Cuban Affairs from the Department of State, 9 August 1961. Obtained from the Department of State Public Information Library. Rollason replaced Dr. Carlos Piad, the Washington representative of the Cuban Revolutionary Council, who was resigning. Reported conversations between Piad and Robert Hurwitch, head of the Cuba desk for the State Department's Caribbean and Mexican Affairs Office, revealed that Piad resigned because a day earlier, Jose Miró Cardona, (who had become the coordinator of the council) had complained about mismanagement of the visa waiver program. In a letter to Antonio de Varona, head of Rescate, an underground organization, Hurwitch urged: "We would prefer that all matters regarding visa waivers of interest to the Council be forwarded to this office by one person in order to administer the Council's requests most efficiently." Varona appointed Rollason.

62. Taped interview with Evora Arca, Miami, June 1993.

63. Letter from José Mandado to Frank Watterson, postmarked March 14, 1962. Follow-up memo to Wendell Rollason from Frank Watterson asking for whatever action he felt needed to be taken, 20 March 1962.

64. Telephone interview with Robert Hale, May 1992.

65. Correspondence regarding an application for visa waivers for Petra M. García García, signed by Hugh Whitaker, Acting Chief, Public Inquiries Branch, Visa Office, Department of State.

4. Children and the Bay of Pigs Offensive

1. Interview with Father Bryan Walsh, June 1994.

2. Howard Hunt, *Give Us This Day* (New Rochelle, N.Y.: Arlington House, 1973), p. 26. Phillips would also resurface in the investigation into Kennedy's assassination; see, for instance, Gaeton Fonzi, *The Last Investigation* (New York: Thunder's Mouth Press, 1993).

3. Taylor Committee Report, 1 May 1961, National Archives, John F. Kennedy Assassination Files.

4. Although the specifics of the propaganda plans have not been declassified Hunt discusses these themes in his book; see, for instance, Taylor Committee Report interview with David Atlee Phillips, 1 May 1961.

5. Gaeton Fonzi, *The Last Investigation* (New York: Thunder's Mouth Press, 1994), p. 129.

6. Quoted in Margaret Power's Ph.D. dissertation, "Right Wing Women in Chilean Politics: 1964–1973," University of Illinois at Chicago, 1996, p. 58.

7. In Latin the concept is *patria potestas*. But in Spanish-speaking countries it is referred to as *patria potestad*. This is what is used in documents of this time period.

8. Lee Strickland, CIA information officer, refused to answer questions about Radio Swan during a deposition we were allowed to conduct as a result of my lawsuit. A year later the CIA released documents pertaining to the Taylor Report. These documents indicate that Radio Swan was a CIA project, and that Dave Atlee Philips was in charge of it. Propaganda Plans for the Bay of Pigs Invasion, portions of Taylor Report excised, released to the National Security Archives, Washington, D.C.

9. Quoted in Juan Carlos Rodríguez, *The Bay of Pigs and the CIA* (Melbourne, Australia: Ocean Press, 1999), p. 55.

10. Ibid., p. 56.

11. Reported in Warren Miller, *90 Miles from Home* (Greenwich, Conn.: Crest Book, 1961), p. 18.

12. Ibid.

13. Document #65: Memorandum of Conversation. Date: 29 July 1960. Participants: Manuel López de Quintana Sartorio; Harry M. Lofton, American consul; Donald R. Neuman, vice consul. Subject: Views of Cuban citizens on Cuba and political problems in Caribbean area. Dept. of State, Public Affairs Library.

14. Ibid.

15. Nicholas Cullather. Operation PBSSUCCESS, The United States and Guatemala 1952–1954, History Staff, Center for the Study of Intelligence, Washington, D.C., 1994.

16. Memorandum from the Secretary of Defense's Deputy Assistant for Special Operations (Lansdale), 7 November 1960, p. 1116, Foreign Relation of the United States, 1958–1960, Volume 6.

17. Jay Mallins, *Covering Castro: Rise and Decline of Cuba's Communist Dictator* (New Brunswick, N.J.: Transaction Publishers, 1994), p. 48.

18. Interview with Arturo Villar, 1994, and a phone interview in May 1998.

19. Taped interview with Antonio Veciana, May 1998.

20. Document #20: Foreign Service Despatch. From: Amembassy Santiago. To: The Department of State, Washington. 14 December 1960. Subject: Three Cuban Lady Exiles Touring Continent Describing Conditions Under Castro. Reporter: EpKardas:mfr.

> According to a usually reliable press report; three Cuban lady exiles are currently traveling throughout Latin America to lecture about the Communist-type takeover of their island by the Castro regime. The ladies are Caridad Sabates del Valle, Georgina Freire de Alemán and Ester Rams de Rodríguez de la Torre. They arrived in Santiago on December 10, 1960 from Buenos Aires, Argentina, after having visited Rio de Janeiro and Sao Paulo, Brazil, and have

just left for Lima, after which they plan to proceed to Miami, their present place of residence. Another similar group of Cuban ladies is reportedly touring the Central American republics.

21. Ibid.

22. And Bogota, Colombia, in which Viron Vaky reported their visit.

23. CIA Memo Dated: April 1963, John F. Kennedy Assassination System, record number 176-10010-10161, NSF: Co Cuba, Subject Exiles, Box 48. Also, in a phone interview with Isabel Bequer in November 1993, she confirmed that their trip was paid for by the U.S. government.

24. Document #70. Foreign Service Despatch. From: Amembassy San José. To: The Department of State, Washington. Desp. No. 377. 19 December 1960. Reporter: H. Franklin Irwin: ac. Subject: Cuba: Anti-Castro Activity.

25. Damián Hernández, ¿Tienen los padres el derecho de educar a sus hijos?, *La Quincena*, 31 December 1960; and "El estado asumira en Cuba la patria potestad dentro de poco tiempo," *República*, martes 13 de diciembre, 1960;

26. December 21, 1960, U.S. representative to the Organization of American States addressed the delegates on "The Problems of Cuban Refugees," National Archives, State Department Files, 737.0011, December 1960.

27. Correspondence between Margarita Ballestero and Mr. Mayo, 13 January 1961. Correspondence between Mayo and Katherine Oettinger, 28 February 1961. National Archives, Children's Bureau, 0-2-0-7-1 (2).

28. H. Franklin Irwin, "Cuba Propaganda Activities of Anti-Castro Groups." American embassy, San José, Despatch #493, Department of State, February 20, 1961. National Archives, State Department, 737.00/2-2061.

29. "The Communist Totalitarian Government of Cuba: As a Fact or Situation Endangering the Peace of America." 1 March 1961, John F. Kennedy Presidential Library, White House Files, Arthur Schlesinger Jr. Papers, Box 35.

30. Ibid.

31. Ibid., p. 98.

32. Telegram from Bell to JM WAVE, 3 March 1961, National Archives, John Kennedy Assassination Records, Group Record, 233, Box 11, Reel 16–17.

33. *Newsweek*, 3 April 1961.

34. *America*, 1 April 1961, p. 2.

35. Memo to the CIA director, Allen Dulles, from JM WAVE station, 12 April 1961, National Archives, publicity files of the Cuban Revolutionary Council, John F. Kennedy Special Collection, CIA, Files.

36. Press handout prepared by CIA official Tracy Barnes and sent to Arthur Schlesinger Jr., 22 March 1961, John F. Kennedy Presidential Library, White House Files, Arthur Schlesinger Jr. Papers, Box #5.

37. Press handout of the minimum program of the provisional government, 3 April 1961, p. 1. John F. Kennedy Presidential Library, White House Files, Arthur Schlesinger Jr. Papers, Box #5.

38. Peter Kornblugh, ed., *Bay of Pigs Declassified* (New York: New Press, 1998), p. 120.

39. Ibid., p. 131.

40. Richard Welch, *Response to Revolution: The United States and the Cuban Revolution, 1959–1961* (Chapel Hill, N.C.: University of North Carolina Press, 1985), p. 77.

41. For accounts of the invasion see Peter Wyden, *Bay of Pigs: The Untold Story* (New York: Simon and Schuster, 1979). Haynes Johnson with Manuel Artime, José Pérez San Román, Erneido Oliva, and Enrique Ruiz-Williams, *The Bay of Pigs: The Leaders' Story of Brigade 2506* (New York: W. W. Norton, 1964).

42. Taped interview with Raquelín Mendieta, June 1998, Miami, Florida.

43. Tomas Fernández-Travieso, "Los Ocho Fusilados," *El Nuevo Herald*, 17 April 1991.

44. Robert Stevenson, Oral History Series, Department of State, p. 36.

45. Taped interview with María Teresa Cuervo, March 1993.

46. Yvonne Conde, in *Operation Peter Pan: The Untold Exodus of 14,048 Cuban Children* (New York: Routledge, 1999), p. 193, reports an interview with a Pedro Pan who returned to Cuba during the Mariel boatlift and met with Tony de la Guardia, at the time one of Fidel Castro's top intelligence officers (in 1989 he was executed along with three other officers, including General Arnaldo Ochoa) who told him that they had had spies in the camps all along.

47. Interview with Cuervo, 1993.

48. Taped interview with Ester de la Portilla, Miami, Florida, November 1992. She continued to have contact with the FBI and would report on activities of the Fair Play Committee for Cuba. She also became an advocate for her daughter's friends who were still in the orphanage and were being mistreated by a nun there.

49. Congressional Hearings July 12–14, 1961, World Refugees Problems, Washington, D.C., U.S. Government Printing Office.

50. Letter from Penny Powers to Ambassador Philip Bonsal, 3 April 1961. National Archives, Children's Bureau Files, Central Office, p. 1.

51. Penny Powers's description in ibid.

52. Ibid., p. 2.

53. Letter from Frank Craft, director of the Florida Department of Public Welfare, dated 24 April 1961, to Mildred Arnold, Children's Bureau, HEW, Children's Bureau Files.

54. Letter from Penny Powers to W. H. Mitchell, HEW and State Department, 3 April 1961. National Archives, HEW, Children's Bureau, 1961, p. 2.

55. Ibid.

56. Ibid.

5. Parents and the Decision to Send the Children

1. For an excellent discussion on the role of memory, particularly of the voiceless, see Edith Wyschogrod, *An Ethics of Remembering: History, Heterology, and the Nameless Others* (Chicago: University of Chicago Press, 1998).

2. Taped interview with José Arruza, 13 March 1993.

3. Julie Marie Bunck, *Fidel Castro and the Quest for a Revolutionary Culture in Cuba* (University Park, Pa.: Pennsylvania State University Press, 1994), p. 24.

4. Richard Jolly, "Education," in Dudley Seers, Andres Bianchi, Richard Jolly, and Max Nolff, *Cuba: The Economic and Social Revolution* (Durham, N.C.: University of North Carolina Press, 1964), p. 192.

5. Quoted in Richard Fagen, *The Transformation of Political Culture in Cuba* (Stanford, Calif.: Stanford University Press, 1969), p. 41.

6. Telegram from JM WAVE, 3 March 1961, National Archives, John F. Kennedy Assassination Files, Group Record 233, Box 22, Folder D.

7. John Kirk, *Between God and the Party: Religion and Politics and Revolutionary Cuba* (Tampa, Fla.: University of South Florida Press), 1989.

8. *La Voz de la Iglesia en Cuba: 100 Documentos Episcopales* (México, D.F.: Obra de la Buena Prensa, 1995), pp. 64–69.

9. Cuban Catholicism was very eclectic. Many Cubans called themselves Catholics but were not devote practitioners of Catholicism.

10. *La Voz de la Iglesia en Cuba*, pp. 70–74.

11. Kirk, *Between God and the Party*, p. 71.

12. Art. 55, Tit. V. "De la familia y la cultura segunda parte." Ley Fundamental de la República de Cuba de 7 de febrero de 1959, se promulgó el propio 7 de febrero. Leondel de la Cuesta, ed., *En edición extraordinaria de la Gaceta Oficial Constituciones Cubanas: Desde 1812 Hasta Nuestros Días* (Madrid: Ediciones Exilio, 1974).

13. Taped interview with Emilio Cueto, 3 December 1992.

14. See, for instance, State Department, Policy Information Statement on Latin American Youth Congress to be held in Havana the summer of 1960, 17 June 1960, National Archives, State Department Records, Cuba, p. 49.

15. Dolgoff, as quoted in Bunck, *Revolutionary Culture*, p. 27.

16. Fidel Castro, speech at the sixth national meeting of Schools of Revolutionary Instruction. Quoted in Fagen, *Transformation of Political Culture*, p. 105.

17. *Revolución*, Monday, 26 December 1960, p. 1.

18. Bunck, *Revolutionary Culture*, pp. 30–31.

19. Jorge Domínguez, *Cuba: Order and Revolution*. Cambridge: The Belknap Press of Harvard University Press, 1978, p. 279.

20. Taped interview with Monsignor Agustín Román, Miami, Florida, September 1998. This interview helped me understand the depths of the tensions Catholics felt on a day-to-day level.

21. Foreign Service Despatch. From: American Consulate of Santiago de Cuba to the State Department, 27 October 1960, National Archives, State Department Central Files, Cuba, 737.00/10–2760.

22. Foreign Service Despatch. From: Amembassy, SANJOSE. To: The Department of State, Washington. Desp. No. 97. August 25, 1960. Reporter: H. Franklin Irwin Jr:ac.

23. Foreign Service Despatch, U.S. Embassy in Havana, #893. From: Amembassy

HABANA. To: The Department of State, Washington. Desp. No. 893. October 20, 1960. Reporter: WGBewiler:rjg.

24. "El Pueblo de Cuba Reclama la Acción Colectiva": *Documento presentado a la Organización de Estados Americanos por el Frente Revolucionario Democrático en representación del pueblo de Cuba.* . The statement was signed by the Frente's Executive Committee, which by now had expanded to include Manuel A. de Varona, Coordinador General, Dr. José I. Rasco Bermúdez, Dr. Justo Carrillo, Dr. Ricardo R. Sardina, Dr. Antonio Maceo, and Dr. Manuel Artime, 14 November 1960.

25. Taped interview, January 2000.

26. Document #84: Department of State Memorandum of Conversation, 18 May 1960. Subject: Cuban Situation and Solutions Thereto. ". . . stated that he can foresee the support of three elements in the overthrow of Castro: (1) the labor unions, (2) the Catholic Church, and (3) certain elements of the Auténtico Party. . . ."

27. Document #83: Foreign Service Despatch No. 1663. 16 May 1960. From: U.S. Embassy, Habana. To: The Department of State, Washington. Reporter: Wayne Smith. Copied from the Public Information Archives of the Department of State.

28. *La Voz*, p. 98–106. Also, Document #17: Foreign Service Despatch, 24 May 1960. From: U.S. Consulate, Santiago de Cuba. To: The Department of State, Washington. Reporter: P. F. Wollam:pfw.

29. Embassy Despatch No. 1719, 27 May 1960.

30. Manuel Maza, "The Cuban Catholic Church: True Struggles and False Dilemmas," master's thesis, Georgetown University, Washington, D.C., 1982, p. 96.

31. Foreign Service Despatch No. 1719, 27 May 1960. From: Embassy, Havana. To: The Department of State, Washington. Ref: Embassy telegram 3444 dated June 2, 1960; June 8, 1960. Reporter: W. S. Smith. Public Information Archives, Department of State.

32. Document #16: Foreign Service Despatch. From: American Embassy, Habana. To: The Department of State, Washington. May 27, 1960. Ref: Embassy's Despatch 1691, May 24, 1960 and Deptel. 1795, May 19, 1960. Subject: Further Reaction to Archbishop of Santiago's Pastoral Letter. Reporter: W. S. Smith/rps.

33. Document #11: Foreign Service Despatch. From: Amembassy, Habana. To: The Department of State, Washington. July 28, 1960. Subject: Castro Regime's Reaction to Recent Catholic Anti-Communist Demonstrations. Daniel M. Braddock, Deputy Chief of Mission, WSSMith:cs.

34. Maza, "The Cuban Catholic Church," p. 95.

35. National Archives, State Department Records, Embassy Files, Religion 570.3, October 3, 1960, reported by Wayne Smith.

36. Document #23: Foreign Service Despatch. From: Amembassy Habana. To: The Department of State, Washington. December 9, 1960. Subject: Open Letter from Cuban Roman Catholic Hierarchy to Prime Minister Castro: Bishops Come to

Issue with Castro Government on Communism and Religious Freedom. Reporter: HRWellman:rjg.

37. Foreign Service Despatch, 1499, Wayne Smith reporter, "The Catholic Church in Cuba as a Force in the Struggle Against Castro," 2 January1961. National Archives, 570.3, x–350.

38. *La educación en la Revolucion* (La Habana, Cuba: Instituto Cubano del Libro), 1974, p. 40.

39. Jolly, "Education," p. 192.

40. James Baker, hearings on proposed plan submitted to the Congress of the United States, December 1961.

41. Quoted in Fagen, *Transformation of Political Culture*, p. 242.

42. José Martí, *On Education: Articles on Educational Theory and Pedagogy, and Writings for Children in the Age of Gold*, ed. Philip Foner (New York: Monthly Review Press), 1979.

43. Quoted in Fagen, *Transformation of Political Culture*, p. 105.

44. Ibid., p. 107. For an extensive discussion of the role played by multiple organization in the insurrection see Julia Sweig, *Inside the Cuban Revolution* (Cambridge: Harvard University Press, 2002).

45. Lionel Soto, "Las escuelas de instrucción revolucionaria y la formación de Cuadros," *Cuba Socialista*, November 1961, pp. 28–41.

46. The concept of boarding schools was started by the Jesuits in Europe. Various Catholic orders had boarding schools throughout the island.

47. Bunck, *Revolutionary Culture*, p. 28.

48. Karen Wald, *Children of Che: Childcare and Education in Cuba* (Palo Alto, Calif.: Ramparts Press, 1978), p. 49.

49. Bunck, *Revolutionary Culture*, p. 28.

50. Cables between U.S. Embassy in Havana and Visa Office of the State Department make multiple references of waivers to nuns and priests being expelled from Cuba. Outgoing Telegram to Secretary of State, 7 March 1961, State Department Visa Office Files, 161.1Q1/3 761.

51. Kirk, *Between God and the Party*, p. 103.

52. Interview with Adelaida Everhart, Florida, May 1958.

53. Taped interview with Rafael Ravelo, Chicago, Illinois, April 2000.

54. Original affidavit giving permission for Rafael to travel abroad to study, dated May 19, 1961.

55. Memo on the Routine Life of an Ordinary Person Who Lives in Port of Nuevitas, National Archives, John F. Kennedy Assassination Files, Originating Agency CIA, Box #15, Folder F47, dated 4/19/62, Manuel Salvat Files.

56. Taped interview with Valentin Díaz, Miami, Florida, November 1992.

57. James Baker, informal memo, 25 May 1998.

58. Taped interview with Valentin Díaz, Miami, Florida, November 1992.

59. Taped interview with Emilio Cueto, Washington, D.C., December 1992.

6. *Rescate de la Niñez:* The Aftermath of the Invasion

1. *Foreign Relations of the United States (FRUS), 1961–1963,* vol. 10, ed. Louis Smith, general editor, David S. Patterson (Washington, D.C.: United States Government Printing Office, 1997), p. 315.

2. Ibid., p. 666.

3. William Lederer and Eugene Burdick, *The Ugly American* (Greenwich, Conn.: Fawcett Publications, 1958).

4. See Evan Thomas, *The Very Best Men, Four Who Dared: The Early Years of the CIA* (New York: Simon and Schuster, 1995), p. 271.

5. Appendix d to Memorandum from Joint Chief of Staff to Secretary of Defense McNamara, 26 April 1961, FRUS, vol. 10, p. 377.

6. Memorandum for the Record, May 5, 1961, in FRUS, vol. 10, p. 486.

7. Memo from. McGeorge Bundy to Secretary of HEW and Director of CIA, 25 April 1961. National Security Action Memorandum No. 42. National Archives, John F. Kennedy Presidential Library, National Security Files, Box 329.

8. U.S Policy Toward Cuban Exiles, Annex III, Department of Defense, 3 May 1961, John F. Kennedy Presidential Library, Theodore Sorensen Papers: Classified Subject Files: 1961–1964: Cuba. General, 5/03/61–5/24/61, Box 48.

9. Cuban Refugee Problems: Hearings before the Subcommittee to Investigate Problems Connected with Refugees and Escapees. Committee on the Judiciary, United States Senate, 87th Congress, First Session, 6, 7, 13, 1961 (Washington, D.C.: United States Government Printing Office, 1962).

10. Ibid., Baker proposal to Congress, 1961.

11. Annex A, May 4, 1961, National Archives, John F. Kennedy Assassination Files, Rockefeller Commission Files.

12. Department of State, Secretary of State to U.S. embassy in Caracas, March 7, 1961. Obtained under Freedom of Information Act from the FBI, "Cuban Refugee Problems Files. Also Outgoing Telegram Department of State, Madrid, October 9, 1961, National Archives, State Department Central Files, Cuba, 737.000/10–661.

13. Memorandum of Conversation, 19 May 1961, Maurice Mountain, Director of Policy Planning Staff, Department of State, in FRUS, vol. X, p. 549.

14. John F. Kennedy Library, National Security Files, National Security Council, Box 329, Tab 42.

15. Annex B, U.S. Policy Toward Cuban Exiles. John F. Kennedy Presidential Library, Theodore Sorensen Papers, Classified Subject Files: 1961–1964: Cuba. General, Box 48, Item #1b.

16. Memo from Mildred Arnold, Director of Division of Social Services, to Regional Child Welfare Representatives, National Archives, Children's Bureau Files, 24 April 1961.

17. Cable from Carlyle Onsrud to Mildred Arnold, 8 May1961, National Archives, Children's Bureau, 0-2-0-7-1 2.

18. Mildred Arnold, Director of Division Services, 8 May 1961, National Archives, Children's Bureau, 0-2-0-7 2.

19. FBI memorandum, 24 July 1961, re: Cuban Refugee Problem in the US Internal Security, obtained by Freedom of Information Act request to the FBI.

20. Taped interview with Wendell Rollason, Ft. Myers, Florida, November 1993.

21. I knew of my cousin's story, but I stumbled on the official record while conducting research at the National Archives.

22. National Archives, John Kennedy Assassination Files, CIA Records, Group Record, 233, Box 40, Folder B, August 3, 1961, telegram from Bell 10, to JM Wave.

23. National Archives, John Kennedy Assassination Files, CIA Records, Group Record, 233, Box 40, Folder B, August 10, 1961, telegram from JM Wave to the director of the CIA.

24. Interview with Pancho León and Masita Delgado, September 1998.

25. Phone interview with Ignacio Arruza, 5 November 2002.

26. As part of the lawsuit we received material the CIA was using to prepare its defense, including newspaper articles. One was a story about Mongo.

27. Taped interviews with Ramón Grau, August 1992 and May 1998. This story is told in Grau's book with Valerie Ridderhoff, *Mongo Grau: Cuba Desde 1939* (Madrid, España: Agualarga Editores, 1997), chapters 12 and 13.

28. Sergio López-Miró, "El lado oscuro de Pedro Pan," *El Miami Herald*, 29 November 1990.

29. David Wright, "Daring Hero Helped 14,000 Children Escape Castro's Cuba and Gain Freedom in America." *National Inquirer*, 3 March 1987.

30. Ramón Grau Alsina, arrest records, Ministry of the Interior, Cuba, papers received from the University of Havana's Center for the Study of Alternative Policies, 1993.

31. "Glorificación de un crimen," *Granma*, 19 September 1986.

32. A letter sent by Father Walsh to Brother Maximiliano, August 16, 1962, regarding false visa waivers suggests that he had his own church contacts. From Operation Pedro Pan Archives.

33. When Mongo was jailed, he had wanted her to "double" (i.e., tell the Cubans she would spy for them when in reality she was still working for British intelligence), but she continued taking care of the families of the political prisoners. At one time he tried to send Powers a gift from jail, a hand-painted fan, but she refused it.

34. Taped interview with Penny Powers, March 1993.

35. Taped interview with Antonio Comellas, March 1993.

36. Taped interview with Bill Moriarte, March 1993. After I filed the CIA lawsuit, he refused to speak to me again, although he had been forthcoming in the first interview.

37. This name appears both in an article written by Polita Grau in the book *Unfinished Revolution* and in the *CIA Handbook of Counterrevolutionary Organizations*, released pursuant to a lawsuit, *Torres v. CIA*, filed 1998.

38. Taped interview with Albertina O'Farrill, March 1993. Also see Victor Pino Yerovi, *De embajadora a prisonera política* (Miami, Fla.: Ediciones Universales, 1991).

39. Taped interview with Nenita Carrames, Miami, March 1993.

40. Taped interview with Alicia Thomas, Miami, March 1993.

41. Memorandum from Chief of Operation Mongoose, Operation Mongoose (Lansdale), 7 December 1961, in FRUS, vol. X, p. 691.

42. *Time,* 8 September 1961, p. 38.

43. *Time,* 6 October 1961, p. 41.

44. Interview with Carrames, March 1993.

45. Arrest records obtained from the Center for Alternative Policies at the University of Havana, Summer, 1991. These records were retrieved from the Ministry of the Interior archives.

46. Fidel Castro speech, 19 September 1961. Reprinted in *Hoy,* 20 September 1961, along with a copy of the supposed legal proposal to transfer parental rights over children to the state. Also in *El Mundo,* 20 September 1961, p. 1.

47. *Foreign Relations of the United States (FRUS), 1961–1963,* vol. X, ed. Louis Smith, gen. ed., David S. Patterson (Washington, D.C.: United States Government Printing Office, 1997), p. 670.

48. Ibid., p. 675.

49. Cuba Daily Summary, 15 November 1961, National Archives, John F. Kennedy Library, Arthur Schlesinger Jr. Papers. White House Files, Box 5, File 1961.

50. Cuban Refugee Problems. Hearings Before the Subcommittee to Investigate Problems Connected with Refugees and Escapees. Committee on the Judiciary, United States Senate, 87th Congress, First Session, 6, 7, 13, 1961 (Washington, D.C.: United States Government Printing Office, 1962). Testimony of Arthur Patten, Member, County Commission, Dade County, Florida, p. 49.

51. Cuban Refugee Problems Hearings, Testimony of Ralph Renick, news director, WTVJ, Miami Florida, p. 136.

52. Cuban Refugee Problems Hearings, Testimony of Rev. Bryan Walsh, National Conference of Catholic Charities, p. 225.

53. Cuban Refugee Problems Hearings, Testimony of Wendell Rollason, director, Interamerican Affairs Commission, p. 153.

54. Ibid.

55. Cuban Refugee Problems Hearings, Testimony of Most Reverend Coleman Carroll, Bishop, Catholic Diocese of Miami, Florida, p. 13.

7. The Children

1. Taped interview with Nenita Greer, Miami, Florida, 1998.

2. For instance, see *The Flight of Pedro Pan* documentary directed by Joe Cardona and Mario de Varona, 1999; and Yvonne Conde's *Operation Pedro Pan: The Untold Exodus of 14,048 Cuban Children* (New York: Routledge, 1999) includes stories from

the surveys she conducted. These were not scientific samples; nonetheless, they offer important pieces to the Pedro Pan puzzle.

3. Field Report submitted to HEW Children's Bureau by Lucille Watson, consultant, 21 October 1963. National Archives, Children's Bureau Central Files.

4. This was revealed at a conference sponsored by Barry University in November 2001. Some of the children who came into the United States with visa waivers signed by Father Walsh were not logged into the official file if relatives or friends picked them up. We don't know the number of children who entered the United States unaccompanied.

5. "Cuba's Children in Exile," U.S. Children's Bureau report submitted to U.S. Department of Health, Education and Welfare by Katherine Oettinger, "The Story of the Unaccompanied Cuban Refugee Children's Program," (Washington, D.C.: U.S. Government Printing Office, 1967).

6. The role of the Children's Bureau had already been defined in 1958 as a caregiver for the children not as a screening agency for minors seeking entrance to the United States. It was reiterated in February 1961 that this office would coordinate the provision of child welfare services within the Cuban refugee program. Memo on Role of the Children's Bureau, 16 February 1961, National Archives, HEW Children's Bureau Central Files.

7. Contract for Provision of Foster Care for Unaccompanied Cuban Refugee Children, National Archives, HEW Children's Bureau Central Files.

8. Kathryn Close, "Cuban Children Away from Home," Children 10 (January-February 1963).

9. Marjorie L. Fillyaw, "Cuba's Child Refugees," Ave Maria, 7 April 1962, p. 22.

10. FBI memo dated 25 July 1962, subject: Cuban Refugee Problem in the United States Internal Security-Cuba, obtained via Freedom of Information Act.

11. See J. Bruce Nichols, The Uneasy Alliance: Religion, Refugee Work, and U.S. Foreign Policy (New York: Oxford University Press, 1988), chapter 6.

12. Betty Barton, Assistant to the Chief for Cooperation and Planning 31 January 1961, National Archives, HEW Children's Bureau Central Files, 0-2-0-7-1 2.

13. Katherine B. Oettinger, chief of HEW Children's Bureau, 23 March 1961, National Archives, HEW Children's Bureau Central Files, 0-2-0-7-1 2.

14. Erwin Potts, Miami Herald, 8 March 1962, p. 1.

15. Gene Miller, "Peter Pan Means Real Life to Some Kids," Miami Herald, 9 March 1962.

16. Memo from Martin Gula to Mildred Arnold, Director of Social Services, HEW Children's Bureau, 19 December 1960. National Archives, HEW Children's Bureau Central Files, 0-2-0-7-1 2.

17. Memo, Frank M. Craft, director, Florida State Department of Public Welfare, 14 March 1961. National Archives, HEW Children's Bureau Central Files.

18. Memorandum to state public welfare administrators and child welfare directors from Mildred Arnold, director, Division of Social Services, 24 May 1962, National Archives, HEW Children's Bureau Central Files.

19. Letter to Joseph Kirkpatrick, Confidential Law Assistant Librarian, Supreme Court Chambers, Buffalo, N.Y., 27 March 1961, National Archives, HEW Children's Bureau Central Files, Box 761. Also, letter to Abraham Ribicoff, Department of HEW, 13 March 1961. National Archives, Social Services Administration.
20. Letter to President Johnson from Mrs. Earl Michelle, 20 December 1963, National Archives, HEW Children's Bureau Central Files.
21. Memo to Frank Craft from Mildred Arnold, 30 October 1962, National Archives, HEW Children's Bureau Central Files, p. 4.
22. Ibid., p. 3.
23. Ibid., p. 3.
24. Ibid., p. 6.
25. Letter from J. Arthur Lazell, Director, Cuban Refugee Center to Roy Wynkoop, Executive Officer, Welfare Administration, 5 August 1963, National Archives, HEW Children's Bureau Central Files.
26. Memo to Mildred Arnold from Frank Craft, 17 April 1961, National Archives, HEW Children's Bureau Central Files.
27. The number of unaccompanied minors may be much greater than what has been reported, since many of the children who were picked up directly by friends or relatives do not appear in the official Walsh register. Interview with Elly Chovel, president of Operation Pedro Pan and who has had access to the airport list, July 2001.
28. Fillyaw, "Cuba's Child Refugees," pp. 20–25; also Close, "Cuban Children Away From Home," pp. 3–10.
29. Elena García Wagner, www.streamnologics.com.
30. There are inconsistencies in the various official and unofficial reports about the receiving centers. This may be due to the time period reported. The following descriptions draw from the history section of Operation Pedro Pan website, www.pedropan.org; Monsignor Bryan O. Walsh, "Cuban Refugee Children," *Journal of InterAmerican Studies and World Affairs* 13 (July–October 1971): 378–415; Fillyaw, "Cuba's Child Refugees," 1962, pp. 20–25; Close, "Cuban Children Away from Home," pp. 3–10; Katherine B. Oettinger, John Thomas, "Cuba's Children in Exile" (Washington D.C.: U.S Department of Health, Education and Welfare, 1967). Also Conde, *Operation Pedro Pan*, chapter 5 has an excellent description of the various receiving centers and the mixed experiences.
31. Letter from Alfred Schwartz to HEW Secretary Abraham Ribicoff, 5 July 1962, National Archives, HEW Children's Bureau Central Files, Box 761.
32. Quoted in an AP story, "Cuban Children Helped in Florida," *New York Times*, 27 May 1962.
33. Taped interview with Margarita Castro, Miami, Florida, March 1993.
34. Letter from Luis García to Jacqueline Kennedy, 6 November 1963, National Archives, HEW Children's Bureau Central Files.
35. Series of letters from boys at Camp Matecumbe to President Kennedy, August, October, 1962, National Archives, HEW Children's Bureau Central Files, Box 761.
36. Taped interview with Alfredo Lanier, Chicago, Illinois, May 1996.

37. Phone interview with Carlos Erie, October 1999.

38. Taped interview with Lanier, May 1996.

39. Gene Miller, "Cuba Priests Fly into Miami," *Miami Herald*, 25 May 1961; also *Diario de Las Américas* carried the news on the same day.

40. Taped interviews with Rafael Ravelo, May 1996 and March 1999.

41. Letter in Sara Yaballí Pedro Pan Collection, No. 0350, Box 2, University of Miami Special Collection, Cuban Archives.

42. See Matthew A. Crenson, *Building the Invisible Orphanage: A Prehistoy of the American Welfare System* (Cambridge: Harvard University Press, 1988), pp. 1–6; see also Marvin Olasky, "The Rise and Fall of American Orphanages," in *Rethinking Orphanages for the 21st Century*, ed. Richard B. McKenzie (Thousand Oaks, Calif.: Sage Publications, 1999), pp. 65–78.

43. After I filed the CIA lawsuit I received dozens of phone calls from Pedro Pans throughout the country. These are just some of the stories they shared with me.

44. Ministry of the Interior, documents obtained from the Centro de Estudios de Políticas Alternativas.

45. Phone interviews with Xavier and Ignacio Arruza, November 2002.

46. Phone interview with María Conchita Cádiz, 10 November 1999.

47. In a report to John Thomas, Director of Cuban Refugee Program, from Lucille Batson, October 1963, National Archives, Children Bureau Central Files, p. 56.

48. See Robert Katz, *Naked by the Window: The Fatal Marriage of Carl Andre and Ana Mendieta* (New York: Atlantic Monthly Press, 1990), for details about her death.

49. Taped interview with Raquelín Mendieta, Miami, June 1998.

50. According to Polita Grau, Lizette's letters to her parents about the treatment at the orphanage made them worry and not be as effective in their underground work. Taped interview with Polita Grau, 1998.

51. Interview with Raquelin Mendieta, June 1998.

52. Letter from Mildred Arnold to Anna Sundwall, child welfare representative, Denver, Colorado, 8 March 1962, National Archives, HEW Children's Bureau Central Files, Box 761.

53. Oscar Torres and Francisco Emeterio were the two boys mentioned in the letters. Edith Miller, 1 July 1962, National Archives, HEW Children's Bureau Central Files.

54. Letter to Senate Majority Leader Mike Mansfield from Russell Giesy, principal, Whitefish High School, 7 June 1962, National Archives, HEW Children's Bureau Central Files.

55. Letter in Sara Yaballí Pedro Pan Collection, No. 0350, Box 2, University of Miami Special Collection, Cuban Archives.

56. Ibid.

57. Letter from Mansfield to Ribicoff, 1962, National Archives, HEW Children's Bureau Central Files.

58. Report written by Anthony Celebrezze, HEW representative, to Senator Mansfield, 20 August 1962, National Archives, HEW Children's Bureau Central Files.

59. For a discussion of Catholicism and sexual abuse, see Nancy Scheper-Hughes,

"Institutionalized Sex Abuse and the Catholic Church," in *Small Wars: The Cultural Politics of Childhood*, ed. Nancy Scheper-Hughes and Carolyn Sargent (Berkeley: University of California Press, 1998), pp. 295–317.

60. Letter from Oscar Torres, 12 July 1962, National Archives, HEW Children's Bureau Central Files.

61. Close, "Cuban Children," p. 196.

62. Ricardo Núñez-Portuondo, "The Cuban Refugee Program: The Early Years," is available through the website of www.operationpedropan.org.

63. Taped interview with María Concha Bechily, Chicago, 20 May 1996.

64. Taped interview, Candy Sosa, Miami, 6 June 1996.

65. Division of Social Services Filed Report, 29 October 1961, National Archives, HEW Children's Bureau Central Files.

66. Hearings of the House of Representatives Subcommittee of the Judiciary, June 1963, Study of Population and Immigration Problems, pp. 23 and 52.

67. Lucille Batson, memo for the record, 1 November 1962, National Archives, HEW Children's Bureau Central Files.

68. Letter to Michael Mansfield from Russell Giesy, Principal, Whitefish High School. June 7, 1962. National Archives, HEW Children's Bureau Central Files.

69. John Thomas, "U.S.A. as a Country of First Asylum," in *Cuban Refugee Problems*, ed. Carlos E. Cortés (New York: Arno Press, 1980).

70. Memorandum for General Landsdale, subject: Membership of the Psychological Warfare Committee; dated January 5, 1962.

71. USIA Report, Current USIA Programs on Cuba, 6 February 1963, National Archives, USIA Country Files. Also see Dispatch from Chief of Station, JM Wave, June 1963, report on Unidad Revolucionaria propaganda activities that includes an open letter to Cuban mothers. National Archives, John F. Kennedy Assassination Special Files, Group 233, Box 63, Folder F.

72. Official Memorandum of the Caribbean Survey Group, 23 March 1962, National Archives, John F. Kennedy Assassination Files. The first comic book was to portray communism as the enemy of religion, and the following comic book would depict communist control of the Havana University. Monies were set aside for the comic books and purportedly they were published, though none have been located so far.

73. Memo from Lt. Col. Patchell to Gen. Lansdale, Office of the Secretary of Defense, 17 July 1962, John F. Kennedy Assassination Files, National Archives.

74. Memo from Lt. Col. Patchell to Gen. Lansdale, Office of the Secretary of Defense, 24 July 1962, John F. Kennedy Assassination Files, National Archives.

75. Report by Deputy Director Donald Wilson of the USIA on agency participation in Phase I of Operation Mongoose, 20 July 1962, John F. Kennedy Assassination Files, National Archives.

76. Psychological Support plan for Operation Mongoose, 20 February 1962. The CIA gave me a copy that had many sections blacked out. A fuller version was found in the John F. Kennedy Assassination Files.

77. Taped interview with Father Walsh, Miami, Florida, May 1998.
78. Letter from Katherine Oettinger to Robert Hurwitch, 2 August 1962, National Archives, Children's Bureau, 0-2-0-7-1-2. Hurwitch had asked Oettinger to send him her article on the children to be translated so that the State Department could send it to Latin America.

8. Doors Are Shut

1. Lucille Batson and Martha Hynning, Field Report, 4 December 1962, National Archives, HEW Children's Bureau Central Files, Box 761.
2. Kathryn Close, "Cuban Children Away from Home," *Children* 10 (January–February 1963).
3. Clippings in Children's Bureau Central Files, 020701–020703, Box 761, National Archives.
4. Letters from the Children's Bureau Central Files, National Archives, Box 761.
5. Memo for the record, Mildred Arnold, Children's Bureau Central Files, 020701–020703, Box 761, National Archives.
6. Interview with James Baker, Ormand Beach, Florida, June 1992.
7. Hugh Thomas, *The Cuban Revolution* (Harper and Row, 1971), chap. 43, 44, 45.
8. Memorandum for the Interdepartmental Committee on Cuban Affairs, 3 April 1963, Lyndon B. Johnson Presidential Library, National Security Files, Gordon Chase, Box 5.
9. Brig. General Landsdale, Memo of Meeting with the President, 16 March 1962, National Archives, John F. Kennedy Assassination Files, Defense Department Files.
10. Memo from Dean Rusk to U.S. embassies, 10 March 1965, LBJ Presidential Library, National Security File, Box 18, Vol. V, 9/64–2/65.
11. John F. Thomas, "Aiding Children and Youth," report of the Department of Health Education and Welfare, Cuban Refugee Program, written by 10 March 1964, gives these figures. Also see data on Unaccompanied Refugee Children, Department of Health, Education and Welfare, 31 December 1962, mentions only National Archives, Children's Bureau Central Files, 0-2-0-7-1. The figure on the number of children with relatives is an estimate.
12. A memo for the record from Lucille Batson, 1 November 1962, National Archives, Children's Bureau Central Files, 02071.
13. Memo to John Thomas from Mildred Arnold, 21 February 1963, Unaccompanied Cuban Refugee Children-Consultant's Recent Field Trip to Miami, National Archives, Children's Bureau Central Files.
14. Testimony to Senate Subcommittee Hearings on Cuban Refugees, 3 December 1962 (Reprinted by U.S. Government Press, Washington D.C., 1963), p. 341.
15. Memo for the Record, Lucille Batson, Notes on Meeting of National Voluntary Resettlement Agencies, 23 October 1962, p. 3, National Archives, Children's Bureau Central Files, Box 761.

16. Written communication with Pancho León, October 2002.

17. Monsignor Bryan O. Walsh, "Cuba Is Not Another Poland," *Miami Herald*, Viewpoint, 7 December 1997.

18. Memorandum from Arthur Lazell, director of the Cuban Refugee Emergency Center, to Roy Wyncoop, executive director, Welfare Administration, on Procedure for CREC registration of persons leaving the Unaccompanied Child Program, 5 August 1963, National Archives, Children's Bureau Central Files.

19. Memorandum written by Gordon Chase to Mr. McGeorge Bundy, 23 March 1963, National Archives, Lyndon B. Johnson Presidential Library, National Security Files, Gordon Chase, Box 5, Cuban Coordinating Committee Program; also an other memo written January 29, 1963.

20. Memorandum for the Special Group, from Brig. General Lansdale, Operation Mongoose, 19 April 1962, Defense Department, National Archives, John F. Kennedy Assassination Files, Agency, Matheny, Record Number 178-1-4-10267, SSC Series.

21. CIA Current Intelligence Memorandum, 25 April 1962, in FRUS [Foreign Relations of the United States], vol. X, p. 798 (Washington, D.C.: U.S. Government Printing, 1997).

22. Memorandum of Discussion, Attorney General and John McCone, 3 July 1962, in ibid., pp. 842–43.

23. Memorandum for the President from Bromley Smith, 18 January 1963, PPK, POF, C Box 114.

24. Taped interview with Concha Bechily, Miami, 22 June 1992.

25. Taped interview María Bechilly, Chicago, September 1996.

26. Ralph Dungan memo, White House Papers, John F. Kennedy Presidential Library, 21 March 1963, Box 56, Department of State. AID memo to Ralph Dungan, White House Papers, Box 56, October 10, 1963. Memo to Ralph Dungan, Executive Office of the President Bureau of Budget, 10 October 1962. Miriam Ottenberg, "Behind the Rescue: A Step by Step Account of How Castro's Captive's Were Rescued," *Evening Star*, 24 December 1962.

27. Taped interview with Concha Bechily, Miami, 22 June 1992.

28. Ministry of the Interior, documents obtained from the Centro de Estudios de Políticas Alternativas, University of Havana.

29. Department of State, Bureau of Security and Consular Affairs, "Summary of Department of State's Participation in the Cuban Refugee Program and in the Repatriation of U.S. Nationals and Their Families from Cuba," 19 August 1963. Obtained via Freedom of Information Act. National Archives, State Department Records, 1993. Also included in a memo from Abba Schwartz to various offices in the State Department, John F. Kennedy Presidential Library, National Security Presidential Papers, Box–39–40.

30. Incoming Telegram from the Swiss Embassy to U.S. Secretary of State, 18 May 1963, Control no. 14975. Obtained via Freedom of Information Act.

31. Letter from Ralph Odum to Mr. John Barrett, Justice Department, 26 February

1963, National Archives, John F. Kennedy Presidential Library, Files of Robert Kennedy, Attorney General, General Correspondence, Box 14.

32. Memo from Mr. Woodward, State Department to Secretary of State, 21 November 1961, tab B, in Memo from Gordon Chase to McGeorge Bundy, Cuban Visa Waiver Program, 30 August 1963, John F. Kennedy Presidential Library, National Security Files, Box 39–40.

33. Memo from Gordon Chase to McGeorge Bundy.

34. Years later he would refuse my request for an interview because he claimed to have no knowledge of the project. Letter to author from Barbara Christiana, Haig's assistant, 8 June 1998.

35. Memo from Alexander Haig to John Crimmins, Interdepartmental Coordinating Committee of Cuban Affairs, 30 August 1963, National Archives, John F. Kennedy Assassination Files, Califano, Box 5, Folder 1.

36. Memo to John Thomas from Mildred Arnold, 21 February 1963, Unaccompanied Cuban Refugee Children-Consultant's Recent Field Trip to Miami, National Archives, Children's Bureau Central Files.

37. Letter from Wendell Rollason to Mr. George Phelan, Visa Office, Department of State, 28 August 1962, National Archives, State Department Files, ARA/CMA, Visa Waiver Matters.

38. Letter from Wendell Rollason to Allen Moreland, 23 August 1962Director of the Visa Office, Department of State, National Archives, State Department Files, Visa Office Files, Visa Waivers matters.

39. Briefing paper for the President's press conference, 20 August 1963, John F. Kennedy Presidential Library, National Security Files, Box 39–40.

40. Memo to John Thomas from Mildred Arnold, 21 February 1963, Unaccompanied Cuban Refugee Children-Consultant's Recent Field Trip to Miami, National Archives, Children's Bureau Central Files.

41. Incoming Telegram from Cuban Coordinator, 12 January 1965, Lyndon Johnson Presidential Library, National Security Files, Cuban Cables, Vol. IV, Box 17, 9–64 to 7–65.

42. Department of State cable written by Officer Freeman, from Mexico City, 27 November 1964, Lyndon Johnson Presidential Library, National Security Files, Gordon Chase Files, Box 5.

43. Letter from Wendell Rollason to McGeorge Bundy, Lyndon Johnson Presidential Library, National Security Files, Cuba, Vol. V, Box 18, 9/64 to 2/65, #30, 30a, 30b.

44. Prevention of Intervention in the Hemisphere, 23 May 1963, Lyndon B. Johnson Presidential Library, National Security Files, Cuba, Gordon Chase Files, Box 3, #33.

45. Memo from Gordon Chase to McGeorge Bundy, Cuban Visa Waiver Program, 30 August 1963, John F. Kennedy Presidential Library, National Security Files, Box 39–40.

46. Memorandum from Desmond Fitzgerald to the Director of Central Intelligence, 9 December 1963, National Archives, John F. Kennedy Assassination Files, Record #1781000310199.

47. Memorandum for the National Security Council Standing Group, Annex 7, Exile Problems, April 1963, National Archives, John F. Kennedy Assassination Files, National Security Files, Cuba, General Standing Committee, 4/63: Box 38.

48. Memorandum from Gordon Chase to McGeorge Bundy, 30 January 1963, Lyndon B. Johnson Presidential Library, National Security Files, Box 349–40.

49. Department of Defense document, Annex C, National Archives, John F. Kennedy Assassination Files, National Security Files, Cuba, Subject Exiles, 1961, Box. 48. Also draft letter from Dean Rusk to the President, 29 March 1963, Lyndon B. Johnson Presidential Library.

50. Annex C, D, E, Defense Department, National Archives, John F. Kennedy Assassination Files, National Security Files, Cuba, Exiles, 1961, Box 48.

51. Memorandum for the Director of the FBI, January 1962; subject: Processing of Cuban Exiles into the U.S Armed Forces. Obtained through Freedom of Information Act

52. Memorandum for the National Security Council Standing Group, 1963, Annex 7, p. 2.

53. Address by George Ball, Under Secretary of State, "Principles of Our Policy Toward Cuba," p. 5, to the Omicron Delta Kappa Convention, 23 April 1964, National Archives, Lyndon B. Johnson Presidential Library, National Security Files, Cuba, Box 26, 27, 28, 29, Cuba US Policy, Vol. 1, 2/64–5/64.

54. Gordon Chase, notes of a December 19, 1963, meeting with President Johnson, National Archives, John F. Kennedy Assassination Files, Record Number, 17810000310128.

55. State Department memo sent to embassies, 18 May1965, Lyndon B. Johnson Presidential Library, National Security Files.

56. Letter from Lucille Batson to María Miranda, 24 April 1963, National Archives, Children's Bureau Central Files.

57. Letter to Allen Moreland, visa officer, Department of State, from Phyllis Watson Cuban Resettlement Program, 28 April 1965, copy in Lyndon B. Johnson Presidential Library, White House Central Files.

58. Airgram from U.S. Embassy in Mexico to the Department of State, 15 December 1964, Lyndon B. Johnson Presidential Library, Gordon Chase, Box 30.

59. Interview with Hugo Chaviano, Chicago, Illinois, July 2000.

60. Memo prepared for President Johnson by Gordon Chase, LBJ Presidential Library, April 9, 1964, National Security Files.

61. Memo written April 9, 1965, National Security Files, Country, Cuba, Box 30, memo #16.

62. Gordon Chase to McGeorge Bundy, 11 June 1965, National Security Files, Cuba, Refugees, 10/63-7-65, Box 30, #10.

63. Airgram from USUN, 16 April 1965, Lyndon B. Johnson Presidential Library, National Security Files, Cuba, Cuba Refugees, #15.

64. "Talking Points to Use with the UNHCR Representatives Concerning Reunion of Parents in Cuba with Unaccompanied Children in the United States," Lyndon B.

Johnson Presidential Library, National Security Files, Cuba, U.S. Policy, Vol. II, 12/63–7/65,1a.

65. The Cuban Communist Party, Special report, Central Intelligence Agency, November 1965, National Archives, Lyndon B. Johnson Presidential Library, National Security Files, Cuba, Box 18, Cuba, WG Bowdler File, Vol. 1, 4/64–1/66, #15.

66. John Virtue, Cuba Today, UPI, Nov. 25th, National Archives, Lyndon B. Johnson Presidential Library, National Security Files, Cuba, Box 17, #17.

9. Reconstructing Home

1. www.Teresita.org.

2. Noon briefing, 30 September 1965, National Archives, Lyndon B. Johnson Presidential Library, National security Files, Cuba, Bill Bowdler, Vol. 1, 4/64–1/66, , Box 18, #39f.

3. Castro Statement, 30 September 1965, National Archives, Lyndon B. Johnson Presidential Library, National security Files, Cuba, Bill Bowdler, Vol. 1, 4/64–1/66, Box 18, 39–h.

4. U.S. Coast Guard History, www.uscg.

5. Memorandum from Benjamin Read to McGeorge Bundy, 1 October 1965, National Archives, Lyndon B. Johnson Presidential Library, National Security Files, Cuba, Bill Bowdler, Vol. 1, 4/64–1/66, Box 18, #40.

6. To Mrs. Hynning from Lucille Batson, 5 March 1964, "Unaccompanied Cuban Refugee Children," p. 2, National Archives, Children's Bureau Central Files, October 1964.

7. Telegram sent by Mario and Clara Sarduy to President Johnson, 9 October 1965, Lyndon B. Johnson Presidential Library, White House Central Files, Cuba.

8. Memorandum from Bill Bowdler to McGeorge Bundy, , 14 October 1965, National Security File, Country File Cuba, Vol. 1, (Bowdler File) Box 18. Memorandum for the President from McGeorge Bundy, 14 October 1965, National Archives, Lyndon B. Johnson Presidential Library, National Security Files, McGeorge Bundy Papers, Daily Regional Staff Report for the President file, Box 19. Memorandum of Conversation, Department of State, 20 March 1964, National Archives, Lyndon B. Johnson Presidential Library, National Security Files, Cuba, Bill Bowdler, Vol. 1, 4/64–1/66, Box 18, #34.

9. Memorandum from Bill Bowdler to McGeorge Bundy, 14 October 1965, National Security File, Country File Cuba, Vol. 1, (Bowdler File), Box 18.

10. Memorandum for the President from McGeorge Bundy, 14 October 1965, National Archives, Lyndon B. Johnson Presidential Library, National Security Files, McGeorge Bundy Papers, Daily Regional Staff Report for the President file, Box 19.

11. Memorandum of Conversation, Department of State, 20 March 1964, National Archives, Lyndon B. Johnson Presidential Library, National Security Files, Cuba, (Bill Bowdler), Vol. 1, 4/64–1/66, Box 18, #34a.

12. Telegram sent to President Johnson, 4 October 1965, Lyndon B. Johnson Presidential Library, White House Central Files, Cuba.

13. Memo of Understanding sent to Bill Moyers, 4 Novemeber 1965, LBJ Library.

14. Ramón Sánchez Parodí, whose three younger brothers had been sent through Operation Pedro Pan, stayed in Cuba. He would come to the United States in 1977 in charge of the Cuban Interests Section and negotiate an immigration treaty for the United States that would help normalize immigration.

15. *Miami Herald*, 5 October 1965.

16. American Opinion Summary, Department of State, 10 November 1965, "Cuban Refugees," Lyndon B. Johnson Presidential Library, White House Files, Bill Moyers Files.

17. Letters and Telegrams to the President, Lyndon B. Johnson Presidential Library, White House Central Files, Cuba, October 1965.

18. Letter from the governor of Florida to President Johnson, 15 October 1965, Lyndon B. Johnson Presidential Library, National Security Files, Cuba, Box 30, #2a.

19. Telegram from Rev. Fred Fox, director of Catholic Social Services, 11 October 1965, Lyndon B. Johnson Presidential Library, White House Central Files, Cuba.

20. Letter from the governor of Florida to President Johnson, 15 October 1965, Lyndon B. Johnson Presidential Library, National Security Files, Cuba, Box 30; Letter from Donald Wheeler Jones, 13 October 1965, #1f and 1e.

21. Letter from Wayne Phillips, director of news and information for the Democratic National Committee, to Chuck Daley, White House, 16 June 1964, Lyndon B. Johnson Presidential Library, National Security, Central Files, Subject, Cuban Exiles.

22. Field Report, Dwight Ferguson, 25 October 1961, National Archives, Children's Bureau Central Files.

23. Letter sent by Manuel Perez to HEW Secretary Abraham Ribicoff, 14 November 1961, National Archives, HEW Children's Bureau Central Files, Box 761.

24. Memo from Lucille Batson to Mildred Arnold, 16 August 1963, Children's Bureau Central Files, 0-2-0-7-1 2.

25. Memo from Mildred Arnold, director of Division of Social Services, to John Thomas, director of the Cuban Refugee Program, , 21 August 1963, National Archives, Children's Bureau Central Files. But by August 1, 1963, travel to Miami had been approved for only three children.

26. Memorandum from Roy Wynkoop to John Thomas, director of the Cuban Refugee Program, 13 August 1963 National Archives, HEW Central Files, Box 1.

27. Taped interview with María Bechily, Chicago, May 1996.

28. Interview with Elly Chovel, Miami, June 2000.

29. For instance, see Martha Hynning letter to Frances Davis, 13 August 1962, National Archives, Children's Bureau Central Files, Box 761.

30. I write about the politics of this period in *In the Land of Mirrors: Cuban Exile Politics in the U.S.* (Ann Arbor: University of Michigan Press, 1999), chapter 4.

31. Grupo Areíto, *Contra Viento y marea* (La Habana: Casa de las Américas, 1978).

32. Ibid., p. 44, author's translation.

33. A longer version of my return and disillusionment appears in my essay, "Where Ghosts Dance el Guaguancó," part of an anthology I edited, *By Heart/De Memoria: Cuban Women's Journeys In and Out of Exile* (Philadelphia: Temple University Press, 2002).

34. Luis Adrian Betancourt, *¿Por qué Carlos?* (La Habana, Cuba: Editorial Letras Cubanas, 1981).

35. Taped interview with Rafael Ravelo, Chicago, Illinois, March 1999.

36. Ibid.

37. Main statement made by Fidel Castro in Matanzas, 2 August 1999, on the subject of "Illegal Migration from Cuba to the U.S.," Press Release of the Cuban Mission to the United Nations.

38. In 1977, fifty-five young exiles returned to Cuba. Their trip was documented by Jesús Díaz, in a documentary called *55 Hermanos*. A closing statement by one of the group's leaders called for recuperating for the nation all the children who had been taken out of Cuba.

10. Pedro Pans Search for Memory

1. Ana Mendieta, 8 January 1981, Santiago de Cuba, from her personal diary, courtesy of Raquelin Mendieta.

2. Edith Wyschogrod, *An Ethics of Remembering: History, Heterology, and the Nameless Others* (Chicago: University of Chicago Press, 1998).

3. Tina Rosenberg, "Salvador's Disappeared Children," *New York Times Magazine*, 7 February 1999.

4. *Chicago Tribune*, 18 April 1999.

5. For instance, Victor Andres Triay, *Fleeing Castro: Operation Pedro Pan and the Cuban Children's Program* (Gainesville, Fla.: University of Florida Press, 1999) relies mainly on the account of Monsignor Walsh's account of the first thirty days of the program. Throughout, Triay defends the program as "humanitarian." There is little probing of the national security context that defined the moment during which this operation unfolded or any reference to government documents. Other books include fictional accounts such as Josefina Leyva, *Operación Pedro Pan: El éxodo de los Niños Cubanos: Una Novela Histórica* (Coral Gables, Fla.: Editorial Ponce de León, 1993); María Armengol Acierno, *Children of Flight Pedro Pan* (New York: Silver Moon Press, 1994).

6. Ramón Torreira Crespo and José Buajasán Marrawi, *Operación Peter Pan: Un Caso de Guerra Psicológica contra Cuba* (La Habana: Editora Política, 2000).

7. James Blight and Peter Kornbluh, *The Politics of Illusion: The Bay of Pigs Reexamined* (Boulder, Colo.: Lynne Rienner Press, 19980.

8. Gail Reed, "Operation 'Peter Pan'—Flight of Fear," *Cuba Update*, February 1994, pp. 7–8. I had not yet met Wendell Rollason or anyone who knew exactly what his name was or occupation. Someone had told me he was a lawyer and his name was Rawleson; this is the way it appears in Reed's article.

9. Miguel González Panda died in 1999. He left an unfinished film to Joe Cardona who subsequently finished it with Mario de Varona, "Flight of Pedro Pan," 1999.

10. *Del Otro Lado de la Pecera*, 1994.

11. It is interesting to note that Fidel Castro trusted an American living in Cuba before he trusted Cuban filmmakers.

12. Ramón Torreira Crespo and José Buajasán Marrawi, *Operación Peter Pan: Un caso de guerra psicológica* (La Habana: Editora Política, 2000).

13. Wayne Smith, interview, National Public Radio, 3 May 2000.

14. I have two pending requests, one to the CIA includes a list of specific items and an other to the National Archives asks to open the records of the Bureau of Security and Consular Affairs with regard to Cuba during this period.

15. The press coverage in the United States and in Cuba surprised me. It coincided with the pope's visit to Cuba. I received dozens of phone calls: Pedro Pans who did not know how they had come to the United States; others who had lost contact with their parents. There was one call from New Orleans: a Cuban child who had been separated from his friends because they were put in a home for white delinquent children while he was placed in one for black children called the Lafayette Home for Bad Boys. Calls from operatives came as well: former stringers for the CIA who felt that the truth should be told; a commander of the Bay of Pigs invasion who supported my quest for documents. I received a letter from Cuba, relatives responding to an article published in *Granma*. They were trying to find a niece who had been sent out by her parents in 1962; the parents had died before being reunited with her.

16. We deposed the CIA's Freedom of Information Officer at length and found that the CIA's initial search for my request ran the term "Peter Pan" through a data system called Orris, which contains already released documents. The CIA knew that "Peter Pan" was not a cryptogram for any of their operations, something I could not have known because the list of cryptogram names is confidential. Predictably, this search yielded no documents.

17. I reviewed internal CIA memos about my lawsuit that indicated the agency's initial search was a mockery. As a routine practice, the CIA does not search operational files for Freedom of Information requests because much of their contents are too sensitive for release. Unfortunately, there is little willingness to sort out specific documents from within those files that would not compromise the well-being of any individuals. The CIA's outright refusal to search operational files at all clearly demonstrates the agency's lack of commitment to making available documents the public may be entitled to review.

The second search was not guided by my request, however, but rather by the CIA's revision of my request. Instead of looking for documents pertaining to the exodus of more than 14,000 unaccompanied children, using the numerous terms and possible events I provided, they cast their nets in the direction of documents that could show that there had been a government program to instigate the exodus. Again, none were found.

18. Report of the Central Intelligence Agency, 21 June, 1962, Cuban Refugee Children.

19. Judith Edgette, "Domestic Collection on Cuba," *Studies in Intelligence*, Fall 1963, pp. 41–45, describes the extent of the intelligence gathering during this time period. In addition, Robert Kennedy would ask for periodic reports from this source, John McCone. Memorandum for the Record, Cuba, National Archives, John F. Kennedy Assassination Files, General Subject Files, Document ID 1781000410129.

20. Memo from Mrs. Hynning, assistant director, Division of Social Services, Children's Bureau to Lucille Batson, Consultant, "Conference with Father Walsh, director of Miami Catholic Welfare Bureau, 29 June 1962, National Archives, Children's Bureau Central Files.

21. Cuban Counterrevolutionary Handbook, HRG Reference Copy, Box 19, Volume 37, written in October 1962, obtained through litigation.

22. Phase I of Mongoose Report, General Lansdale, July 1962, provided by the CIA.

23. The fire, by the way, is studied today as an example of how not to store government documents.

24. See Daniel Patrick Moynihan, *Secrecy: The American Experience* (New Haven: Yale University Press, 1998).

25. Edmund Cohen, "Cold War Documentation, National Security, and the Fullest Possible Accounting: Restriction vs. Access," paper presented at the Cold War Conference on the Power of Free Inquiry and Cold War International History, 25 September 1998, National Archives, p. 9.

26. Angus Mackenzie, *Secrets: The CIA's War at Home* (Berkeley: University of California Press, 1997).

27. It is this kind of philosophy that results in the CIA's refusal to release propaganda plans and broadcasts to Cuba from the early 1960s despite the fact that they were publicly broadcast. To do so would be to admit that Radio Swan was a CIA project. And although other governmental entities have recognized it as a government project, the CIA to date has not done so publicly.

28. Letter from Jacob Esterline to Lee Strikland, then Information and Privacy Coordinator, in response to a request from the CIA about information regarding the children. Released during the course of my lawsuit, *Torres vs. CIA*. The date on the letter is redacted, p. 400, of packet of background information.

29. Early in my research, David Lambert, an archivist of State Department records, suggested that perhaps the collaboration with the British is what made these records so hard to obtain.

30. Jay Weaver, "Peter Pan Sex Abuse Lawsuit," *Miami Herald*, 9 November 2002.

31. Walsh, "Cuban Children Refugees," p. 395.

32. John Thomas, "The Cuban Refugee Problem: Aiding Children and Youth," National Archives, Children's Bureau Central Files, 10 March 1964.

33. R. Hart Phillips, *The Cuban Dilemma* (New York: Ivan Obolensky, Inc., 1962), p. 277.

34. Taped interview with Monsignor Walsh, May 1998.

35. For children of other conflicts, coming together has been an important part of

their reconstruction; see for instance "At World War II Refuge for Children: A Re-union," *New York Times*, 11 October 1998.

36. Yvonne Conde, *Operation Pedro Pan: The Untold Exodus of 14,048 Cuban Children* (New York: Routledge, 1999).

37. www.teresita.org.

38. Flora González Mandri, "A House on Shifting Sands," in *Bridges to Cuba*, ed. Ruth Behar (Ann Arbor: University of Michigan Press, 1995), p. 79.

39. Román de la Campa, *Cuba on My Mind: Journeys to a Severed Nation* (New York: Verso, 2000), p. 41.

40. Ibid., p. 43.

41. Caros Eric, *Waiting for Snow in Havana: Confessions of a Cuban Boy* (New York: The Free Press, 2002).

42. Dennis Jarrett reviews his work in the *Santa Fe Reporter*, July 29–August 4, 1998, p. 22. In addition, I had a telephone interview with the artist who later provided me with slides of his work.

43. Reprinted in *Ana Mendieta* (Santiago de Compostela, España: Centro Gallego de Arte Comtemporánea, 1996), p. 216.

44. Ibid., p. 228.

45. Taped interview with Elly Chovel, Miami, Florida, March 1992.

46. Letters written on October 3, 1965, and April 1, 1965, Operation Pedro Pan Collection, Barry University, Eliza Chovel File.

47. Lourdes Rodríguez-Nogues, "Psychological Effects of Premature Separation from Parents in Cuban Refugee Girls: A Retrospective Study," Ph.D. dissertation submitted to Boston University School of Education, 1983; Alejandrina Onelia Estrada, "The Children of Peter Pan: A Retrospective Study of the Migration of Unaccompanied Minors," Ph.D. dissertation submitted to the Wright Institute Graduate School, December 1987; José Manuel Goyos, "Identifying Resiliency Factors in the Adult 'Pedro Pan' Children A Retrospective Study," Ph.D. dissertation submitted to Barry University Ellen Whiteside McDonnell School of Social Work, 1996.

48. Interview with Ravelo, Chicago, 1999.

49. Ibid.

Conclusions

1. Cuban Constitution Family, Family Code, Chapter II, Articles 92 and 95, 1978.

2. Taped interview with James Baker, May 1978.

3. For a longer discussion of this romantic self-image see Andrew Burstein, *Sentimental Democracy: The Evolution of America's Romantic Self-Image* (New York: Hill and Wang, 1999).

4. In *Patos, Elefantes y Heroes* (Mexico: Ariel, 1997), Ariel Dorman makes an interesting argument that "marginal" nations and peoples are infantalized, seen as incomplete, to justify bringing them into the empire.

5. Ché Guevara, "Man and Socialism in Cuba," pamphlet published by Students for a Democratic Society, 1969, p. 24.

6. Elizabeth Jane Tans, "Cuban Unaccompanied Minors Program: The Wisconsin Experience," *Child Welfare* 62 (May/June 1983): 269–79.

7. Before Elián González, there had been Daniel Bussot.

8. Press release, Ileana Ros-Lehtinen, *Congresista Ileana Ros-Lehtinen Exorta a Miembros de Pedro Pan que tomen en sus hogares Niños refugiados Cubanos Detenidos en Krome*, 29 August 1994.

9. Elly Chovel, "Church Is Concerned for Detainees," *Miami Herald*, 29 October 1994. Chovel responded to a plea from Alina Fernández, Fidel Castro's daughter who had gone into exile, who advocated bringing in the children.

10. Letter from the Operation Pedro Pan Archives, dated August 31, 1994.

11. Meg Laughlin, "Textbook Is a Guide for Kids at Elián's School," *Miami Herald*, 20 January 2000.

12. Armando Codina, article written for the *Miami Herald*, 30 January 2000.

13. For an extensive discussion on the modern childhood, see *The Children's Culture Reader*, ed. Henry Jenkins (New York: New York University Press, 1998) *and Childhood in America*, ed. Paula Fass and Mary Mason (New York: New York University Press, 2000).

14. Hunter Hurst III, "Juvenile Court at 100 Years of Age," National Center for Juvenile Justice, 1996; Margaret Talbot, "What's Become of the Juvenile Delinquent," *The New York Times Magazine*, 10 September 2000.

15. Vicki Goldberg, "The Child, the Adult Within and the Blur Between the Two," *New York Times*, January 1996.

16. In recent years there has been growing journalistic concern with the changing nature of childhood; see, for example, Lisa Belkin, "The Backlash Against Children," *The New York Times Magazine*, 23 July 2000.

17. For varied discussions on the themes see the following articles, Peter Appleborne, "No Room for Children in a World of Little Adults," *New York Times*, 10 May 1998; Edward Rothstein, "How Childhood has Changed! (Adults, Too)," *New York Times*, 14 February 1998.

18. Jason Ziednberg, Report: "Drugs and Disparity: The Racial Impact of Illinois's Practice of Transferring Young Drug Offenders to Adult Court" (Washington, D.C.: Justice Policy Center, 2000).

19. See for instance, Roger Rosenblatt, *Children of War* (New York: Doubleday, 1983).

20. Anne Higonnet, *Pictures of Innocence: The History of the Crisis of Ideal Childhood* (London: Thames and Hudson, 1998), p. 78.

21. Gary Cross, *Kids' Stuff: Toys and the Changing World of American Childhood* (Cambridge: Harvard University Press, 1997).

22. Shirley R. Steinberg and Joe Kincheloe, eds. *Kinderculture: The Corporate Construction of Childhood* (Boulder, Colo.: Westview Press, 19980.

23. Robert Coles, *The Moral Intelligence of Children: How to Raise a Moral Child* (New York: Plume, 1997).

24. Climent's work can be viewed at Mary Anne Martin's online catalog, www.mamfa.com.

25. Robert Bennett has discussed the curious absence of children in the liberal democratic project. Although they are counted for the purposes of reapportionment, they cannot vote. See his essay, "Should Parents Be Given Extra Votes on Account of Their Children: Toward a Conversational Understanding of American Democracy," *Northwestern University Law Review* 94 (Winter 2000): 503–66.

26. Jane Rutherford, "One Child, One Vote: Proxies for Parents," *Minnesota Law Review* 82 (June 1998): 1464–1525.

27. See the works of Fred Greenstein, *Children and Politics* (New Haven: Yale University Press, 1965); Robert Hess and Judith Torney, *The Development of Political Attitudes in Children* (New York: Doubleday Anchor Books, 1968).

28. Robert Coles, *The Political Life of Children* (Boston: Atlantic Monthly Press, 1986).

29. Bonnie Honig, *Political Children, Feminist Interpretations of Hannah Arendt* (University Park, Pa.: 1995), pp. 263–84.

30. David Halberstam's book on the civil rights movement, *The Children* (New York: Ballantine, 1998), suggests that the now grown children who participated remember their activism as empowering.

31. Joseph Goldstein, Anna Freud, and Albert Solnit, *Beyond the Best Interests of the Child* (New York: The Free Press, 1973).

32. Fidel Castro's speech at the Closure of the Fourth Congress of the Union of Young Communists, 1982, reprinted in *Granma*, April 1982.

33. See Jacqueline Bhabha and Wendy Young, "Through a Child's Eyes: Protecting the Most Vulnerable Asylum Seekers," in *Interpreter's Releases* 75 (June 1, 1998). Also Human Rights Watch Children's Project, "Slipping Through the Cracks: Unaccompanied Children Detained by U.S. Immigration and Naturalization Service," Washington, D.C., 1997.

34. Center for the Study of Migration, "Repatriation and Reintegration of Unaccompanied Refugee Children," *Migration World Magazine* 26 (Jan.–Feb. 1998): 5.

35. William J. Del Castillo, "Cuba: The Aftermath of the Pope's Visit," quoted in *Daily Catholic*, vol. 9–10, 28 January 1998.

Acknowledgments

Ten years have passed since I began researching events that led to the unprecedented exodus to the United States of so many Cuban children, including myself. It has often been a frustrating and painful journey, but it has also been intellectually and personally transformative. It was ultimately possible because of the loving and generous support of relatives, friends, and colleagues.

My husband, Matthew Piers, and our daughters, Alejandra and Paola Piers-Torres, have been with me throughout the entire journey. Alejandra and Paola continue to teach me how vulnerable and wise children and young adults can be; they have listened patiently to the stories, and in turn have made me smile at their tender, and occasionally irreverent, retelling of them. Matthew took on the impossible legal challenge of suing the CIA, and, most important, gave me his love, even in the most difficult times when the past almost threatened to consume the present.

I am particularly indebted to Elly Chovel, whose intelligence and humanism has guided our search for explanation; Ileana Oroza who so lovingly helped me tell the story; and Gayatri Patnaik at Beacon Press whose enthusiasm, thoroughness, and knowledge shepherded this project into becoming a book. You three have been the guardian angels of *The Lost Apple*.

I have been one of the many lucky writers who has benefited from Charlotte Sheedy's lifetime commitment to publishing alternative voices. There is a special thanks for her and Carolyn Kim. I am grateful to the Beacon staff as well.

Every researcher should be fortunate enough to find Milton Gustafson. Milt taught me how to use the National Archives and took a personal interest in the project. Without him many of the documents I unearthed may still be hidden away in unopened, dusty file boxes. The commitment of Ron Whalen (John F. Kennedy Presidential Library) and Regina Greenwell (Lyndon B. Johnson Presidential Library) to making governmental records available to the public has made it possible for us to have a more comprehensive understanding of this time period. Esperanza de Varona's assistance at the University of Miami, Cuban Archives Special Collection, provided important pieces to the puzzle.

Peter Kornbluh of the National Security Archives and Sheryl Walters, my first lawyer on this project, counseled me on how to use Freedom of Information Act requests. Joan Grimson, formerly of the staff of the Senate's Intelligence Committee, worked diligently to pry open the CIA's files. When all failed, Matthew Piers, Jonathan Rosenblum, Dana Sukenik-Kornfeld, and Theresa Amato contributed their legal skills and analytical eyes to this project.

Rosy Valenzuela, Alina Mulet, Yadira Calderon, Christina Jackiw, Helena Beckett, Shanti Drake, Stephanie Gladden, Charles Browning, Phoebe Connelly, and Alejandra Piers-Torres all helped with the research and preparation of the manuscript. Jon Elliston's archival dexterity unearthed critical documents. Lisa Milam, Eduardo Aparicio, and Javier Figueroa's reviews have sharpened this manuscript. Thank you all for your work and insights.

John D. and Catherine T. MacArthur Foundation's Research and Writing program provided the first grant that initiated the project. Ruth Adams and Kim Stanton supported it. Grants from the John F. Kennedy Presidential Library's Abba Schwartz Award and the Lyndon B. Johnson Presidential Library made possible research trips there.

DePaul University's Research Council granted me a research leave in 1995. The Humanities Center fellowship provided the time and intellectual comradeship to help develop the philosophical underpinnings of this project. Thanks to Jackie Taylor and to the staff, and to my fellow "fellows," Jonathan Gross, Eric Murphy Selinger, and Dolores Wilber.

In addition, the time they provided allowed me to bring together scholars who are also involved in rethinking childhood: Jacqueline Bhabha, Bernadine Dohrn, Robert Bennett, and Jane Rutherford. Jim Block deserves a special mention for his generosity of spirit and his insightful comments.

John Coatsworth and Wayne Smith provided reviews of the project in its earliest stage. Frank Bonilla, Richard Meister, Julia Sweig, Frances Aparicio, David Frey, Ruth Behar, Marifeli Pérez-Stable, María Cristina Herrera, Félix Masud-Piloto, Jerry Poyo, Pat Callahan, Lourdes Torres, Bibiana Suárez, Bryan Sikes, and Gilberto Cárdenas are some of the many colleagues who have nurtured my thinking about this project—some by sharing their research, others by commenting on mine, and still others by providing forums in which I could share mine. I am especially grateful to Yvonne Conde, author of a book on Operation Pedro Pan, for her willingness to swap information and insights.

Denise Mattson, Robyn Florzak, Roxanne Brown, Valerie Phillips, Mirta Ojito, Frances Sellers, Rich Bard, Roane Carey, and Charlie Madigan have all helped get my ideas into the public. I am especially grateful to Cecilia Vaisman for her friendship and collaboration in producing the radio documentary on Operation Pedro Pan.

For the last twenty years, Achy Obejas and I have sustained a conversation about Cuba, exiles, and our generation. If this were fiction one of the characters would be named after her. Many friends have been very supportive: Pastora San Juan Cafferty, Joan Hall, and George Cotsirilos, Tania Bruguera, Woody Wickham; Joe Cardona became a friend while making *The Flight of Pedro Pan*; José de Córdoba helped with some of the earlier interviews; and Liz Balmaseda has been a friend in perhaps the most difficult way one can be a friend, by asking the hard questions and not letting me get away with easy answers.

Magical moments I have shared with my music buddies María Romeu, Steve Saltzman, Neil Tesser, Michael Orlove, Caleb Dube, and Jim DeJong have helped me through the long hours of writing. I am grateful to live in a city in which our souls can be nourished by so much music.

From my father, Alberto Torres, I inherited a love of music and from my mother, María Isabel Vigil, a love of ideas. My separation from them was painful, but it was made more manageable because of the love and understanding I received from Nenita and Pucho Greer, and by the kindness and generosity Frances Bauta showed me by bringing me into her own family. Without them, my fate may have been very different. To Paula Fuqua, I owe special appreciation for helping me understand my emotional journey.

In 1997, Maria Piers, my mother-in-law, died. She was a psychoanalytically trained anthropologist and child psychologist. She was cofounder of the Erikson Institute in Chicago and author of various books on children. In part because of her work, Chicago has the country's highest concentration of professionals who work with children. Many books from her library found their way into our home. In an effort to sustain a conversation with her, I began browsing through them. Because of those books, I was able to expand my understanding of our exodus to a broader philosophical inquiry of how children became vehicles for nation building. I also began to see that Maria's lifelong work had been a creative and courageous philosophical struggle to counteract modernism's reduction of children to a political function. For her the education of children was critical, particularly early childhood education. But most crucial to the building of a more humane future is how well we understand children's unique sensibilities and needs, and from that principle came her lifelong work to educate us about children. It is to her work and memory that I dedicate this book.

Index

Made in the USA
Lexington, KY
13 November 2013